Approaches to Local History

General Editor: David Hey

Local history has been a spectacularly successful growth area in recent years, amongst professional historians and enthusiastic amateurs alike. In this new seris, Longman will be publishing books on particular themes and aspects of the subject, written by experts for a student and lay readership. It will include practical volumes that explore the methodology of local research, and volumes that themselves illuminate the hidden lives of ordinary people in times past.

Already published:
A History of British Surnames   Richard McKinley

A History of British Surnames

Richard McKinley

Longman
London and New York

Longman Group UK Limited
Longman House, Burnt Mill, Harlow,
Essex CM20 2JE, England
and Associated Companies
throughout the world

Published in the United States of America
by Longman Inc., New York

First published 1990

British Library Cataloguing in Publication Data
McKinley, Richard, 1921–
  A history of British surnames. – (Approaches to local history).
  1. British surnames. Etymology
  I. Title   II. Series
  929.4'2'0941

ISBN 0-582-01870-6 CSD
ISBN 0-582-01869-2 PPR

Library of Congress Cataloging in Publication Data
McKinley, R. A. (Richard Alexander)
  A history of British surnames/Richard McKinley,
    p.   cm. – (Approaches to local history)
  Includes index.
  ISBN 0-582-01870-6 – ISBN 0-582-01869-2
  1. Names, Personal–Great Britain. 2. English language-Etymology–Names.
  I. Title. II. Series.
  CS2505.M36 1990
  929.4'2'0941–dc20   89-12303
                                                                      CIP

Set in 10/12 Times
Printed in Singapore
by Longman Singapore Publishers (Pte) Ltd.

Contents

Editorial preface

It is a hundred years ago now since Dr H. P. Guppy published his *Homes of Family Names in Great Britain*, that pioneering attempt to analyse the geographical distribution of British surnames and to point to their origins. Other amateurs, notably C. W. Bardsley, followed in his path, but it was not until Professor P. H. Reaney published his *Dictionary of British Surnames* in 1958 and *The Origins of English Surnames* nine years later that the results of systematic scholarly research were made available in print. Reaney was a Professor of English Language interested in the meaning, formation and development of names. His publications marked a great advance in our understanding of the subject. For a time it seemed that we could go no further.

Many a local historian, however, must have felt dissatisfied on reading the explanation of a surname offered in Reaney's dictionary. The purely linguistic approach seemed inadequate. Detailed knowledge of the topography and documentary history of a parish or a neighbourhood often pointed to a different interpretation, especially in those areas of scattered settlement where the names of farms and hamlets are the same as surnames peculiar to the district. The approach of the local historian was needed to complement that of the specialist in old languages. It was particularly fortunate then that when Dr Marc Fitch endowed a research fellowship for the study of surnames in the Department of English Local History at the University of Leicester Richard McKinley should have been appointed to the post.

In the days before the computer was brought to the aid of historical investigation Richard McKinley's card indexes and his painstaking methods of recording and analysing were regarded with some awe by his colleagues. He brought not only a thorough technical expertise but a wide general knowledge to bear on the interpretation of his material. He proceeded county by county, through Norfolk and Suffolk to Oxfordshire, Lancashire and Sussex, and now in semi-retirement he is working on Devon. Meanwhile, his postgraduate student, Dr George Redmonds, published his study of the surnames of the West Riding of Yorkshire. In this way, widely-scattered parts of the country, with very different patterns of settlement, illuminated the subject as a whole.

In this present work Richard McKinley brings together the fruits of these years of labour. Interest in the origins and spread of surnames is higher than ever before. To the ranks of local historians have been added armies of family historians for whom the origin of a name is the ultimate quest. This book is written in non-technical language that the informed amateur historian and genealogist can understand. It follows older works in the ways in which it categorises surnames, but adds considerably to the linguistic dimension by using surnames to shed light on many aspects of social history. In particular, it draws attention to the complex patterns of population mobility that have always characterised British society. Despite this considerable movement, however, core families have remained remarkably attached to their places of origin. Even today certain types of surnames help to provide a distinctive flavour to local societies throughout the land. It is clear from Richard McKinley's work that the study of surnames is of interest not only to those who are tracing their ancestors but to historians who wish to identify the peculiar character of local societies. An understanding of the ways that surnames have arisen and ramified since the middle ages is now a prime requirement for the social historian as well as the linguist.

DAVID HEY

Introduction

The aim of this book is to provide a history of British surnames and of their development for the reader without any specialised knowledge of the subject. An exploration of the processes by which surnames evolved will enable genealogists, family historians, and local historians to put into context, against a general background of surname development, evidence collected about individual surnames or families, or about the body of surnames present in individual localities. A further object of the book is to explain how to investigate the meaning and etymology of surnames, and the complications involved in the process. Surnames of some types were at first largely confined to particular regions, and some individual surnames arose only in one area of Britain. These factors provide some clues about where, geographically, to look for some surnames, and the evidence for this will be discussed. It is not intended to provide either a dictionary of British surnames, though many individual names will be mentioned, or a guide to tracing pedigrees. Works of both kinds exist already, and are discussed in the advice on further reading at the end of the book. The scope and nature of the book have been much influenced by research into surnames over many years and by contacts with genealogists and family historians, including a large body of correspondence, from which the need for a work on the subject has become evident.

This book will cover the history of surnames in Great Britain. The history of Irish surnames is not dealt with here, and such names are only referred to in so far as they are found at various periods in Great Britain. The history of surnames in the Isle of Man and in the Channel Islands has also been excluded. Each of these had its own distinctive body of surnames, and each had a separate and complex linguistic history of its own.

The quantity of historical evidence about the origins and evolution of surnames is very large, and extends over a long period. For England in particular, much information about the position in the Middle Ages can be obtained from taxation lists, title deeds, manorial records, and so forth. For Scotland and Wales the information is rather less full, and tends not to extend back quite so far in time, but it is still very extensive. For later periods, there is an increasingly copious mass of material in the shape of parish registers, census returns, poll books and electoral registers, the records of civil registration of births, deaths, marriages, and so forth. Out of all this evidence, some is well arranged and easily accessible, some is not. It is in particular very laborious to scrutinise large quantities of evidence which is still in the form of manuscripts, and for which no printed editions are available. The sheer volume of evidence in existence has always prevented the compilers of dictionaries of surnames, and of other reference works, from looking at every single item of source material in existence. One consequence of this is that there is still much useful work to be done on the origins of individual surnames and on family histories, especially by using material in local record offices. For the purposes of this general survey of British surnames it has been possible to draw on the detailed studies of surnames in some counties or areas, already carried out, and to make use of much work which has already been done on family history. It has, however, not been possible to examine every piece of manuscript evidence, and a good deal of work could still profitably be done on individual surnames, and on the body of surnames in use at various periods in individual counties or smaller areas.

Despite the extensive evidence which exists, the names of some sections of the population are badly documented, especially for the period before parish registers became available. This was particularly true of such people as landless labourers, or unskilled workers in towns. One result of this is that there are some surnames which do not appear in any written records now extant before about 1600, although many such names had probably existed for several centuries unrecorded. These circumstances, and the changes in spelling and pronunciation which surnames undergo over a period, inevitably cause difficulties in discovering the origins and early histories of some names, and it would be a mistake to assume that even the most diligent research can always uncover the facts about the history of every British surname, let alone those about names brought into this country at one time or another from overseas.

Much effort has been devoted by many researchers to studying the history of individual families, and to collecting information about pedigrees. More recently, there has been increasing interest in the study of particular surnames, and there are now many one-name societies. There has also been much academic study of surnames by linguistic scholars, who have used surnames as evidence for the history of the English language (many occupational terms, for instance, are found as surnames much earlier than they can be found in any other connection) and for such purposes as studying the phonetics of dialects. These investigations have thrown much light on the etymology and origins of many surnames. All this work, both by academics and amateur researchers, has created a large body of information about surnames; but some of this information is not very accessible, and it is not easy from all this to form any general view of how surnames have developed in this country or to set the facts which emerge from research into pedigrees, or into the surnames in use within individual towns or villages, against any general background.

Although a great amount of valuable research has been accomplished, and although the quantity of evidence available is very extensive, there are some limitations on what can be discovered about the surnames of families. One is the point, already made, that some names only appear in written records after having existed unrecorded for some time, often for centuries. Another is that despite much investigation by linguistic experts, the meaning and etymology of some surnames still remains either very uncertain or completely unknown. The number of surnames of which this is true is rather greater than might be supposed from consulting the standard reference books on the subject. Further, some surnames as they exist today have more than one possible origin. To give one example, the modern surname Dean may be derived from holding the office of dean (possibly a cathedral dean or rural dean, but the senior officials of some guilds in the Middle Ages were known as deans); it may be from the topographical term 'dene', with the meaning of 'valley'; it may be from another topographical term, 'denne' (swine pasture), the surname derived from which became confused with Dean from some early period; and there is a possibility that it might be from a pet form of the first name Denis, though the fact that the surname is in any particular case derived in this way does not seem to have been proved. Or, to take another case, the surname Winder is in some instances from one or other of the places called Winder in the north west of England, and when the surname originates in Cumbria or north Lancashire it is likely to be from one of the place-names concerned; in Sussex, however, the surname developed from the topographical term 'wynde' (for a winding street, road, or stream), and was a name for somebody who lived near a winding road, etc.; in addition, it seems possible that the surname is sometimes from an occupation, perhaps that of winding woollen yarn. Generally it will not be possible to deduce, simply from the present day form of the surname, which of these possible origins applies.

These ambiguities are a considerable obstacle to the full understanding of British surnames and their history, and no one should approach the subject with the idea that all the basic questions about the meaning and origins of surnames have been resolved, and that all the answers can be found in some work of reference. Much research remains to be done, even about the origins of surnames, and there is still much scope for the amateur investigator who is prepared to pursue the history of one particular surname back into early periods to unearth facts which do not appear in the standard dictionaries of surnames. Even more remains to be done in inquiring into the distribution of surnames at various dates, which is still a very obscure subject. A lot of valuable work can be done by one name societies, and similar bodies, in mapping the distribution of names at various periods, and much information for the purpose can be obtained from the increasingly numerous printed editions of taxation returns, and of other records listing large numbers of the population, such as the 1641–42 Protestation Returns, or the nineteenth-century census material. Much of interest can be discovered, too, by making detailed studies of the surnames present in some limited area, such as a borough, district, or hundred, over a long period.

The lack of any account of how hereditary surnames evolved in Britain makes it difficult for anyone interested in pedigrees, in family history, or in the growth of individual surnames, to set the facts which they discover against any general view of surname history. It also makes it difficult for anyone interested in local or economic history to appreciate the evidence which can be gained by studying the surnames in use in particular localities. When the surnames or by-names present in any township or parish are first examined, for almost any period after such names first start to appear in numbers, the impression gained is usually that the surnames or by-names involved are numerous, very varied in character, and display no particular pattern. Except perhaps in some of the Gaelic-speaking parts of Scotland, it is unusual in Britain to find cases where one locality or parish is wholly or mainly inhabited by people bearing one surname, or surnames of any one type. It is also often the case that if the history of, say, a parish is traced over a period of several centuries, the turnover of the surnames found seems to be very large, so that even over a moderately short time, such as a hundred years or so, there appears to be little continuity. In fact, these impressions are misleading. A scrutiny of the names to be found in a small unit, such as a parish or township, seems at first sight to show constant change and instability in the surnames present, because movements by families of only a mile or two will take them into or out of the area under examination, and such short range moves were common at all times. It is a mistake to suppose that during the Middle Ages and the early modern period village populations consisted largely of peasant families which scarcely moved from their native villages, remained settled in one place over centuries, and perhaps were closely inbred. Frequent movement within a limited area is much more typical of family histories for any period before the Industrial Revolution. If a larger area than a parish, such as a county, a hundred or wapentake, or a group of a dozen adjoining parishes, is taken, it will generally be seen that there was a marked degree of continuity where surnames are concerned. Indeed, any study of the surnames to be found over a considerable period in, say, a county will show that there was present locally a stock of surnames which persisted there over centuries. In many counties large numbers of surnames survived from the thirteenth century, or even in some cases the twelfth, up to the time of the Industrial Revolution, or, often, up to the present day.

Typically, it will be found that in any English county (Scotland and Wales each have their own, rather different, histories of surname development) a large number of surnames which first appear at a relatively early time, say between about 1200 and 1350, persist all through the later Middle Ages and the early modern period, right up until the industrial upheavals which began in the late eighteenth century, and very frequently up to the end of the nineteenth century, or later. The general impression left from a systematic study of the surnames in almost any county is of the existence of a stable body of surnames, persisting locally through the centuries, only very partially disrupted by the population shifts of the Industrial Revolution, and still to a large degree surviving at the present time. It is of course not the case in any county, or at any period, that the body of surnames in use was completely changeless. There were always instances of surnames, some well-established locally, disappearing altogether, and being lost from the local stock of names. There were always examples of new surnames being introduced by migration within Britain, sometimes from distant regions, and in some cases such introduced surnames have ramified over a period and become common in their new homes. It is also true that there are few parts of the country which have remained for any long period totally untouched by any influx of surnames from outside Britain. Such developments in the case of individual names have, however, usually left the general body of surnames in any county little changed.

Not only is the appearance of instability and change in the surnames of any area misleading, but the impression which may be gained from the study of surnames within, say, a parish, that there is no particular form or pattern to the surnames found in any one area, is also false. If the surnames in any one region or county are divided into categories, and studied as a group, it will be found that there are marked differences in character between the surnames found locally, and those present in other counties or regions. Further study will enable at least some of the features of local surnames to be linked to economic conditions, settlement patterns, demographic trends, and local dialects. These differences occur at an early stage in surname evolution, often being perceptible as far back as the thirteenth century, and are very persistent.

It is usually possible to point out what the distinctive features are of the surnames in any county, or in a larger area such as a whole region, and to contrast them with those of other parts. Some of the factors which lie behind these local characteristics can be discerned without too much difficulty, as has been suggested above, but others are much more difficult to explain. For instance, from the whole body of names then existing, it can easily be observed that from the thirteenth century onwards surnames derived from topographical terms for features of the landscape (a type of name discussed in detail in Chapter 3) formed a much larger proportion in the south-eastern counties than in any other region; and that within that region, Sussex – a more isolated county in the Middle Ages, and later, than might be supposed from present-day conditions – had a higher proportion of such names than the other south-eastern counties. In fact Sussex harboured a very large and varied collection of names in that category, many of them still existing in the county today, but it is a matter of great difficulty to discover why this situation arose. In some instances the influences at work can be detected; for example, at the period when surnames were evolving regions that had many small dispersed settlements, such as the Pennines or parts of Devon and Cornwall, had a much higher proportion of surnames derived from place-names than did areas where much of the population lived in nucleated villages. Frequently, however, the reasons for the marked differences that can be seen where surnames are concerned between counties and between regions escape investigation. It would appear that each region has its own habits and practices in the formation of surnames, often ones for which there is no obvious explanation, and it would probably be wrong to suppose that all such practices can be related to economic and social conditions, settlement patterns, and similar factors. Something must have been contributed by local methods of speech and turns of phrase.

Much the same is true where individual surnames or by-names are concerned. Factors such as settlement patterns or dialect may explain why some names are common in certain regions, while being scarce, or totally lacking, in others, but there are features of the distribution of surnames which cannot be explained on these lines. Once surnames became hereditary, both their distribution, and whether they remained scarce, or became numerous, depended upon the fortunes of the family or families with each individual name. Some families were clearly prolific, so that over a period they ramified to a great extent, and the surnames which they bore became numerous. Other families failed to increase significantly, and over a long time failed to proliferate, so that their surnames remained rare. The reasons why some families ramified greatly, while others in the same areas did not, are not usually detectable, at least for the periods before the nineteenth century. No doubt families in a superior economic position would stand a better chance of rearing offspring who would survive into adult life, and genetic factors may have had some influence. Again, many cases can be found of families who ramified to a notable extent, without dispersing very much geographically from their points of origin. The effect of one family proliferating very considerably over a period, without spreading much, was of course to produce a situation where the family's surnames became very common in one area, while remaining scarce, or absent, in other parts. On the other hand, members of some families, perhaps through an active involvement in trade, tended to migrate over long distances, taking their surnames into other regions. It is also the case that some towns situated on main trade routes gave rise to locative surnames which became dispersed from an early date, no doubt because of the connections created by the constant passage of travellers through them. (This is discussed further in the chapter on locative surnames. See Chapter 2.) Such factors as those just mentioned start to influence both the numbers and the distribution of surnames from the point at which they become hereditary onwards.

Beyond the influence exercised on individual surnames by such developments, the general demographic history of regions, and of the whole country, together with the nature of population changes, had an obvious effect upon surnames. A very large number of surnames or by-names can be found in the period between about 1200 and 1350 which have been lost by 1400. No doubt some of these were by-names which never became hereditary, but some were certainly names which had been hereditary for several generations. The loss of most of these names must have been due to the heavy mortality of the middle and late fourteenth century. At a time when there was a drastic fall in population (caused by the series of epidemics usually known as the Black Death), it is not surprising that many less common surnames failed to survive. At a later period–during the seventeenth and eighteenth centuries and into the nineteenth–the phenomenon can be observed in parts of Lancashire and Yorkshire of many locally-originating surnames each becoming very numerous within a restricted area, without spreading out to any significant extent. Such developments, however, are explicable in terms of the demographic history of the areas concerned, where the population was rising mainly through natural increase, with only a limited contribution from immigration. The result was that families already well-established locally tended to proliferate considerably over a period, and their surnames became correspondingly numerous. The distribution of surnames has of course been influenced by the movements of people in or out of any region, and traces of such movements can often be found by investigating regional surnames. It is, however, generally difficult to obtain accurate and comprehensive evidence about such movements for any period before the nineteenth century.

The skills of the genealogist and family historian are essential for the study of surnames and for a full understanding of the subject. Genealogical evidence is important even for discovering the etymology and origins of surnames existing at the present day. One of the essential points in establishing the origin and meaning of any existing surname is to trace its history as continuously as possible back to the earliest forms which can be found, and genealogical evidence is one of the principal means of doing this. If care is not taken to trace the history of surnames continuously, it is all too easy to connect a modern surname, erroneously, with forms from the Middle Ages from which the modern name is not in fact derived. Mistakes of this kind have at times been made in the past, even occasionally by experienced etymologists. In dealing with many other aspects of surname history, genealogical skills are needed. The distribution of surnames in the past, and even at the present day, owes much to the ramification of particular families (though other factors are involved too), and it is important to trace such ramifications in as much detail as the evidence permits. Many issues about the development of surnames–such as, for example, whether all the persons found with a given surname all ultimately share a common ancestry–can only be investigated by genealogical methods.

A very large and potentially valuable mass of evidence about the history of surnames, about the variant forms of names, and about the processes which lead to the proliferation and the migration of names, has been produced by investigations carried out by genealogists, family historians, and members of one name societies. Though the difficulties of assimilating the results of a multifarious, and often unpublished, body of research are formidable, less use has been made of this information in the study of surnames than should have been the case. Correspondingly, research into the history of families, or of individual surnames, has often been carried on in isolation, with usually no attempt being made to set the history of particular families, or surnames, in the context of any general view of surname evolution. It is natural for researchers to concentrate on the history of the particular family or name which is the subject of their interest, but frequently some extra understanding would be gained if what can be discovered about individual names could be seen against some more general background, just as the history of a family can often be illuminated by some knowledge of social and economic history. The lack of any general book on the development of surnames in this country has made it difficult for amateur genealogists or family historians to appreciate how the facts uncovered by their researches fit into any general trend. It is hoped that this book will enable people without any specialised knowledge to put the results of their investigations against some overall picture of the development of British surnames.

DEFINITION OF TERMS

The use of any specialised or technical vocabulary will be avoided as far as possible, but certain terms widely used in connection with surnames need to be explained.

For the purpose of discussion surnames may conveniently be divided into certain broad categories. The divisions listed below are fairly generally used in discussions about surnames, though there may be doubts as to how some individual names ought to be classified.

(a) *Locative surnames.* These are derived from the names of specific places. For instance, the surnames London, Doncaster, Pickering, Kendal, Baldock or Grantham are all locative names. Some surnames of this type can be derived from more than one place. For example, the place-names Norton, Kirby, Drayton, Ashby, and Acton all exist as the names of a fair number of different places, and where the surnames Norton, Kirby, Drayton, Ashby, or Acton are found, it may well be impossible to be sure which of the various places concerned has given rise to the surname of any particular family.

(b) *Topographical surnames.* These are surnames from terms for features of the landscape, whether natural (such as Hill, Brooks, or Marsh) or man-made (such as Fields, Styles, Mills, or Bridge). Surnames such as Fielder, Bridger, Bridgman, Hillman, or Brookman have been included here. So have names which are derived from residence near some topographical feature, such as Atchurch, Bywater, Green, Atlee, or Townsend.

(c) *Surnames derived from personal names.* These are surnames derived from 'first' or 'Christian' names. The term 'personal name' will be used throughout to mean a 'first' name. Surnames in this category include those from personal names without any modification, such as Paul, Peter, James, Donald, Llewellyn, and so on; many such surnames are from personal names which have long been generally disused in this country, so that their character is not instantly recognisable, such as Godwin, Ailwin, Allard, Parnell, or Thurkell, all of which are from personal names now either quite obsolete or very little used; the category also includes surnames from personal names with '-son' added, such as Williamson, Harrison, Parkinson, and so forth, and surnames formed from a personal name with a genitive, or possessive, '-s' added, such as Williams, Roberts, Harris, or Dix; the type further includes surnames beginning with 'Fitz' (Fitzwilliam, Fitzrobert, etc.), Scots surnames prefixed by 'Mac', and some surnames of Welsh origin, such as Probert, Pritchard, Price, and so on.

Surnames from masculine personal names are known as patronymics, and those from feminine ones as metronymics. For instance, the surnames Godwin, Peters, Ferguson, and Maddocks are patronymics, being all from masculine personal names; the surnames Maud, Maudson, Maudling (from Magdalene), Marriott (from a pet-form of Mary), Parnell (from a personal name now not generally used, and derived from the Latin Patronilla), Eve, or Margetson (from Margaret), are metronymics. Pet-forms, diminutives, and 'short' forms of personal names are known as hypochoristic names. Many surnames are derived from such forms: for example, the surnames Wilkin, Wilkins, Wilkinson, Wilcock, Wilcox, Willmot, Wilkie, Wills, and Willis are all from hypochoristic forms of the personal name William, while Parkin, Perkins, Parkinson, and Purkins are all from hypochoristic forms of the personal name Peter. Readers can no doubt think of very many other surnames from hypochoristic forms of personal names.

(d) *Occupational surnames*. These are surnames from crafts or trades, such as Cooper, Weaver, Webster, Palfreyman, Taylor, Smith, Gough or Gow. Surnames from rank or status, such as Burgess, Freeman, Yeomans, Franklin, or Squire, have been included here, and so also have surnames from offices, such as Bailliff, Reeve, or Hayward. It is in practice very difficult to draw any clear-cut distinction between these groups. Names from high positions in state or church have also been included, such as King, Earl, Bishop, Cannon, Archdeacon, Prior, Abbot, Sheriff, Baron, or Knight, since it is often not possible to be sure how they originated, though many seem to have begun as nicknames.

(e) *Surnames derived from nicknames*. These include names from obvious physical characteristics, such as Long, Black, White, Reid, Gwynn, Llwyd, Cruickshank, and so on, ones from moral character- istics, such as Malvoisin, Fairmaner, or Tiplady, ones from express- ions habitually used, such as Goodenough, Godsalve or Pardew, surnames from words for birds, fish, or mammals, such as Hawke, Fox, Steer, Bull, or Herring, and a considerable number of others too varied to be easily described briefly.

(f) *Surnames of relationship*. Names such as Cousins, Brothers, Fadder, or Ayer. This is only a small category.

There are a few surnames which do not fit into any of the above categories. There are also some surnames of which the origins are unknown, or debatable.

SURNAMES ORIGINATING OUTSIDE BRITAIN

There is a tendency among researchers into family history and genealogy to assume that any surname which does not have an obvious origin in the English language must have arisen outside

Britain. English speakers are often insufficiently aware of the possibility of surnames being derived from Gaelic, Welsh, or Cornish, though such names are nowadays liable to be encountered anywhere in Britain. There is, in particular, an inclination to connect any surname with obscure origins to alien immigrations which are widely known about by people with a good general knowledge of British history. For instance, the fact that there was an immigration into East Anglia from Flanders at times during the sixteenth century has sometimes led to suspicions that some surnames found in that region in later periods are likely to be Flemish in origin. Some families in East Anglia have traditions, passed down for several generations, that their surnames are Flemish or Dutch in origin, and while there may be some basis for such traditions in some cases, in others the surnames involved are plainly English. Similarly, it is well known that there was a considerable settlement in this country from France of Huguenots during the late seventeenth century, and this has sometimes led people engaged in tracing their own pedigrees to conjecture that their surnames might be Huguenot. In fact, the majority of inquiries made about the possible Huguenot origins of surnames concern names which are not Huguenot at all. There are a certain number of surnames in Britain today of which the origins cannot be satisfactorily explained, but it would be rash to jump to the conclusion that all of these must be foreign imports. As already explained, some surnames existed in England for long periods before appearing in written records, and during such a lapse of time surnames can undergo changes which are impossible to trace, and sometimes difficult to account for.

It is in practice not possible to distinguish between surnames originating in Britain, and those arising outside it, simply from the present-day spelling or pronunciation. Many alien surnames have been pretty thoroughly Anglicised, to the extent that they appear to be made up of English surname elements. The result is that many alien surnames are no longer recognisable as such, while on the other hand some surnames originating in Britain have at first sight a somewhat foreign look about them. For example, the surnames Beacham, Boone, Boswell, Cantellow, Dabney, Dangerfield, Lacy, Manners and Menzies, Nugent, Scarfield, Scotney, Vipond, and Vian are all from French place-names (Beauchamps and Beauchamp, Bohon, Beuzeville, Cantelu and Canteloup, Aubigny, Aungerville, Lassy, Mesnières, Nogent, Scardeville, Etocquigny, Vieux Pont, and Vienne respectively). Bruce seems to be usually from the French place-name Le Brus (Calvados), though it has become confused with other surnames with a similar sound, Brewes, Brewse, and Browse, which are from another French place-name, Briouze (Orne). Apart from the obvious cases of Fleming and Flanders, the surnames Bremner, Brabner, Brabazon, Brabson. Brabyn, and Brabham are all from terms for inhabitants of the Duchy of Brabant (in what are now Belgium and the Netherlands); Burgoyne, Burgin, Burgon, Burgan all denote people from Burgundy, Champness and Champney someone from Champagne; the surname Wasteneys, now rare but once the name of an important landowning family in the east Midlands, is from the district of Le Gatinais, south east of Paris. Some of these surnames have a very English appearance, but they are all from the names of provinces or districts outside Britain. On the other hand, Tordoff is an old-established Yorkshire surname, the surname Renville is from a Kent place-name; Baccus is a variant form of the topographical name Backhouse; Loftus is from Lofthouse, either from one of the Yorkshire places called Lofthouse or Loftus, or simply a name for somebody who had a house with a loft, Orlebar is from an English place name, Orlingbury (Northants); and Bolitho is from a place-name in Cornwall. Bonally, Wasbister, and Patullo are all surnames derived from place-names in Scotland.

It is always unsound to decide upon the origin of a surname merely from the present day form of the name, and it is unsafe to conclude, as is sometimes done, that a surname must be alien because its origins are not readily apparent, and because it has what seems to be a foreign appearance about it. Most difficulties that arise about the origins of surnames can be resolved by consulting one of the standard dictionaries of British surnames (listed in Chapter 9, 'Advice for further reading'). None of these is entirely comprehensive, and surnames may be encountered occasionally which do not occur in any of them. For most of the main European languages, dictionaries of surnames now exist, but these are not generally available in this country, even in the main public libraries, and most researchers will not find it easy to get access to them. In any case, such dictionaries do not always give surnames in the form in which they are found in this country. There are, however, some steps which can be taken to check whether surnames present in Britain are alien in origin or not.

Between the Conquest and about 1200 a considerable number of surnames from France were introduced into Britain, many of them derived from French place-names. Many of these surnames have been substantially modified in the course of time, as shown by some examples already given. Most of these names are listed in the main dictionaries of surnames. Many of these were the names of landed families, and their beginnings, pedigrees, and later history have often been the subject of extensive research. Apart from what is in the dictionaries, some further information can be obtained from L. C. Loyd, 1951, *Origins of some Anglo-Norman Families* (Harliean Society, vol. 103), which identifies many of the place-names from which French locative surnames were derived. Small numbers of people appear in Britain in the period 1066 to about 1200 with surnames or by-names originating in countries other than France, and when they have locative surnames it is often not easy to identify the place-names from which such surnames are derived. There seems to have been a constant trickle of migration into Britain between about 1200 and 1500, mostly from France and the Low Countries, with smaller numbers of migrants from Scandinavia, Germany, Italy, and the Iberian peninsula, and occasional individuals from further afield. A Henry of Constantinople, for instance, occurs in Norwich in the thirteenth century. This influx does not appear to have been very large at any time, and in general seems to have been due to individuals migrating singly or in families, rather than to the settlement in this country of large groups. Occasionally during this period groups of aliens settled in this country, such as, for example, the Germans who from the late fifteenth century onwards settled in Cumbria to work the metal mines there, and who brought a clutch of German surnames into the county. Immigration during this time had only a small effect on the body of surnames in use in Britain. In many cases, the surnames or by-names of immigrants were thoroughly Anglicised. This was sometimes done by translating aliens' surnames or by-names literally into English, something easily done with names from occupations, from topographical terms, or from the more obvious physical characteristics. Many immigrants are likely to have been without hereditary surnames, and perhaps even without any settled by-names, and to have acquired names after arriving in this country.

The result is that many aliens who entered this country during the Middle Ages appear with names which seem to be wholly English. So far as England is concerned, there are various means which give a view of the names used by foreigners in the country during the period under discussion. In the fifteenth century aliens resident in England were taxed at a higher rate than the king's natural born subjects, and separate assessments were made of foreigners for taxation purposes. The taxation assessments of foreigners, usually referred to as the 'alien subsidies', are preserved in the Public Record Office, though the surviving records are not altogether complete. It is a pity that very little of this material has been printed, as it would be a good deal of use to genealogists. As might be expected, many aliens evaded taxation, so that the alien subsidies do not provide a complete list of all the foreigners resident in the country at any date. At this period, Scotsmen ranked as foreigners in England, whereas Welshmen and Irishmen did not. They do, however, supply much evidence about both the names of aliens, and their places of residence, for normally the township where each foreigner resided is noted.

The alien subsidies show foreigners living dispersed throughout the country, with many in villages, often singly or in twos and threes, and without their being confined to ports and the main cities. They also show that many aliens had surnames or by-names indistinguishable from English ones. Many had English occupational names (perhaps translated from names in other languages, or perhaps reflecting the trades actually being pursued by aliens). Some, more surprisingly, had names derived from English place-names. These had probably in most cases been acquired after arrival in England, though in some instances foreign names may have been transmuted into English locative names with a somewhat similar sound.

A certain amount of further information about aliens' names during the Middle Ages can be obtained from other sources preserved in the Public Record Office, especially the Patent Rolls. No process of exactly the same character as naturalisation existed during the Middle Ages, or later in the sixteenth century, but it was possible for a foreigner permanently resident in England to obtain 'letters of denisation', which put him in the same position as a native Englishman for some purposes. Copies of such letters were entered up on the Patent Rolls, which are preserved in the Public Record Office. A search through the manuscript Patent Rolls would be burdensome, but most of the essential information can be found in the printed *Calendars of Patent Rolls*, issued by the Public Record Office, and to be found in most major public libraries. (Rather confusingly, the Patent Rolls for Henry VIII's reign are not printed in the normal series of calendars, but are included in another series of printed volumes issued by the Public Record Office, *Calendars of the Letters and Papers, Foreign and Domestic, Relating to the Reign of Henry VIII.*) Letters of denisation frequently give the birthplace, or less often the province, of aliens to whom such letters were issued. If people tracing pedigrees discover that some ancestor, in, say, the sixteenth century, seems likely to have been a foreigner who settled in England, it will generally be worthwhile to check whether any useful information can be discovered from the Patent Rolls.

Some further information about aliens and their names is scattered about the Patent Rolls. For instance, in 1436 the Crown required all men resident in England who were natives of the duke of Burgundy's dominions, which included most of what is now the Netherlands and Belgium and parts of France, to take an oath of fealty to the king, and a list of those who took the oath is preserved on the Patent Roll for 1436[1]. In most cases the county in which each of the Burgundians was resident is given in the list, which does provide a useful view of the surnames or by-names used at the time by one important group of aliens in England.

Some Tudor taxation returns, mostly those for the reign of Henry VIII, do note that some taxpayers were foreigners. Unfortunately this does not seem to have been done in any systematic or complete manner, and in any case it only gives information about those foreigners, probably a minority, who were sufficiently well off to pay direct taxes.

The late sixteenth century saw the arrival, mostly in London and the south-coast ports of large numbers of people fleeing from the wars of religion in France. Many of these refugees only lived in England for short periods, and returned to France when conditions improved, so that the impact of these movements on the body of surnames in use in Britain was less than might be supposed from the numbers of people involved. Some separate congregations of French Protestants came into existence at places where there were sizable numbers of French refugees, such as at Rye in Sussex, but little seems to have survived of any records kept by such bodies. Some French families did, however, establish themselves in this country during this period: for example, the Bongard family, who became involved in the Sussex glass industry, and whose surname, in the form Bunger, survived in that county for many years. There were other immigrations of aliens during the sixteenth century, including the settlement of considerable numbers of Flemings, mostly engaged in the textile industry, in London, Essex, and East Anglia – movement which brought some new surnames into eastern England. Some other immigrations of aliens took place during the sixteenth century, such as the further settlement of German miners in Cumbria, and some of these movements led to batches of foreign surnames appearing in certain areas.

When immigrants entered the country in the period before 1500 their surnames, if they had any, were very frequently Anglicised to such an extent that, as already described, they are not easily recognised as foreign. This was much less the case for names brought into the country after about 1500. Some aliens who settled in Britain from the sixteenth century onwards adopted English surnames which had no connection with the names which they had previously used, and some alien names were fairly easily altered by minor changes in spelling and pronunciation into English forms, but from about 1500 many foreign surnames introduced into this country survived there without substantial change.

Many subsequent migrations have of course taken place, from those in the sixteenth century to the large flow into Britain of Asians and West Indians after 1945. Some of these movements are well known, like the Huguenot immigration from France in the late seventeenth century, or the settlement of Jewish families from the continent of Europe during the nineteenth century. Both these migrations led to the permanent settlement of a good many families in Britain, and to the presence here of a number of new surnames. Much information about Huguenot families and their names can be found in the publications of the Huguenot Society, which has issued a long series of volumes containing a great deal of valuable evidence. People who suspect that their families may have Huguenot origins should start by consulting this printed material. In some places where Huguenot communities of some size came into existence separate Huguenot churches were established which kept their own registers, and these provide much useful information. Compilers of pedigrees and family histories seem inclined to suspect Huguenot origins without at times much justification, perhaps because the migration of Protestants from France is something generally well known, and it is desirable to at least check the available printed material before coming to any conclusions about origins.[2]

For the nineteenth century much information can be obtained from the original census returns from 1851 onwards, though this may require a good deal of searching through a type of record which is very voluminous. Many local record offices hold microfilms of the 1851 census returns. Indices of the surnames in the 1851 and later censuses have been printed for some counties, and the increasing quantity of such indices being published will greatly ease the task of using the census material, as census returns usually give the place of birth of each person listed, and something can be discovered about people who migrated into this country during the nineteenth century.

One very large group of surnames which originated outside Great Britain, but which are now to be found in almost all parts of the country, and often in considerable numbers, are of course Irish ones. Very few Gaelic names from Ireland can be found in either Wales or

England before about 1500. (One feature of mediaeval taxation records, or other sources which list large numbers of surnames for England and Wales during the Middle Ages, or even during the Tudor period, is the scarcity, or often the total absence, of any surnames beginning with Mac. A glance through the index to almost any printed edition of such sources will demonstrate this, and it is a pointer to the rarity of Gaelic surnames from either Scotland or Ireland in England and Wales.) Those inhabitants of Ireland who appear in England or Wales before about 1500 have mostly French, English, or Welsh surnames or by-names, and were presumably the descendants of settlers in Ireland. A few people appear with names derived from places in Ireland, mostly ports on the east coast. It is likely that these were by-names acquired after arrival in Britain. The surnames or by-names Irish and Ireland were widespread in England from the thirteenth century onwards, though not very common in any region, so that migrants from Ireland cannot have been scarce in England, but very few Gaelic surnames from Ireland can be found. It must be assumed that many Irish migrants to Britain during the period to 1500 gave up any Gaelic names they may have had, and acquired English or Anglicised ones.

The Gaelic language was of course first brought to Scotland through the migration of Scots from Ireland into western Scotland. Because of this it is difficult in some instances to distinguish between Irish surnames and those originating in the Gaelic-speaking parts of Scotland. Some surnames have possibly arisen separately in both countries, and dividing Scots and Irish names is made more difficult by the fact that Gaelic surnames, wherever they originate, often underwent sharp changes in spelling and pronunciation after migrating into English-speaking areas. In the circumstances it is difficult to form any accurate idea about the scale of any influx of Irish names into Scotland in the period between about 1100 and 1500, a time when in England, and in the Scots-speaking parts of Scotland, hereditary surnames were evolving. Even at later periods it is not always possible to separate Scots surnames and those brought into Britain from Ireland. However, there does not seem to have been any great flow of names from Ireland into Scotland in the period under discussion.

As far as England and Wales are concerned, there was no really large-scale migration of Gaelic surnames from Ireland between about 1500 and 1700. In Lancashire there is a notable scarcity during that time of Gaelic surnames from either Scotland or Ireland, though the county is easily accessible from Ireland, with which regular trade was carried on through such ports as Liverpool and Preston, and though Lancashire was later to be an area which received many Irish migrants. The county, too, is not very far from the Scottish border. Before 1700 there does not seem to have been any large inflow of Gaelic surnames, either from Scotland or Ireland, into England or Wales. Most Irishmen who appear in England during the sixteenth and seventeenth centuries, and even during much of the eighteenth, did not have Gaelic surnames, but had surnames which, though sometimes long established in Ireland, were linguistically in origin French, English, or rather less frequently, Welsh.

In the eighteenth century, and especially in the later years of that century, Irish surnames tended to become considerably more numerous in Britain, and during the nineteenth century some parts of Britain, such as south Lancashire or the Clydeside area of Scotland, experienced large-scale settlement from Ireland, which brought in large numbers of new surnames. At the same time, surnames from the Gaelic-speaking areas of Scotland were spreading in increasing numbers into other parts of Scotland, and into England and Wales. As a result of these movements some Gaelic surnames were substantially altered by being Anglicised in various ways, a process about which something is said later in the book. Surnames of Irish and Scots origin are now widely distributed in almost all parts of Britain. A look through any source of information, such as a telephone directory or electoral register, which lists large numbers of the inhabitants of, for example, the resorts on the south coast of England, will reveal the presence of many people with Scots and Irish surnames, and this is not a new phenomenon in such places, though they were not the recipients of large scale migration direct from either Scotland or Ireland in the nineteenth century. Most Irish surnames can be found in the reference works given in the 'Advice on further reading' at the end of the book (Chapter 9). Where many surnames are concerned the same reference works give some information about the parts of Ireland where surnames originated. If the appropriate dictionaries or Irish and Scots surnames are consulted, it will usually be possible to separate Scots names from Irish ones. It must, however, be remembered that there have been complex moves between the two countries over the centuries. There was a significant migration of Scotsmen, mostly from the south west of the country, into the north of Ireland in the seventeenth century. Many surnames from various parts of Ireland became established in some areas of Scotland during the nineteenth century. Such migrations, and the fact that surnames have undergone modifications in the course of time, may mean that establishing the origins of some surnames presents difficulties.

REGIONAL DIFFERENCES IN THE CHARACTER OF SURNAMES

It is impossible to examine the surnames present in several counties, from different parts of England, without being struck by the very sizable differences which existed in the Middle Ages, and which in large measure persisted into later periods, between the different English regions (leaving aside for the moment Wales and Scotland). Thirteenth- and fourteenth-century sources show that there were then marked differences between the English regions in the proportions of surnames and by-names falling into each of the main categories, so that, for example, some areas, such as Yorkshire or Cornwall, had an exceptionally high proportion of surnames derived from place-names, while the south east of England had an exceptionally large body of surnames from topographical terms. There were also major differences in, for instance, the vocabulary used for occupational or topographical surnames or by-names. Sixteenth- and seventeenth-century sources show that such regional, or county, characteristics persisted, with only slight modifications, into the early modern period, and despite all the migrations and social and economic changes of the last two hundred years, significant traces of such differences can still be found in the distribution of surnames in many parts of England at the present day. It is not easy to demonstrate the differences between counties and regions by any method which is statistically sound, and which at the same time brings out in a clear way what the differences were. One method is to calculate the proportion of names falling into each major category, given in a selection of sources. For this purpose it is obviously better to choose source material such as taxation returns, which list a substantial part of the inhabitants in various counties. There are disadvantages in this method: no such sources list absolutely all the inhabitants of any county at any single date; the proportion of the population given is liable to vary from one source to another; it is hardly ever possible to find any source which covers the whole of England on a uniform basis, and taxation records, in particular, tend to omit the poorer sections of the community, whose names are badly documented generally; many sources, such as the mediaeval 'lay subsidy' rolls, have sections which are illegible, or the returns for a few places are missing. Most of the sources which might be used for such a purpose have their limitations. The Protestation Returns for 1641–42, for example, which ought to list all the adult male inhabitants of England at that date and which, in practice, do provide a very full list of the surnames then in use, are unfortunately lacking for many counties or parts of counties.

Despite all these drawbacks, the method remains the best available for showing the main differences between counties or regions where surnames are concerned, and it has been employed for Table 1 which shows the essential points of difference between a selection of counties.

It should of course be added that apart from the broad distinctions between regions of the kind under discussion here, there were, and even today to some extent still are, other more detailed differences between the surnames to be found in each county. Some remarks are made about this in discussing the various main categories of surnames. Various factors, including the vocabulary and phonetics of local dialect, the pattern of human settlement in each area, and local habits or fashions in the formation of surnames, have all played their part in creating a characteristic body of surnames in each region, which in spite of great alterations in society still survive to some extent, more completely in some regions than in others. Even today, there are certain surnames which are generally thought of as being particularly characteristic of, say, the north of England, or the south west. Many of the characters who appear in the television series 'Coronation Street', for example, have surnames which many viewers would regard as being typical of Lancashire, and indeed many of them are old Lancashire surnames, often derived from places in the south of the county.

The purpose of Table 1 is to show the differences between the English regions, where surnames in each of the main categories are concerned, at two different periods. Statistics are given for a selection of counties, distributed through the various parts of England. It is not possible to give similar figures for all counties at any one date, because of gaps in the source material. The statistics are based on taxation returns and similar sources, which list large numbers of the inhabitants of each county concerned. Many of the records used to provide evidence for the table are available in printed editions, but in order to fill gaps in the printed material it has been necessary to use manuscript sources in the Public Record Office. The circumstances in both Wales and Scotland are substantially different from those in

England, so that it is difficult to make meaningful comparisons with English counties. None of the sources used covers the whole population of the counties concerned, but the figures given do provide a reasonably accurate view of the differences between regions.

The table gives, for each county dealt with, the percentages of people with surnames or by-names falling into each of the main categories, at the dates as shown, and in the sources used. The figures are for percentages of individual persons, listed in each source, and not for percentages of the names occurring there (so that if, for example, ten persons all named Brown are listed, this will be counted ten times, and not just once). The table is divided into numbered columns, each giving the figures for the names in one principal category. The way in which surnames are divided into categories for the purposes of this book has already been explained. The categories represented in the columns are:

1. Locative names
2. Topographical names
3. Surnames and by-names from personal names
4. Occupational names
5. Surnames and by-names from nicknames
6. Names in other categories, or of uncertain origin

Figures are given for a selection of counties, for two periods. The first set of figures is drawn from fourteenth-century sources, and shows what the position was in the counties concerned at a time when most names had either been hereditary but for a short time, or were not hereditary at all. The second set of figures are from sixteenth- and seventeenth-century sources, and show what the position was at a period when the evolution of hereditary surnames in England was virtually complete, but before the shifts of population caused by the Industrial Revolution.

NOTES AND REFERENCES

1. Public Record Office, *Calendar of Patent Rolls, 1429–36*, pp. 537–9, 541–88.
2. For guidance on sources for Huguenot ancestry, see N. Currer-Briggs, and R. Gambier, 1985, *Huguenot Ancestry*, Phillimore.

Table 1

County	1	2	3	4	5	6
Buckinghamshire, 1332	24	14	24	21	7	10
Devon, 1332	28	15	14	22	12	9
Dorset, 1327	15	16	19	21	16	12
Gloucestershire, 1327	32	12	24	16	13	3
Kent, 1334–5	27	15	22	19	11	6
Lancashire, 1332	52	15	3	15	6	7
Leicestershire, 1327	27	17	21	10	10	18
Oxfordshire, 1327	21	7	24	23	9	14
Shropshire, 1327	40	9	23	5	16	7
Staffordshire, 1327	30	15	17	18	7	13
Suffolk, 1327	15	11	30	23	5	15
Surrey, 1332	27	18	14	24	9	8
Sussex, 1332	23	26	15	18	12	6
Warwickshire, 1332	30	11	21	23	8	9
Worcestershire, 1327	19	11	31	14	12	13
Yorkshire, 1379	29	3	13	24	8	23
Buckinghamshire, 1524	23	7	33	21	5	11
Cornwall, 1664	19	12	37	14	12	5
Devon, 1524–25	20	18	27	17	12	6
Gloucestershire, 1608	20	14	21	28	11	6
Lancashire,						
Salford Hundred, 1524	59	11	11	13	2	4
Nottinghamshire, 1641–42	28	13	31	16	9	3
Oxfordshire, 1641–42	22	13	32	22	8	3
Rutland, 1522	28	9	26	22	12	3
Shropshire, 1672	21	13	42	11	9	3
Staffordshire, 1666	29	12	25	21	6	7
Suffolk, 1524	14	7	30	30	3	16
Surrey, 1664	22	11	20	26	4	17
Sussex, 1524–25	17	15	27	23	4	14
Worcestershire, 1603	29	15	29	17	10	3

CHAPTER ONE
The evolution of hereditary surnames

BEGINNINGS OF HEREDITARY SURNAMES IN ENGLAND

The system of hereditary surnames prevailing today in Britain, in Western Europe generally, and in many other parts of the world, is so familiar, so convenient, and so long established that few people ever give any thought to how or when it arose, or what forces and impulses gave rise to it in the first place. In fact the development of hereditary surnames in this country was a prolonged and complex business, not operating uniformly over the whole of Britain, but subject to marked regional variations and to differences between one social class and another, and propelled into existence by a variety of forces, some of which are not easy to perceive.

As far as can be seen from the very incomplete evidence about the names of the population during the Anglo-Saxon period, stable hereditary surnames, descending over a large number of generations, were not then present in England. There do seem to have been instances where what began as non-hereditary nicknames or by-names eventually descended from father to son, and this might have led to the evolution of hereditary surnames in the course of time, even if the Norman Conquest had not taken place. At the time of the Conquest some of the more important and wealthier noble families in Normandy already possessed hereditary surnames. The evidence for the state of affairs in Normandy before 1066 is not very copious, but hereditary surnames were evidently at that time a relatively new phenomenon, extending back for no more than one or two generations before 1066. It also seems that they were confined to the upper reaches of the landowning class, and that even in that section of society they were by no means universal. Roger de Montgomery, for example, one of the most important landholders in Normandy in 1066 and subsequently a great feudatory in England, had a by-name which does not seem to have been hereditary, though there is some evidence about his father, an earlier Roger. Roger de Montgomery had at least five sons, two of whom are known to have used the name de Montgomery (which in their cases might be reckoned a hereditary surname), while the remaining three used three different by-names, not inherited from their father. This important noble family lacked a surname at the time of the Conquest, or even later. The counts of Eu and Mortain were major landholders, related to the ducal house of Normandy, but both seem to have been known by their titles, and to have lacked surnames, in 1066 and later. The counts of Meulan, landholders in Normandy before the Conquest, later important tenants-in-chief in England, and earls of Leicester, lacked a hereditary surname at the time of the Conquest, and remained without one all through the twelfth century. (The earls of Leicester are sometimes referred to by historians as the Beaumont family; the name de Beaumont was used by Robert, the first earl of Leicester, and it may have been used by his father, who was also the lord of Beaumont, so that to an extent the name was hereditary, but the second, third, and fourth earls all used other by-names.) Other examples could be given of Norman landholders being without surnames at the time of the Conquest. A further indication of the infrequency of surnames among the Norman nobility at the time of the Conquest is the widespread tendency after 1066 for Normans holding land in England to adopt by-names derived from the names of places on their newly-acquired English estates. There is much evidence of this from the names of tenants listed in Domesday Book, and it concerns tenants at various levels. For example, Robert de Stafford, a major tenant-in-chief with large holdings in Staffordshire and elsewhere, is styled de Stafford in Domesday. He had a by-name derived from a place on his English lands, probably his most important residence. He was a son of Roger de Toeni and had obviously not inherited his name, though it was inherited from him by his son, and became the hereditary surname of a leading aristocratic family. At a lower level, subtenants of Norman origin can be found in 1086 with by-names from English place-names. For instance, in Sussex, two of the subtenants listed in Domesday were Robert de Hasting and Robert de Olecumbe, with by-names from Hastings (Sussex) and Ulcombe (Kent), respectively. Clearly these names were not existing hereditary ones brought in from Normandy, but by-names acquired after the Conquest. Domesday records many similar cases of tenants who, judging from their personal names and other evidence, were from Normandy or elsewhere in France, and who had by 1086, twenty years after Hastings, already adopted by-names from places in England, by-names which were in some cases transmitted to their descendants, and became hereditary surnames. The tendency for landholders to have by-names or surnames from the names of places where they held property should be noted.

Despite this evidence, which shows that many of William I's followers who obtained land in England plainly did not have hereditary surnames, there is evidence that by 1066 some noble families in Normandy had surnames which had descended hereditarily for a generation or two. William de Warenne, for instance, a large tenant-in-chief with lands in Sussex, Surrey, Yorkshire, and Norfolk, and the founder of a family long important in English history, was the son of Rodolfus de Warenne; the name is from a small settlement, Warenne (Seine-Maritime). This is one source of the surname Warren, though it has other origins as well. Henry de Fereires, a tenant-in-chief in Derbyshire, Staffordshire, and elsewhere, was the son of Walkelin de Fereires; the surname was transmitted to Henry's descendants, who were major landowners in England for the next two centuries and are traceable in this country to a later date. The present surname Ferrers is from one or other of the French places called Ferrières. Walter Giffard, a tenant-in-chief in the south Midlands, had inherited his name from his father. Giffard, a surname which still survives, is from a nickname, with the meaning 'fat cheeks', and is one of several surnames or by-names of the nickname type found among landholding families of Norman origin in England after the Conquest. William de Aubigny, who acquired lands in Norfolk at a rather later date, probably under William II, and later became earl of Arundel, had a father and grandfather named de Aubigny, and had a surname traceable to the early or middle eleventh century. William's surname was from St Martin d'Aubigny (La Manche); the present day surname which occurs as Daubeney, Dabney, Dobney, and so on is from one of the several places in France named Aubigny, not necessarily the one just mentioned. There are a fair number of other examples of landholders from Normandy, holding land in England by 1086, or at a slightly later period, who possessed surnames which had been hereditary for a generation or two.

These instances nearly all concern really large landowners, who were of course the section of the community for whom there is the most information. If there was more evidence about the names of lesser landholders, like many of the Domesday subtenants, it might reveal the presence of hereditary surnames in moderate numbers among them too, but this is very uncertain. In fact, very few Domesday subtenants had surnames or by-names which were borne later by people certainly identifiable as their descendants. It seems clear that only a minority of Norman landholders had hereditary names at the time of the Conquest, and that where hereditary names existed, they had only been hereditary for, usually, a generation or two by 1066.

On this strictly limited scale, hereditary surnames were imported from France into England after 1066. In the two centuries or so after the Conquest, hereditary names were acquired by most families of major landholders, and by many landed families of lesser import- ance. The great landholding families are usually well documented, and there is generally no difficulty in discovering what the position is as regards their surnames. Many major landholding families acquired hereditary surnames between the time of Domesday, and about 1200. In some cases, as already mentioned, Domesday tenants-in-chief transmitted their by-names to their descendants, who used them as hereditary surnames. By about 1250 the great majority of great landholding families had hereditary surnames, though there were exceptions, like the FitzWalter family, who were important landhol- ders in Essex and East Anglia, but who did not possess a hereditary surname until the early fourteenth century. As far as this social group was concerned, there appear to have been no differences in the adoption of hereditary surnames between one region of England and another, and in fact the position in Scotland was not very different from that in England. This is what would be expected, for the great landholders formed a single social class across the whole country, often intermarrying; many major landholders had estates in several different regions, and some had lands in both England and Scotland. Marked regional differences are not to be expected in such circumstances.

Below the really great landowners, who were roughly the group who would later constitute the peerage, lay the much larger and considerably more varied class of knights and other landholders of moderate wealth (forming the class which would later be called the gentry). The wealth of individual families in this class varied considerably, ranging from those which held a single manor, or even just part of one, to the holders of estates which were similar in size and value to those of the less wealthy barons. The early development of hereditary names in this class is not easy to trace. Evidence for the period between the time of Domesday and about 1150 is for many such families very incomplete. When fuller information becomes available from about 1150 onwards, it can be seen that some families have histories for the period 1100 to about 1150 which can be discovered fairly fully, but this applies to a minority of such families. Some landed families had descents from subtenants mentioned in Domesday, but the number of cases where this can be satisfactorily proved is not very great, taking England as a whole. Many landed families which can be found during about 1150 to 1200 have no antecedents which can be discovered, and may well not have been descended from Domesday subtenants. Many instances can be found of landed families at this level who had acquired hereditary surnames by about 1200, but it is not easy to say with precision what proportion of families in this class had hereditary names by any particular date.

Some evidence about the circumstances of particular groups of knightly families can be put forward. Among the tenants by knight service of the Honour of Wallingford, a large group of estates in the south Midlands, nearly four-fifths of the families had acquired hereditary names by 1200[1]. The position among the remaining one fifth is in some cases uncertain; only a small minority were still without hereditary surnames by 1200. Turning to another part of England, there is some information from a document which lists most of the major landholders in Lancashire in 1212. Out of these, more than a third certainly had hereditary surnames by 1212. This is something of a minimum figure, since the position about the remaining two-thirds is uncertain in some instances.[2]

Evidence such as this, and an investigation into the names of many individual families, suggests that in the south of England, the Midlands, and East Anglia, many knightly families had acquired hereditary names by about 1200, and that by about 1250 the great majority of such families had hereditary names. In the north of England the development was perhaps slightly later. The evolution of hereditary names was not a uniform or regular process, and there were exceptions; some English knightly families were still without surnames in the fourteenth century.

It does, however, seem that by the middle thirteenth century a majority of large and medium landowners in England had acquired hereditary surnames. As is apt to be the case where surnames are concerned, it is easier to observe the developments that took place, than to explain why they happened. Some considerations which influenced landholders into adopting surnames can be detected. A look at any of the lists of feudal landholders compiled by the Exchequer and Chancery during the twelfth and thirteenth centuries will show that, of those listed with surnames or by-names, a high proportion have names derived from place-names. In Scotland, the list of those who did homage to Edward I in 1296 (the 'Ragman Roll'), is notable for the high proportion of persons with locative names.[3] Most of these people were landholders, though some were burgesses, and the status of others is not known. It was extremely common for a landholding family to possess a surname which was derived from a place-name, usually from a place which was the family's main residence, or which was the most important part of its estates. (Indeed, the chief characteristic which distinguishes the surnames of landholders at an early period from those of other classes is just that landholders tended to have a much larger proportion of surnames derived from place-names than did any other section or the community.) There is obviously a fairly direct connection between the possession of a hereditary surname of this kind, and the possession of a hereditary landed estate. For about a century or so after the Conquest, there was possibly a degree of uncertainty about the position of landholders who held from the king. William I had made many large grants of lands, and many landholders in the period after the Conquest were the heirs, or the successors in title, of the recipients of his grants. How far his grants were grants of property in fee and inheritance was perhaps not clear. In these circumstances, anything which helped to stress the hereditary character of tenure was likely to be viewed with favour by landowners, and the acquisition of a hereditary surname, especially one derived from a landed family's estates, would obviously have this effect. It would seem that this must have been one reason, perhaps the principal one, for landholding families adopting hereditary surnames. It was part of a general trend for them to consolidate their position as hereditary property owners.

The close connection between hereditary surnames and hereditary land ownership by primogeniture can be seen further from the way in which, in some families, the senior line of a family continued to use a hereditary surname, while junior branches, not of course possessing the main family estate, began at various periods to use new surnames. This practice was fairly common in the twelfth and thirteenth centuries, and is sometimes found later. To mention two examples, the de Trafford family of Trafford (now part of Manchester), had a hereditary surname from the twelfth century, derived of course from the place which was the centre of their estate. In the late thirteenth century, by which time the family's name was well established, Sir Richard de Trafford gave lands at Chadderton, in south Lancashire (now in Greater Manchester) to a younger son, who assumed the name of de Chadderton, a surname which his descendants, owners of land at Chadderton, continued to employ, as a hereditary surname. The elder branch of the family continued to use the surname of de Trafford. Similarly in Sussex, in the late twelfth and early thirteenth centuries, land at Socknersh (near Brightling) came into the hands of younger sons of William de St. Leger, who had a hereditary surname by then in use for several generations and derived from a locality in France where the family had held land; a younger branch of the de St. Leger family then adopted the name of de Sokenerse, which descended in that line of the family as a hereditary surname, while the senior line continued to use the name of de St Leger. Researchers who push their investigations back into the Middle Ages will have to reckon with the fact that landed families with settled hereditary surnames sometimes threw out younger branches which chose entirely new names.

There was an obvious link between the possession of hereditary surnames by landed families and their possession of hereditary estates, descending for the most part by primogeniture, but beyond this little can be said about the motives which led such families to acquire and retain surnames. It does not appear that the possession of a hereditary name was at any time a mark of high status, even though the habit of using such names began with the larger landowners. Something may be due to influences from France, where landowners were acquiring hereditary names at much the same time as those in England, or perhaps rather earlier. A good many landholders in England still had property in France, mostly in Normandy, during the twelfth century, and must have been aware of what the trends in France were. A parallel can be seen in the spread of coats of arms, which were hereditary, from France to England in the twelfth century.

Landholding families were, generally speaking, the best documented part of the population during the Middle Ages, and there is a good deal of evidence about their surnames and by-names, even if at points the evidence is not as full as might be wished. It is much more difficult to see what is happening among other social classes, for whose names there is much less evidence, especially during the two centuries or so after the Conquest. It would seem that in the south of England and East Anglia, very few families, apart from substantial landholders, had hereditary surnames before about 1150. Between about 1150 and 1250 instances where families outside the ranks of sizable landholders had hereditary surnames begin to appear, but remained few. Between about 1250 and 1350, many families belonging to various classes acquired surnames. It is not possible to give precise statistics, but it is likely that, in the regions in question, rather more than half the population had surnames by about 1350. The late fourteenth-century poll tax returns, which give a more complete view of the names then in use than any other source for the same period, show that about 1380 there were still numbers of people without any surnames or by-names at all. By the early fifteenth century, however, it seems to have been unusual in these regions not to have a surname. In the north of England, developments occurred about a century later than in the south and Midlands. Wales and Scotland each had their own course of development.

Something can be said in rather more detail about the growth of hereditary names among some sections of the population, but it is worth considering how and why families-came to have surnames. It has sometimes been suggested that names were given to people by officials, such as the clerks who drew up manor court rolls and other manorial records such as rentals, or by the taxers who drew up the lists of taxpayers assessed for the lay subsidies, but there is little evidence for this. It is true that the keeping of written records increased noticeably during the thirteenth century, so that the ordinary man was much more likely to have his name put down in writing in 1300 than in 1200, and it is true that the use of written title deeds increased during the same period, which would affect small freeholders (a considerable part of the population in most areas), and might have led to clerks who drew up deeds bestowing by-names on parties to property transactions for the sake of legal precision, and to prevent confusion between individuals with the same first name. Certainly by 1300 direct taxation was reaching a long way down into society, and title deeds were coming to be used even for small pieces of property. It might be supposed that the increased use of documents for one purpose or another, and the tendency for all classes of society except the very poor to appear in written records, would make it convenient for most people to have permanent by-names, if not hereditary surnames, but there is little sign of this being the case. Many persons appear in thirteenth- and fourteenth-century documents, such as tax assessments, without any surnames or by-names at all, often listed as simply the son of some person (in the usual formula, 'John son of William', and so forth). This persisted over a long period, and there is no indication that it caused any practical difficulties.

Furthermore, the whole nature of many surnames and by-names which can be found during the thirteenth and fourteenth centuries tells against the theory that they were often allocated by officials. Most surnames or by-names found at those periods do not seem to be of the kind likely to be allotted by an official, even by some local clerk with a personal knowledge of those involved. Many surnames seem likely to have begun as by-names used in speech, which developed into hereditary surnames. One large category of surnames, for instance, are those derived from personal (or first) names (these are dealt with in Chapter 4). In many cases such names are derived from diminutives or pet forms of personal names. Such forms are rarely found in mediaeval documents, which are mostly of an administrative or legal nature, where such familiar and informal variations would not be expected. The surnames in question were obviously from diminutives or pet-forms which were used verbally. No doubt such surnames began as by-names used in speech. Similarly many surnames which originated at this time are ones of the nickname type. Some of these are derived from oaths or ejaculations. Presumably some individuals had expressions which they habitually used, so much so that the phrases concerned were applied to them, in the first instance as by-names. Some such names, such as Godshalf or Godsmark, or names from French phrases such as Wardew, Parfoy, or Pardew, have survived as surnames to the present day. Many others, such as Parmoncorps or Godemefecche, have not survived. The relatively common name Goodenough probably belongs to this group. Again, there are many surnames (and many by-names which have not survived), which refer to philandering, such as Toplady and Tiplady, Toplass (and Topliss which is a form of the same name), Shakelady, Fullielove, Paramore (from 'paramour'), Sweetlove, Spendlove, and some others of which the origin is now less obvious, for example Lemon ('lover, sweetheart'), or Blandamer, from the Old French *Pleyn d'amour*, a name with the same significance as Fullielove. There were also in the Middle Ages a fair number of by-names, then in use but not now surviving, which were definitely obscene. It is difficult to believe that names such as these were originally bestowed by clerks, taxers, and so forth for convenience of reference. Mediaeval clerks were at times capable of inventing facetious or whimsical names, as can be seen from some of the names which were given for fictitious characters such as pledges in court rolls (often given in rhyming pairs, like John Doe and Richard Roe), but surnames of the kind just discussed seem likely to have begun as by-names used verbally, which subsequently developed into hereditary surnames.

It seems probable, therefore, that most of the population had surnames which began as by-names, used at first in speech. no doubt in a purely informal way, and which eventually stabilised and developed into hereditary surnames. Many by-names, of course, never developed into hereditary surnames, including, no doubt, many which were used in a casual, short-lived fashion. In the period 1250 to 1350, in particular, when many families were first acquiring hereditary surnames, and when there is enough evidence to give a fairly good view of the name in use, many by-names existed which never developed into surnames. During this period individuals were sometimes known in the course of a lifetime by two or three different by-names. It is, however, not at all easy to explain why people adopted hereditary surnames, or perhaps had surnames bestowed on them by their neighbours. Imitation of the landowning classes may have been a factor. To people like small freeholders, who possessed property which descended hereditarily, it may have seemed that the possession of a hereditary name strengthened and made more secure the continuity of the family's holding from generation to generation. Between about 1150 and 1300 the number of male first names in general use was declining sharply (a development discussed in Chapter 4), while a few male first names were becoming extremely common. In consequence, the personal names in use were becoming less distinctive, and it may have seemed desirable to have the additional mark of individual identity conferred by a surname. While all these factors may have operated to some degree, they hardly seem adequate to account for such a widespread phenomenon as the general adoption of surnames, even allowing for the fact that the process was spread over several centuries. It would seem that in the course of the thirteenth and fourteenth centuries large proportions of the population acquired hereditary surnames, but it is not easy to see what the basic forces behind this development were. Some weight ought no doubt to be given to the forces in any community which make for conformity. Once the more prestigious and influential members of any group had surnames, there would be a tendency for others to follow the example thus set.

The evidence from original sources gives a good deal of information about the surnames people had, but tells us very little about why particular names were first adopted. It is generally impossible to say why, for instance, a man living about 1300 who was a blacksmith, who had a father called William, and who walked with a limp, came to be called Smith, rather than Williamson or Crookshank. How many nickname-type surnames came to be bestowed is often quite undiscoverable. It is also the case that while the wealthier landed families are usually well documented, this is much less the case for other sections of the population. However, despite these difficulties, something can be said about the evolution of surnames among some portions of the English population.

HEREDITARY SURNAMES OF TOWNSPEOPLE

Some hereditary names can be found among the more affluent parts of the London population during the second half of the twelfth century. It is probable that at this period the wealthier merchants may have been influenced by their contacts with aristocratic families already using hereditary names, and possibly by the knowledge that surnames were in use by some classes in France. During about 1200 to 1250 there were families with hereditary names in most of the larger provincial towns and cities, usually families of some wealth. Even in that section of the urban population, hereditary names were by no means universal, and in the late thirteenth century many of the more substantial citizens and burgesses were still without surnames. In fact, it was still not unusual at that time for townspeople to be without by-names of any kind. Many inhabitants of towns and cities seem to have acquired surnames in the period from about 1300 to 1350. The late fourteenth century poll tax returns show very few inhabitants of such places without any surnames or by-names at all. There was, however, a sizable element in the urban population which very largely escaped being recorded. The names of the richer and more prominent inhabitants can be found in property deeds and in the names of holders of municipal offices, and the names of many middling people can be found in the lists of persons admitted to the freedom of cities and boroughs, but there are few records of those who were too poor to own property, to pay direct taxes, or to be admitted to the freedom. It is difficult to say what the position may have been about the names of unskilled labourers in towns. It can only be said that by the fifteenth century most townspeople who occur in extant records seem to have had hereditary surnames. There were certainly some exceptions to this. Even in the fifteenth century, examples can be found in most boroughs and cities of men with by-names which were not the same as their fathers' surnames or by-names. In York, there still seem to have been many people without hereditary names in the sixteenth century. This was probably exceptional at that period, though hereditary names developed later in the north of England than in other regions. Detailed studies of the surnames and by-names in many English towns have still to be made, and it is probable that such studies would reveal considerable local variation in the ways in which hereditary surnames evolved in towns. However, the great majority of the urban population appear to have hereditary names by 1500.

HEREDITARY NAMES OF SMALL FREE TENANTS

Small free tenants were an important section of the rural population in England, though forming a larger proportion of the inhabitants of some regions than of others. The evidence, though not very copious, suggests that during the eleventh and twelfth centuries most small free tenants did not have surnames or stable by-names. A moderate number of examples can be found in the period from about 1170 to 1250 where families of small freehold tenants had surnames. In the south of England, the Midlands, and East Anglia, such instances become more common in 1250 to 1350, and although it is difficult to obtain any general view of the position, as distinct from noting individual cases, it was probably during this period that the majority of small freeholders in the regions mentioned obtained surnames. In the south east of England the development probably occurred rather earlier than elsewhere, and in that region most small free tenants seem to have had hereditary names by about 1300. In the north of England the development occurred considerably later. Examples can be found where families of small freeholders in northern counties had hereditary names in the thirteenth century, but this seems to have been exceptional, and there are many small free tenants in the north without surnames all through the fourteenth century.It was not until the fifteenth century that the majority of small freeholders in the north came to possess surnames. Even then, the evolution was not complete, and new surnames, mostly patronymics, were still being formed in some northern areas, such as south-west Lancashire, during the sixteenth century.

HEREDITARY SURNAMES OF SERFS

The position about serfs' surnames or by-names is very uncertain for any period before the late thirteenth century, when the availability of manorial records in increasing quantities throws more light on the subject. Such evidence as there is for earlier periods suggests that up to at least about 1250 serfs did not have surnames, and usually had no settled by-names. Serfs formed a significant proportion of the population in many areas, and though many surnames can be found as the names of both serfs and of freemen, some surnames (not only ones connected with servile status) seem to have originated among the unfree part of the population, and not have originally belonged to freemen. Where a good series of manor court rolls exist, the descent of unfree families can often be traced, as the deaths of bond tenants and the names of their successors are regularly noted in the court rolls of most manors. (Anyone who lives at or near a place for which a good series of manorial records have been preserved, perhaps in the local record office, might find it an interesting piece of research to list the names of free and unfree tenants mentioned there, and to see how many of them still survive in the area; serfs' surnames were often very persistent in the areas where they arose, partly because of the way in which serfs were bound to the soil in particular manors.) In Sussex, where developments took place rather earlier than in most of England, many serfs had acquired surnames by about 1300. The spread of hereditary names among the unfree tenants in the county was, however, a long process, and occasionally serfs there were still without surnames as late as the fifteenth century. The position in other south-eastern counties probably resembled that in Sussex. In the Midlands and East Anglia most unfree families seem to have adopted surnames in the period between about 1250 and 1350. In the north, serfs were later in acquiring hereditary names, and most unfree families seem to have adopted them between about 1350 and 1450, though some few cases can be found of bondmen with hereditary names before that time. In general, there does not seem to have been much difference between the dates when serfs adopted surnames in any region, and the dates when small freeholders there adopted them. This is one of several ways in which there was a close similarity between the surnames of serfs, and those of small freeholders.

It can be seen from the account given above that the spread of hereditary names among the various sections of the population was a long drawn out process, and that there were substantial differences between regions. Two further points about the evolution of surnames should be made. One is that there were local variations in the course of the development, which can only be detected by a careful examination of the situation in each county, in detail, and only a small number of counties have so far been thus investigated. In some of the more isolated parts of south Lancashire, for example, new surnames, usually patronymics, were still being formed in the early seventeenth century. More detailed research than it has so far been possible to carry out might well reveal local pecularities in other parts of the country, where the growth of hereditary names is concerned. The second point is that the names of some sections of the population are very poorly recorded during the Middle Ages, and to a rather less extent during the sixteenth century. The names of unskilled workers in towns, and of domestic servants, landless labourers, subtenants of villeins, and so forth in rural areas, figure very little in the surviving documentary sources. The situation is aggravated by the fact that evidence for the surnames in use in England during the fifteenth century is less full than either earlier or later. For that period there are no tax returns listing large numbers of taxpayers, as there are for both the fourteenth century and the sixteenth, and there are no alternative sources which could provide similar lists of surnames and by-names. In the sixteenth century a fair number of surnames appear which have not been recorded before 1500. It is unlikely that these are all new names created during the sixteenth century, or in the years just before 1500. New surnames which are definitely known to have been created after 1500 are in most cases patronymics (often in forms like Johnson, Williamson, etc.). In England, leaving aside Wales and Scotland for the moment, there has not been any period, right up to the present day, when the formation of new surnames has entirely ceased, but the rise of new surnames was rare after 1500, except in a few small areas. It is probable that most of the surnames which first appear after 1500 are ones which had existed unrecorded for some considerable time before that date, perhaps in many cases from the thirteenth or fourteenth centuries. Such surnames may have gone through various migrations from their places of origin, and various changes in spelling and pronunciation, by the time they are first encountered after 1500, and this creates difficulty in determining their origins. Beyond this, it is true of surnames generally, whatever period they originate in, that it is quite exceptional to find any evidence at all about why some particular surname came to be used by any individual or family, or precisely why some by-names fell into disuse while others persisted to become hereditary surnames. On such issues the sources of information are very largely silent, though occasional chance observations in mediaeval documents tell why, for example, some particular person was given a nickname. One source, for example, remarks about an individual nicknamed 'Budde' (beetle) that he was *pro densitate sic cognominatus* ('so nicknamed because of his thickness').[4] This observation, from the eleventh century, tells us what the nickname in question signified to people at the time, but evidence of such a kind is scarce.

EVOLUTION OF SURNAMES IN WALES

In Wales in the twelfth century, when surnames were still at an early stage of development in England, there were already two distinct elements among the population. On the one hand there were settlers from outside, mostly but not all English, who occupied land conquered by the Anglo-Norman marcher lords, most of it to begin with in south Wales. On the other hand there were the indigenous Welsh, with their own language and their own practices about naming. Up until the sixteenth century there continued to be a sharp division between the two sections. The English settlers and their descendants, together with smaller numbers of immigrants from the Continent, such as Flemings, continued for the most part to hold land according to the English law about land tenure and inheritance, and in many places enjoyed privileges denied to the Welsh. Welshmen usually held land according to the traditional Welsh laws about land tenure, and these involved a complex system of partible inheritance, substantially different from systems of partible inheritance which existed at the same period in parts of England. In particular, if a person holding land died without direct male heirs (females and persons descended through females being excluded), his land was partitioned between a group of male relatives who might include distant cousins. In practice, these rules about dividing inheritances seem to have applied to unfree holdings in Wales, as well as to freehold land. Welshmen, therefore, or at all events those belonging to families with any landed possessions, even quite modest ones, were generally in a position of having some expectations or possibilities of inheritance from relatively distant kinsmen. These were circumstances in which it was especially necessary for a man to ensure that his ancestry and relationships were kept in mind, constantly, because at any time a connection, perhaps to some fairly distant kinsman, might constitute a claim to real property. Keeping up the memory of descent was all the more vital because of the absence of any method of systematically recording births, deaths, and marriages in writing. In principle, if not always in practice, all through the Middle Ages and up to the reign of Henry VIII, Welshmen who were Welsh by language, culture, and descent held land according to the Welsh rules of land tenure and inheritance, while English and other settlers and their descendants held land according to English rules. These arrangements survived Edward I's conquest of Wales, and though somewhat disrupted by the heavy population losses from pestilence in the middle and late fourteenth century, and the consequent economic changes in the fifteenth, persisted until 1541 when abolition of the Welsh system of land law by act of Parliament came into effect.

It is not the case that Wales was divided between Welsh-speaking and English-speaking areas in any stable fashion. Until the conquest under Edward I, fluctuating military fortunes in the conflicts between the Anglo-Norman marcher lords and the Welsh princes meant that the control of border areas was liable to change hands. In some areas the population was mixed, part Welsh and part English, and in fact most of the marcher lordships had both Welsh and English tenants. After Edward I's conquest, parts of the conquered territories were given away by the king to various noblemen, while the remainder was formed into the Principality of Wales, a unit which did not at that time cover all of Wales. This, however, did not altogether stabilise the position between Welsh and English. English settlers were at times planted in lands hitherto occupied by Welshmen, and in the fifteenth century some areas which had for long been occupied by English speakers came to be inhabited mainly by Welsh speakers.

As far as the English-speaking population is concerned, their surnames and by-names do not seem to have differed substantially from those current in England, nor do there seem to have been any great differences from the way in which hereditary surnames developed there. As might be expected in an immigrant community, a good proportion of the English settlers had locative names, derived from the places from which they or their forbears had migrated to settle in Wales. It is the names of the Welsh-speaking part of the population which were distinctive.

From the late eleventh century onwards, parts of Wales, especially in the south, were under the control of Anglo-Norman lords, many of whom possessed hereditary names from the eleventh or twelfth centuries onwards. For instance, the families of de Bohun, de Braose, de Valence, Mortimer, and Lacy, all with hereditary surnames from French place-names, gained large estates in Wales at one period or another. Many of the great marcher lords had below them knightly tenants of English or Norman origin, who had hereditary surnames from the twelfth century in many cases. For a long time, however, neither this, nor the increasing use of hereditary names by English settlers in Wales, seems to have had much influence among the Welsh population. A few Welsh landowning families adopted hereditary names, often Anglicised, but before 1400 at the earliest this seems to have been unusual. Even in the fourteenth century, Welsh gentry who held offices in the franchises of the great landowners, and who might be thought to be a group especially exposed to English influence, do not usually seem to have had surnames. A great many Welshmen at all levels of society used names of the genealogical type, which set out their ancestry for perhaps two or three generations back. Such names in use were, for instance, Gruffydd ap Rhys ap Hywel (or, to Anglicise the names in a way perhaps horrifying to Welshmen, Griffith son of Rice son of Howel). There is an obvious connection between names constructed in this way and Welsh laws about land tenure, which made relationships in the male line important in respect of property inheritance. The personal names involved in these genealogical designations were mostly Welsh, but instances where names of other origins were used can often be found. For instance, taxpayers listed in the Merioneth lay subsidy roll for 1292 included Cadugan ap Adkin, Madoc ap Phelip, and Ivor ap Meiler, showing a mixture of Welsh names with non-Welsh ones.[5] Other types of by-names were in use among the Welsh-speaking population, including some from occupations (occasionally from Middle English occupational terms), and others of the nickname type from physical characteristics. As far as can be seen, these were not usually hereditary before about 1500.

During the fifteenth century there was some increase in the tendency for Welsh landed families to acquire hereditary names, but even so, it would appear that until after 1500 the great majority of the Welsh-speaking inhabitants did not have surnames. At earlier periods, however, some Welsh surnames occur in England, as a result of Welshmen migrating. Some border areas, like the western parts of Shropshire, for instance, had quite large Welsh populations, judging from the large numbers of people with Welsh personal names listed in such sources as subsidy rolls. It is likely that in these areas there were many people who were bilingual. There were also numbers of

Welshmen in districts easily accessible from Wales, such as north Devon or south Lancashire, where Welsh migrants would have found themselves in communities which spoke English and followed English practices about surnames. In these circumstances some names of Welsh origin appear in England. For example, the surname Nereberth, from the place-name Narberth, in Dyfed,[6] was present in Devon in the thirteenth century, no doubt as a result of migration across the Bristol Channel. This name was from a place in an English speaking part of south Wales; in general locative surnames are rare or lacking in Welsh-speaking areas. In Staffordshire, a county fairly accessible from Wales, Craddock, Griffin, Meredith, and Oweyn, all from Welsh personal names, occur in the fourteenth century as surnames or by-names, probably though not certainly hereditary. In Oxfordshire, a county rather more distant from Wales, the surname Griffin (from an Anglicised form of the Welsh personal name Gruffydd) occurs both in Oxford itself and in several villages from the thirteenth century, and its persistence suggests that it was hereditary; it survived to become a quite numerous surname in the county by the seventeenth century. In Lancashire, the surnames Carnavan and Denbegh existed at Liverpool from the fourteenth century, and their survival shows that they too had become hereditary. In Dorset Kerdif occurs as a surname or by-name (not certainly hereditary) during the fourteenth century and Cardiff was the surname of a landed family in Gloucestershire at the same period. These are examples of locative names formed from the names of places in Wales, a type of surname rare within Wales, though common in England. No doubt such surnames or by-names were at some time acquired by Welshmen who migrated into England. Between about 1300 and 1500 surnames from Welsh personal names, or from Welsh place-names, can be found scattered in many parts of England, some in regions far from the Welsh border. A moderate number of Welsh names became hereditary in this way in England, at a time when hereditary names were scarce in Wales itself.

The situation as regards surnames began to change in Wales during the sixteenth century, perhaps influenced to some extent by Tudor legislation. Under Henry VIII the separate Welsh land law came to an end, the marcher jurisdictions, which had for long prevented the Crown from exercising much direct influence over considerable parts of Wales, were suppressed, and in general Wales tended to be assimilated to England. These changes, far reaching though they were in many ways, did not immediately revolutionise the nature of surnames in Wales, where many people throughout the sixteenth century continued to use genealogical names of the traditional type. During the same period there was increasing movement from Wales into England, and many people with Welsh personal names, surnames, and by-names can be found as inhabitants of English counties, some distant from the Welsh border. Many people with Welsh names found in England have by-names or surnames in the form Ap Richard, Appryse, and so forth, and these are unlikely to have been hereditary.

In the sixteenth century, however, changes were beginning to affect Welsh names. One of these was a tendency to replace the traditional type of patronymic name with an Anglicised version formed from a personal name with a possessive '-s' added, so that, for example, names such as Ap Robert, Ap Gruffydd, and so on became Roberts, Griffiths, etc. The predominance in Wales of the old type of patronymic names was so great that, as surnames with '-s' gradually replaced the older type of patronymic name, surnames in '-s' eventually became very numerous in Wales, so much so that they are often thought of as a category of name especially typical of Wales. In terms of the origin of the type, this is not true. Surnames and by-names formed from a personal name with a possessive '-s' added had been found in England much earlier, and had been very common in some parts of that country from the fourteenth century onwards (a development discussed in Chapter 4). In fact, the region of England where surnames in '-s' were most numerous, and where they formed the highest proportion of the total body of surnames in use, was the south-west Midlands, where in the sixteenth century very many such surnames were well established. The south-west Midlands is of course a region closely adjacent to Wales, and especially to the well-populated southern region of Wales, and Herefordshire and Gloucestershire, two counties particularly near Wales, were two of the counties which had long had an unusually high proportion of surnames of the type concerned. (The factors causing this regional distribution of the type are discussed in Chapter 4.) During the sixteenth century, many persons with Welsh surnames, by-names, or first names, presumably migrants from Wales, were inhabitants of the counties along the Thames valley, as far east as London, and it must be supposed that there was a good deal of contact between Wales and this area, where surnames with a possessive '-s' had been common for centuries. The geographical distribution of surnames in '-s' in England no doubt explains why this category of name came to be used in Wales as the equivalent of the traditional type of Welsh patronymic by-names, rather than the other type of English surname ending in '-son' (Williamson, Robertson, etc.), which might seem a more obvious replacement for Welsh patronymics.

Changes in Welsh practices about names took place slowly, however, and the adoption of hereditary surnames was spread over a long period. During the sixteenth century some gentry families which had not hitherto had hereditary surnames acquired them. In the period 1550 to 1600 names in '-s' were already fairly common in Wales, but it is impossible to be sure just what proportion were hereditary. In towns, and in the more accessible rural areas, most families seem to have acquired surnames during the seventeenth century. In some mountain areas, especially in north-west Wales. surnames were not adopted by much of the population until the eighteenth or early nineteenth centuries. When hereditary names were adopted at these late periods, they were sometimes drawn from Old Testament names, which had come into use under the influence of evangelical religious feeling, and some Welsh surnames derived from Biblical names originated at this late date. Various factors operating in Wales from the sixteenth century onwards tended to make the stock of Welsh surnames, as it eventually developed, more Anglicised than might have been expected. These included the disuse of a good many Welsh personal names which had been employed earlier. Despite this, many surnames survive in Wales to the present day which are from the Welsh language.

DEVELOPMENT OF SURNAMES IN SCOTLAND

In considering the history of surnames in Scotland, a distinction must be drawn between those areas where Scots (that is, the Lowland form of English) was spoken, and the Gaelic-speaking regions. During the Middle Ages the sources for Scots names are in general less full than the corresponding ones for England at the same period, and it is at least as difficult to make precise statements about the evolution of hereditary names in Scotland as it is to do so about England.

As far as can be seen from the available sources, hereditary names were not in use in the Scots-speaking regions before about 1100. During the twelfth century some families of French or English extraction, who already had hereditary surnames, became established in Scotland, many of them with the support of King David I (1124–53), and some of these became major landholders in the country. These included, for example, such families as Bruce, Balliol,

Fraser, Graham, Lindsay, Somerville, de Hay, Haig, Colville, and de Quincy, most of them with surnames from French, or less frequently English, place-names. The surname of Stuart, later that of the reigning dynasty, arose from the holding by a family, Breton in origin, and related to the Fitzalans, of the hereditary office of steward of Scotland, under a grant from David I. It would be difficult to say, in connection with this family, at what point Steward or Stuart ought to be considered as having become a surname, rather than a title from a hereditary office held by the family. Apart from major landed families such as these, some families of French or English origin, but of rather less standing, settled in Scotland during the twelfth century. David, earl of Huntingdon, for example, a younger brother of William the Lion, king of Scotland, and a large landholder in both England and Scotland, established some tenants from his English estates in Scotland. The result of this was the settlement in Scotland of some landholding families, originating outside the country, with hereditary names – a position rather like that existing in England in the period after 1066.

The presence from the twelfth century onwards of this body of families with hereditary names, some or them among the most influential in the country, no doubt had some effect, but nevertheless the spread of surnames in Scotland seems to have been slow. Some Scots landed families used surnames from the late twelfth century, or the thirteenth. The Douglas family, for example, had a surname (from a Scots place-name) which appears to have been hereditary from the late twelfth century. Most landed families seem to have acquired surnames, often locative ones, by about 1300. It is much more difficult to say what the position was about the names of the rest of the population. In the fourteenth century the surnames or by-names used in the Scots-speaking regions do not seem to have been substantially different in their general character from those employed in England at the same date. Surnames or by-names formed from personal names with the addition of '-son' occur from the thirteenth century onwards, and became fairly common, though less so than in some parts of northern England. Some of these have a Gaelic personal name as the first element, such as Finlayson, Gilchristson, or Malcolmson, and these may be Anglicised forms of Gaelic names which began with the prefix 'Mac-'. Gaelic surnames or by-names were scarce generally in the Scots-speaking regions. However, some people were still without any surnames or by-names at all in the fourteenth century, and new patronymic surnames were still being formed in the fifteenth century and the early sixteenth. It is probable that the acquisition of hereditary names by the bulk of the population was in Scotland, as in England, a slow and patchy process, and that on the whole developments in Scotland took place at a rather later date than in the north of England. The general spread of hereditary surnames was not complete in the Scots-speaking regions until at least the sixteenth century.

There were cases where the tenants or other dependents of major landholders assumed their overlords' surnames as their own. This is said to have happened on a large scale with the surname Gordon in the fifteenth century, when the surname became numerous in north-east Scotland through many tenants and so forth of the Gordon family assuming the family name.[7] Such arrangements may have been influenced by the existence of clan names in the Gaelic-speaking parts of the country. The fact that the surnames of some well-known aristocratic families are today very numerous in some parts of Scotland suggests that there may have been a fair number of cases where the surnames of landed magnates were assumed by tenants. The surname Douglas, for example, is now very common in the Borders and in the south west, while Stewart is a common name in several areas. Both these surnames might in the case of some families have originated without any connection with the well-known noble families which bore them. Stewart, and variants of it such as Stiward, was already a widely distributed name in England in the thirteenth century, and the name of people with no link to the Scottish dynasty. The surname Douglas is from a place-name, and it is quite possible for a place to give rise to the surnames of several distinct families, perhaps at different periods. Nevertheless, it must be suspected that the frequency with which both names are now found owes much to tenants, retainers, etc., taking the surnames of their lords' families.

Surnames have a separate history in the Gaelic-speaking parts of Scotland. As long as the clan system survived – which it did until the eighteenth century – surnames were those of clans rather than of individual families. Such names were often, though not invariably, patronymics with the prefix 'Mac'.[8] Whenever the power and jurisdiction of a clan chief was extended into fresh areas, the inhabitants of those parts would generally assume the name of his clan. There is no evidence that all the members of a clan were descended from a common ancestor, and it is unlikely that this was ever the case.

The position in the Gaelic-speaking areas of Scotland appears to have remained like this until after the rising of 1745, though people with hereditary surnames originating elsewhere occurred there to some small extent. After 1745, and the subsequent disruption of the clan system, clan names were gradually transformed into hereditary surnames. The process was slow, and in the late eighteenth century some families in the highlands had names which were not fully stable and were liable to change. Until after 1745, names from the Gaelic-speaking regions were not very common in the other parts of Scotland, and they were scarce in England and Wales. (Anyone looking through such seventeenth-century records as the 1641–1642 Protestation Returns, or the late seventeenth-century Hearth Tax records, for example, is at once struck by the almost total absence of surnames beginning with 'Mac'.) From about 1750, surnames or by-names from the Gaelic-speaking areas began to appear in increasing numbers in the Lowlands, where Gaelic names, being at this time often not hereditary, were often drastically changed by being Anglicised in various ways. In some cases patronymics were transformed into surnames ending in '-son', so that, for instance, MacDonald became Donaldson. In other cases the personal names which formed the second part of many surnames were greatly modified in a way likely to make them less strange to the ears of those whose native language was English, so that, for example, forms such as Maccambridge (from Mac Ambrois, 'son of Ambrose') were produced. (This subject is discussed in Chapter 4 below.)

SURNAMES USED BY MARRIED WOMEN

The convention whereby women on marriage take their husbands' surnames has existed for so long, and though occasionally challenged by feminists has generally been so well established that the practice is liable to be taken for granted. In fact the convention was created over a period, while hereditary surnames were in the process of evolving. During the twelfth and thirteenth centuries, in England, the usage about married womens' surnames was very flexible. Women on marriage in some instances took their husbands' surnames or by-names, in some cases continued to use surnames inherited from their fathers, and in other instances again they used designations which they had acquired, either before or after marriage, and had not inherited. Cases can be found where a woman who married twice continued, after her second marriage, to use her first husband's surname or by-name. It does not appear that there was any fixed rule, at any level in society, or in any region of the country. This lack of any established practice is not surprising at a time when surnames were still in the early stages of development, and when there were still no definite rules about the inheritance of names.

In addition, two further usages can be found in England during the Middle Ages, both of which survived for a considerable time, but which both eventually fell out of use. In the south and Midlands of England, married women often had by-names formed from their husbands' surnames or by-names with a possessive '-s' added, so that, for example, the wife of William le Couper was called Alice le Coupers. This seems to have been especially common when the husband's surname or by-name was an occupational one, but surnames or by-names in other categories were treated in the same way, though less frequently. This practice is connected with the use of a possessive '-s' in surnames of other types, and is discussed in Chapter 4. In parts of the north of England the habit existed of forming by-names for married women by adding the word 'wife' to their husbands' surnames, by-names, or first names, to produce by-names such as Williamswife. Such by-names for married women are sparsely recorded in written sources for the time before about 1500, but this is at least partly due to the shortage of evidence about women's names generally at that period. Women tend to be noted in mediaeval documents much less frequently than men. Such by-names may well have been used much more in speech than would be deduced from the relatively few references in written material. During the period from about 1500 to 1700, when written sources are fuller and more varied, there is more evidence of such by-names being widely used in some areas, such as south Lancashire or the West Riding of Yorkshire. By the eighteenth century, however, the practice of forming by-names in this way had fallen into disuse. Neither of the two types of by-name just mentioned developed into hereditary surnames. Surnames of the type concerned ending in 'wife' are not now to be found (the surname Housewife, and variants of it such as Hussif, is an occupation name; it appears as a men's surname or by-name as early as the fourteenth century, probably because it was then already hereditary, though just possibly it may have been a derisory nickname when applied to men).

In addition, purely local customs existed on some manors during the Middle Ages about the by-names of wives or widows. At Cuxham in Oxfordshire, for instance, where there is a large surviving body of manor records which have been carefully studied, there was a custom that a man who married a widow and through her became the tenant of a holding in the manor assumed the surname or by-name of the widow's first husband.[9]

Until well after 1350 there was consequently in England no consistency about married women's surnames or by-names, and although married women sometimes took their husbands' names, that was only one possible usage, out of several. From about 1350, however, it became more and more common among landholders for married women to take their husbands' names. The fact that hereditary surnames were by then usual at that social level no doubt helped to favour this development. By about 1400 it was usually the established convention among the landed classes that women on marriage took their husbands' surnames. The practice so created spread gradually to other classes during the course of the fifteenth century, and by 1500 it was general, though still not universal, for married women to use their husbands' surnames at all social levels. In some of the more conservative and more isolated parts of the country, such as south Lancashire, the convention was still not always observed, even after 1500, and there are cases of married women not using their husbands' surnames in the sixteenth century. This, however, was exceptional, and in England it was evidently the usual course from the fifteenth century onwards.

The position in the Scots-speaking parts of Scotland during the Middle Ages appears to have been similar to that prevailing in England, with no single generally observed practice about married women's names. The convention whereby married women used their husbands' names was not fully established in Scotland until a relatively late period, and during the sixteenth and seventeenth centuries it was not rare for wives to employ surnames different from those used by their husbands. In such cases wives generally seem to have used surnames inherited from their fathers.

In Wales, the English-speaking parts of the population followed English usages about married women's names. Among the Welsh-speaking population, there was for long no regular practice of wives using their husbands' surnames or by-names. Even as late as the eighteenth century it was still not the rule for married women to take their husbands' names, and the practice did not become properly established until the nineteenth.

NOTES AND REFERENCES

1. R. A. McKinley, 1977, *Surnames of Oxfordshire*, Leopard's Head

Press, p.12.

2. Public Record Office, 1931, *Book of Fees*, vol. 1, pp. 206–22.

3. J. Bain (ed.), 1884, *Calendar of Documents Relating to Scotland*, National Register of Scotland, vol. 2, pp. 193–213.

4. G. Tengvik, 1938, *Old English Bynames*, Almquist and Wiksells, Uppsala, p. 297 (*Nomina Germanica*).

5. K. Williams-Jones (ed.), 1976, *Merioneth Lay Subsidy Roll 1292–1293*, University of Wales Press, pp. 33, 35.

6. T. J. Morgan and P. Morgan, 1985, *Welsh Surnames*, University of Wales Press, pp. 28, 171.

7. G. F. Black, 1979, *Surnames of Scotland*, New York Public Library, pp. xxv, 319.

8. On such names, see p. 121.

9. P. D. A. Harvey, 1965, *A Mediaeval Oxfordshire Village*, Oxford University Press, p. 117.

CHAPTER TWO
Locative surnames

Locative surnames are defined here as surnames derived from the names of specific places. They are to be distinguished from surnames originating from words for general features of the landscape, which are treated as topographical surnames, and are the subject of the next chapter. Thus surnames such as York, Manchester, Norton, Drayton, or Pickering will be considered as locative, whereas surnames like Brooks, Hill, Bridge, and so forth will be listed as topographical. It will also be convenient to include in locative names surnames which are derived from counties (Kent, Derbyshire, Devenish, Cornwallis, or Lancashire, for instance) and surnames from districts, such as Craven (a name from the district of Craven in West Yorkshire and not one connected with cowardice). Gower (sometimes from Gower in south Wales, though the name has other origins in some cases), Cunningham (from the district so named in Strathclyde), Lennox (from the Scottish district to the north of the Clyde), Murray (from Moray in Scotland), or Norris (from a term for someone from the north of England). Other names included here will be those from terms of nationality, such as English, England, Scott, Welsh, Dench (from Denmark), Tyas (person from Germany), or Allman (often from a general term for people from the Holy Roman Empire), and from provinces, etc., in foreign countries, such as Flanders, Fleming, Brabazon, Bremner, and Brabant (all three for persons from Brabant, in what is now Belgium), Gascoigne (for a Gascon), Bret and Britain or Britton (usually for someone from Brittany), Burgoyne (for a Burgundian), Champness (for someone from Champagne), Portwine (from Poitevin, a man from Poitou), Lombard (usually for somebody from north Italy, though there has been confusion with surnames from the personal name Lambert), or

Pettingale (from Portugal). All these names have in common the characteristic that they relate an individual to a particular place or area, and so provide evidence about geographical origins.

One of the main reasons for interest in locative surnames, of course, lies precisely in the fact that they provide information about the place or region where individuals or families originated. If a single family is being traced, then obviously it may be of interest to identify the place from which it first acquired its surnames; if a community is being investigated, then an examination of the locative surnames to be found in it may reveal something about population mobility, and about the parts of the country from where migrants came into the community, and information of this kind is often difficult to obtain from other sources for any period before the nineteenth century. This, however, raises the question of how the researcher without any specialised knowledge of either place-names or surnames can identify which surnames, out of perhaps a large and varied batch, are derived from place-names. How, in fact, are you to recognise a locative surname when you encounter one? This is all the more important because many locative surnames, a very numerous group in England, though less so in Scotland and Wales, are not listed in the standard dictionaries of surnames.

It must be said that there is no simple formula which will instantly winnow out locative surnames from those in other categories. Some help can be obtained by noting the presence of certain elements which often recur as syllables in place-names, and which are therefore frequently found in locative surnames or by-names. For instance, as many readers will no doubt have observed for themselves, there are certain syllables which often occur at the end of place-names, such as 'ham', 'ton', 'by', 'thorpe', 'ley' or 'leigh', 'ford' or 'forth', 'worth', or 'worthy', 'hurst', 'den', 'combe', 'holme', 'cote', 'cester' or 'chester', 'bourne' or 'burn', 'bury', 'burgh', 'hill', 'field', 'stead', 'mouth', and so on. Surnames from place-names which are from Celtic languages such as Welsh, Gaelic, or Pictish may be more difficult for English readers to recognise, but speakers of Welsh or Gaelic acquired locative surnames much less frequently than English speakers. In Cornwall, on the other hand, the place-names of the county have given rise to an exceptionally large body of locative surnames, which are today not confined to Cornwall, but are to be found in most parts of Britain (and overseas as well). Many of the place-names concerned are Cornish linguistically. The old saying that 'by Tre, Pol, and Pen you may know Cornish men' is still not without some force, for a relatively high proportion of surnames originating in Cornwall are from the county's place-names, and those three syllables do occur quite frequently at the beginning of Cornish place-names. The observation of such features of locative surnames, together with the deployment of a researcher's own knowledge of place-names, will enable a good many locative surnames to be identified as such.

However, attempting to identify all the locative surnames from a list of people such as, say, a list of all the inhabitants, or all the taxpayers, of any sizable place in the country, at almost any period after surnames or by-names came into general use, will never be easy. Some surnames which are in fact locative do not appear at first sight to have that character at all. For instance, surnames which are locative include Blenkinsop (from Blenkinsopp, Northumberland), Blanko (from Blencow, Cumberland), Filkins (from Filkins, Oxfordshire), Danvers (from Anvers, that is, Antwerp), Hoo (from Hoo, Sussex), Trowell (often from Trowell, Nottinghamshire, though sometimes occupational), Arnold (sometimes from Arnold, Nottinghamshire, or Arnold, North Yorkshire, though sometimes from a personal name), Boarhunt (from Boarhunt, Hampshire), Stirrop, (from Styrrup, Nottinghamshire, though sometimes occupational), Frodson (from Frodsham, Cheshire), and Thicknesse (from Thickness, in Staffordshire). The surnames Linklater, Isbister, Greenhead, Keith, Pennycook, Kincaid, Knox, and Logan are all derived from places in Scotland. On the other hand, a few surnames which appear convincingly locative have in fact other origins. The surname Jerningham, for example, is from an old personal name, Gernagan, probably Breton, which was in use sparsely in England during the eleventh and twelfth centuries but was never at all common and fell into disuse. Francombe is from the French *Franchehomme* (the equivalent of the English Freeman), and not from a place-name. Pridham and Prodham are also from a French word, prudhomme, 'honest man'. The surname Saxby is sometimes from one or other of the places so named, and when the name originates in the east Midlands this is the usual source of the surname. In Sussex, however. where the surname has been well established since the sixteenth century, the name has developed from Saxespee ('draw sword'), a form already present in Sussex before 1300, and there it is not a locative name at all. (This example, one of many which could be given, shows how complicated the origins of surnames can be, and how important it is to try to trace their origins back as continuously as possible to their early beginnings.)

It has already been stated that if the points of origin of locative surnames can be reliably identified, then something can be learnt about the beginnings of surnames and of families, but there are obstacles to achieving this objective. One is that locative surnames are derived, not from the present day forms of place-names, but from the forms which place-names had at the time when locative surnames were first being formed. Locative surnames are among the oldest hereditary names, some dating back to the twelfth century or even the eleventh, and many more to the thirteenth century. Most sources which list any appreciable number of people in England during the twelfth century will show that the majority of surnames or by-names then in use were locative. In some instances place-names have undergone such great changes since the twelfth and thirteenth centuries as to make identification of derived surnames very difficult.

Anyone who attempts the task of identifying the origins of the locative names in any list of the inhabitants of some place under investigation will rapidly discover the difficulties this creates. To give a few examples, the surname Adburgham, still in use, is derived from a place in Lancashire which was called Adburgham in the thirteenth century, but which is today called Abram. The surname has preserved the former spelling of the place-name in some cases, usually those where the surname belonged to families which moved away from Lancashire at an early date; the form of the place-name Abram has given rise to the surname Abram which is still current in Lancashire, and it seems that where families with the surname continued to reside in the neighbourhood of the place concerned, their surnames underwent the same changes as the place-name. This particular place-name has, therefore, been the origin of two surnames which, in their present forms, seem very different. Or again, the surname Erdington, when it originates in Oxfordshire, is usually from a place in that county known as Erdington in the thirteenth century, but today known as Yarnton. This is all the more confusing because there is a place called Erdington in the adjoining county of Warwickshire. In Sussex, similarly, the surname Treve (now often spelt Treves) is from an old form of the name of the place now called River. Many other examples could be given of surnames derived from place-names which have changed radically since giving rise to surnames.

If place-names can change in the course of time, surnames are even more liable to modification over the course of centuries. Locative surnames were particularly liable to change if they migrated away from their areas of origin to other regions, where the place-names from which they originated were unknown. To give instances, the surnames Barraclough, Barrowcliff, Berecloth, Berry-cloth, and several other variants are all from a West Yorkshire place-name, which was probably spelt Barecloughe or Barneclogh in the fourteenth century. In the same way the surnames Birkenshaw, Bircumshaw, Burkimsher, Burtinshall, Brigenshaw, Buttonshaw, Brackenshaw, Buttinger, and Bruckshaw are all from the place-name Birkenshaw, in West Yorkshire, spelt Birkenschawe or ·Birkenescawe in the thirteenth century. This surname, a Yorkshire one at first, has ramified considerably, and different variants are now well established in other parts of Britain. The place-name Aspinwall, that of a small locality in south Lancashire, has given rise not only to the surname Aspinall, now widely dispersed outside Lancashire, but to the surnames Asmall, Asmold, and Asmah, while the two well-known place-names Leicester and Worcester have given rise to the surnames now spelt Lassiter and Wooster. Again, many further examples could be given of locative surnames which have changed substantially in the course of centuries, and now have no obvious connection with the place-names from which they originated.

It can be seen from this that any attempt to identify the source of a locative surname merely by trying to match up the modern form of a surname with the modern form of available place-names is beset by dangers, and can easily lead to an inaccurate identification. Some suggestions about how to overcome these difficulties will be made later, but it must be pointed out that there are further complications. One obvious difficulty is that some place-names occur as the names of more than one locality. The place-names Drayton, Burton, Eccles, Bradley, Norton, Ashby, Newton, or Kirby, for instance, each occur as the name of numerous localities, and the same is true of quite a few other place-names. Even place-names which may not strike an observer as being obviously common do in fact occur more than once. There are, for example, four places named Dalby in Leicestershire alone, and several more outside the county. In Devon there are fourteen places called Aller, some of them very small. Salford is not only the name of the well-known Lancashire industrial town, but that of an Oxfordshire village which gave rise to the surname Salford in that county during the Middle Ages. Singleton is a Lancashire place-name from which there originated the surname Singleton well established in the county for centuries, but there is also a village called Singleton in Sussex, which was the origin of the surname there. Butterworth, a very common surname in the area which is now Greater Manchester, is often from a small locality named Butter-worth in that part of the world, and in fact is an example of how locative surnames from small localities can proliferate extensively over a period of time, but there is another place called Butterworth in Yorkshire. In this connection, too, it must be borne in mind that places of which the spelling is now different were in some cases spelt in the same or a very similar way during the twelfth, thirteenth, and fourteenth centuries when locative surnames were developing. For instance, the place-names now spelt as Bowden, Boughton and Buckden often had much the same spelling during the period in question.

An additional difficulty is that some locative surnames are from the names of places which no longer exist. The number of villages and hamlets which existed in the period 1100 to 1350, but which were subsequently deserted is much greater than is generally appreciated. For instance, the number of villages known to have been depopulated in Leicestershire, a medium sized county, is over sixty. In some cases where villages have disappeared, farms or houses survive bearing the names of the lost settlements, but in other instances no such traces remain, and even the sites of lost villages are sometimes undiscovered. Most of the places that have been lost were never more than hamlets or small villages. The number of locative surnames or by-names that can be found in the period from about 1100 to 1350 was, however, extremely large, and during that time the names of most inhabited places, even very small ones, gave rise to locative names. Some of these never became hereditary and failed to persist for that reason, while others became extinct as a result of the heavy population losses of the fourteenth century, but very many locative surnames still exist and some of these are from villages or hamlets which have been deserted. A considerable number of places were depopulated as a consequence of the fourteenth century pestilences, while in some parts of the country there were many further instances of villages being deserted because of depopulation caused by the conversion of arable to pasture and the enclosure of open fields, mostly in the period from about 1450 to 1550.

The result of all this is that, today, many locative surnames are from the names of places which are not listed in gazetteers or similar reference books, and may be hard to trace even on large-scale maps. To give a few examples, Staresmore was a moderate sized village in south Leicestershire, near Lutterworth, which was depopulated as the result of enclosure and conversion to pasture. The name can still be found on the Ordnance Survey map, if you know where to look, but there is now no inhabited place of that name. Nevertheless, the surname Starsmore survived in the same area during the seventeenth and eighteenth centuries, and still persists, as a rare surname, in south Leicestershire at the present day. Another south Leicestershire village, Poultney, long since deserted, is the origin of the surname Pulteney or Poultney, which still survives as one of the more numerous locative surnames in the county today and has existed as a surname in south Leicestershire continuously over a long period. The place-name can still be discovered on a large-scale map in the names of several farms, but these would be difficult to find if the location of the former village was not already known. The village of Stuchbury or Stutchbury in Northamptonshire, already deserted by about 1550, has originated a surname, now spelt variously Stuchbury, Stuchbery, and Stutchbury, which still survives in Northamptonshire now, though it has become more numerous in the London area. The Oxfordshire hamlet of Golder, never a place of any great size, was depopulated as a result of enclosure before 1500. The surname Golder, however (which might perhaps be taken for an occupational name), still exists in the same county. The surname Holyoak, now a fairly common one in south Leicestershire, is there usually derived from the name of a village, Holyoaks, in the south east of the county near Uppingham, which was depopulated in the late fifteenth and early sixteenth centuries as the result of enclosure and the conversion of arable to pasture; the name of the village can still be found on a large scale map as the name of a house, but otherwise the place-name that gave rise to the surname, in this case a fairly commone one, has vanished.

To give another example which well illustrates the need to exercise care in establishing the origin of locative surnames, the surname Ripon can be found in Norfolk during the Middle Ages and later, and was not particularly scarce. It might well be supposed that the surname was from the well known cathedral town in Yorkshire, all the more because surnames from some Yorkshire place-names did occur in Norfolk during the fourteenth and fifteenth centuries, and some of them proliferated locally. There was, however, in Norfolk a small village called Ripon, now depopulated, and the early instances of the surname in the county are clustered around the site of that village in a way that leaves little doubt that the origin of the surname in Norfolk (though not necessarily elsewhere) is from the village in the county, and not from the Yorkshire town.

Readers who have followed the argument this far may have come to the conclusion that the identification of the place-names from which locative surnames are derived is beset by so many complications as to be an impossible task for any amateur researcher to undertake. This is in fact untrue, and the information to be obtained by discovering the points of origin of locative surnames is sufficiently great to make it worthwhile to persist in the endeavour. The first essential in the process of identification is to trace back the surname to the earliest forms that can be found. It is important to try, as far as possible, to establish a continuous history for any name under investigation. This does not mean proving a continuous pedigree over the whole period from the present back to the time when the name originated, a feat which would be impossible for a large majority of surnames, but it does mean pulling together whatever genealogical evidence is available, noting if the surname survives more or less continuously in one area, and if the name seems to migrate from one area to another during its history, then seeking evidence for the movement of individuals bearing the name. It is rather easy to connect a modern surname with one of the very numerous locative names in use during the fourteenth and fifteenth centuries if the modern surname has a spelling which has some resemblance to the mediaeval form, but this is an unsound method. It is also unsound to suppose that any locative surname that is difficult to connect with a British place-name must be from some foreign place-name. Surnames from places in other countries do of course occur; in particular, there are a fair number of surnames from French place-names. However, the number of foreign surnames to be found in Britain is less than might be expected from the scale of immigration, mainly because of the habit which prevailed, at least up to the seventeenth century, of aliens either settled in this country adopting new, British, surnames, or Anglicising their existing surnames in a way which made them indistinguishable from native names.

Once the earliest known forms of a locative surname have been found, the next step is to discover which place-names might have been the origin of the surname, bearing in mind that locative surnames are likely to be derived from the forms of place-names which existed in the twelfth, thirteenth, and fourteenth centuries, and that these may differ significantly from the present forms. In fact, surnames, if they remain near the place from which they originated, are sometimes influenced by changes in the forms of the place-names, and change in a similar way so that locative surnames do not always diverge from the forms of the originating place-names to the extent that might be supposed. The mediaeval form of English (not Welsh or Scots) place-names can be found in the publications of the Survey of English Place-Names, published by the English Place-Names Society, which are available in most of the larger public libraries. This does not at the moment cover all the English counties, though work is proceeding. The society's more recent volumes give details of minor place-names, which often were the origins of surnames, and about field and street names, but the earlier volumes, those published before 1945, do not always deal adequately with minor place-names. For counties still not covered by the English Place-Name Society's works, the most useful book is the *Oxford Dictionary of English Place-Names*.[1] This is a basic work of reference for anyone interested either in the history of place-names or in surnames derived from them. However, it does not deal with Wales or Scotland, and does not deal with the names of places which no longer exist.

So far as Scotland is concerned, though there is at the moment no complete dictionary of Scots place-names, a good deal of information can be found in W. Nicholaisen, *Scottish Place-Names*, and in M. Gelling, W. Nicholaisen, and M. Richards, *Names of Towns and Cities in Britain*.[2] The origins of a good many Scots and Welsh locative surnames are given in the dictionaries of Welsh and Scots surnames, listed in the 'Advice on further reading' (see Chapter 9).

If the works just mentioned are used carefully and systematically, and if the early forms of surnames are compared with the more or less contemporary forms of place-names, a good many problems about locative surnames and their origins can be solved. In addition, one of the published gazeteers, giving modern place-names in their present-day forms, will be useful both in giving the precise locations of places and in, at any rate, suggesting possible places from which surnames might be derived, though the older forms of place-names should always be checked. Finally, if the area of origin of a locative surname is known, or if it seems to have been concentrated in one area as far as early instances are concerned, it may be worthwhile to scrutinise a large scale map for the area in question to see if any place-name is likely to be the origin of the surname under investigation.

These methods, even in the hands of someone experienced in research into surnames and into genealogy, will not always produce answers. In particular, it can be impossible to decide the origin of a surname if the place-name from which the surname comes is that of a number of separate localities. It is also the case that some locative names are from the names of places outside Britain, and that some locative surnames have become so changed in the course of time that their origins are unidentifiable. Nevertheless, the origins of a great many locative surnames can be discovered, and for the reasons stated it is worthwhile making the effort to do this.

RAMIFICATION OF LOCATIVE SURNAMES

A characteristic of locative surnames in some parts of England is a tendency for individual names to ramify and to increase greatly in numbers within a limited district, with only occasional individuals occurring elsewhere. It is the case generally in all parts of Britain, and with surnames in all categories, that instances can be found where one family has, over a period of several generations or even over several centuries, developed a succession of branches and increased considerably in numbers to the extent that the surname borne by the family has become locally quite common, while remaining scarce, or totally absent, in other parts of the country. Examples of surnames which have ramified locally to a moderate degree can be found in most counties from the sixteenth century onwards, and even before 1500 the beginnings of such developments can be observed in the case of a smaller number of surnames.

However, in some parts of Britain, especially in the north of England, there are areas where some locative surnames have proliferated very greatly, to a much larger extent than is usual when families ramify in the way just described. Such developments have been an important feature of surname history in such areas as south east Lancashire, the dales region of West Yorkshire, or the Yorkshire woollen district. In these areas many locative surnames have increased greatly in numbers, and continue to be very numerous there to the present day. Seventeenth-century sources, such as the Protestation Returns of 1641–42 for Lancashire, show that the process was already well advanced at that period. The locative surnames which proliferated are nearly all ones which originated in the parts where they expanded, and most were derived from the names of small inhabited localities, either detached farms or hamlets. The surnames from the names of towns or larger villages very rarely increased in numbers to anything like the same extent. Although the genealogical evidence for the Middle Ages, and even for the sixteenth century, is generally inadequate to enable pedigrees to be traced for families which were not those of large landowners, it must nevertheless be suspected that each such surname began as the name of a single family, whose surname was derived from the name of a farm or hamlet where the family in question were at first the only, or perhaps the principal, inhabitants. The evidence is hardly ever sufficient to provide conclusive proof of this, but it is often possible to establish that relationships existed in the sixteenth and seventeenth centuries between a number of families all with the same surname, and this suggests that at those periods all the bearers of any one of the locative names under discussion are likely to have had a common descent. These circumstances, and the way in which many locative surnames remained for a long period in one small area, centring in each case around the point of origin, creates a strong presumption that many of the locative surnames in question were at first each the surname of one family, even if the genealogical evidence to prove this does not exist.

It is probable that in these circumstances all the people bearing any one of the locative surnames in question were all descended from one common ancestor, living perhaps in the thirteenth or fourteenth century (the periods when most of the surnames concerned first appear). Many locative surnames which originated from place-names in south-east Lancashire, and proliferated there, are still among the more numerous in that region today, despite all the migrations and population shifts of the past two hundred years. Such surnames as Bardsley, Barlow, Butterworth, Clegg, Crompton, Heaton, Heywood, Lomas, Mellor, or Wrigley continue to be very common names in what is now Greater Manchester, but are found much less frequently in other parts of the country. It is likely that each of these surnames originated with a single family, which gradually increased in numbers over a period of centuries. Similarly in parts of West Yorkshire there are locative surnames which have ramified there over a long time, and which are still very numerous there to the present day, while remaining much less common elsewhere. Examples of such Yorkshire surnames are Ackroyd, Armitage, Horsfall, Illingworth, Lockwood, Murgatroyd, and Sutcliffe.[3] A fair number of other locative surnames could be cited as instances of names which have increased greatly in numbers.

The basic factor behind this development is the demographic history of the regions involved. Both south-east Lancashire and West Yorkshire are areas where there was a growth of population from the sixteenth century onwards. Over a long period the expansion was mainly the result of the natural increase of the existing population, with no more than a small amount of immigration from outside. To some extent the situation changed with the Industrial Revolution, so that Lancashire, for example, underwent large-scale immigration from Wales and Ireland. During the nineteenth century, however, despite the continued movement into the county of people from outside, many already well-established surnames, derived from places in south-east Lancashire, continued to increase greatly in that area, with only a relatively small number of instances to be found anywhere else.

The ramification of some locative surnames in Lancashire and Yorkshire appears very striking to anyone who examines the history of surnames in either county, all the more so because the proliferation of surnames, whether locative or in other categories, did not take place on the same scale in most parts of England (and the processes which made some surnames very common in Wales, and in the Gaelic speaking parts of Scotland, seem to have been different). The process of ramification is especially obvious because there are many locative surnames which are derived from unique place-names, and which can have only one point of origin, even though there are some surnames of the type which could be derived from more than one place, and indeed often are. Some surnames derived from occupations such as Smith, Baker, Cook, Tailor, and so on are notoriously very common, and this situation has a long history. Some surnames derived from topographical terms were originally restricted in their distribution to particular counties or regions, but many surnames of this type were always very widespread, and obviously arose independently in many separate places. Much the same is true of surnames derived from the more common personal names. Surnames of the nickname type are rather more likely to have originated in one single place, but even the less common surnames in that category are likely to have originated independently in several different areas (a point discussed later in the book). For these reasons the fact that some surnames increase greatly in numbers, without dispersing very much geographically, is most obvious in the case of locative names, and the process can be seen operating on a particularly extensive scale in some parts of northern England. However, such a proliferation of surnames is not confined to locative names, and this can be found to some extent in many parts of Britain, though generally not on the same scale as in the north of England. In Lancashire, for example, some surnames which are not locative and which are rare in the country as a whole, ramified in much the same way as did locative names, and on much the same scale. For example, the occupational surname Rymer or Rimmer became very numerous in the coastal part of the county, around the location of the modern resort of Southport, during the seventeenth and eighteenth centuries; at that time the surname was very concentrated with most of the individuals bearing the name residing in the coastal area between Liverpool and Preston. Rymer was such a common surname there during the eighteenth and nineteenth centuries that people with the name were often known by nicknames in order to distinguish them. The name is still exceptionally common at the present day in the same part of Lancashire. There are some grounds for supposing that the surname originated in that part of the county with a single family, which migrated there from south-east Lancashire in the fifteenth century.[4] Various suggestions have been made about the meaning of the surname, but it probably signified 'rhymer' in the sense of someone who recited verse for entertainment. The surname does occur independently in several parts of England, and there is no reason to suppose that all the persons who appear with the name, taking the country as a whole, share a common descent. The surname Rimmer, which is found in south Scotland from the thirteenth century onwards and which is still present there today, is probably another form of the same surname, arising independently in Scotland.

Other examples can be given of surnames in different categories which multiplied on a considerable scale in Yorkshire and Lancashire. Another occupational name, Hardman or Herdman, increased in numbers considerably in parts of south Lancashire[5]; in a rather similar way, the topographical surname Crabtree became common in some West Yorkshire districts, and eventually spread over the border into Lancashire.

The ramification of surnames has, therefore, not been confined to locative names. Furthermore, although the way in which, in some parts of Lancashire and Yorkshire, some local surnames have multiplied on a great scale is a very marked feature of the areas concerned, in most parts of England, and in the Scots-speaking parts of Scotland, examples can be found of surnames which have proliferated within a given area, to become numerous there if not on quite the same scale as in Yorkshire and Lancashire. For instance, the surname Busby became quite numerous in the south Warwickshire and north Oxfordshire area by the seventeenth century; this is a locative name, perhaps from the Yorkshire place-name Busby, but more probably from one of the places in the Midlands called Bushby. The surname Belchamber, probably at first the name of a single family, ramified in west Sussex and some nearby parts of Hampshire to become fairly numerous there by the seventeenth century. (The surname probably arose from a family having some connection with a church belchamber, though it is obviously unlikely that anyone could have lived in such a place.) Hoggesflesh (probably a nickname for a pork butcher), again almost certainly at first the name of one family, existed in west Sussex from the fourteenth century, and by the seventeenth had increased in numbers to become moderately common there. Scarfield, a surname from a French place-name despite its English appearance, and as far as can be seen originally the name of a single landowning family, ramified in south-west Sussex, and for a long time was confined to that area; it still survives in Sussex at the present time. Examples of surnames which were already established in one area in the thirteenth or fourteenth century, and which had multiplied in a moderate degree by about 1600, can be found in most if not all English counties, and in all the main categories of surnames.

Similar developments have occurred in the Scots-speaking parts of Scotland, where some locative surnames are concerned. Some surnames have become very numerous in these regions through the adoption of the surnames of major landholding families by their tenants or other dependents, but some surnames from Scottish place-names have ramified in a way which has no apparent connection with such processes, and have remained numerous down to the present day. For example, among the locative surnames now common in Scotland are Drysdale (from Dryfesdale in Dumfries and Galloway), now a widespread surname in south and central Scotland, Moffat (from the town so named in the same county), also now a numerous surname in south Scotland, Bathgate (from Bathgate in Lothian), a surname now common in both Lothian and Fife, Cleghorn (from Cleghorn in Strathclyde), now common in the Borders, Dunlop (from Dunlop in Strathclyde), and Tulloch (from Tulloch in Dingwall parish, near Inverness). All these are locative surnames from Scottish place-names which have ramified considerably. Most of them are not from places whose size, location, or trading connections seem likely to have been the explanation for such an expansion.

These developments, in England and Scotland, give rise to two main issues. One of these is why some surnames ramify, often within a restricted area, while the majority of surnames do not; the other is whether, as a general rule, all the bearers of any one such surname are likely to be related.

The proportion of surnames which have ramified greatly, out of the whole body of names in any area, is always small. Even in the parts of Lancashire and Yorkshire where locative names proliferated remarkably, only a minority of names display this development. Many surnames or by-names which existed up to 1350 or thereabouts had disappeared by 1400, and these include some which seem to have been well-established hereditary surnames. Some surnames which were still surviving about 1500 became extinct during the sixteenth and seventeenth centuries. The surnames which ramified are consequently not only a minority of the surnames existing at the present day, but they are the survivors of a great body of surnames and by-names, many of which have been totally lost. Most locative surnames have remained scarce, and where such names have become common, it is often because each of them has arisen, independently, from a number of localities with the same place-name. The surnames Ashby, Kirby, Burton, and Norton have all been widespread surnames over a long period, but this is because the place-names Ashby, Kirby, Burton, and Norton occur frequently, and the surnames in question each originated in many separate places. This is a different process from the ramification described above. Similarly, there are many surnames derived from one or other of the male personal names which were commonly in use from about 1300 onwards, Williamson, Robertson, Dickson, Harrison, Williams, Richards, Roberts, Rogers, and so on. Where such surnames are concerned, too, it can be seen from the way in which each of them was dispersed throughout extensive regions from an early date and from the way in which examples of such surnames being newly formed can be found at relatively late periods such as the sixteenth and seventeenth centuries, that there is really no question of any one of these surnames having been at first that of one single family. Many such names have been widespread from an early date and have obviously originated separately from a large number of distinct families. Much the same is true of those quite numerous surnames which are derived from topographical terms in use over all or much of the country.

In these circumstances it is obviously pertinent to ask if the surnames which have become relatively numerous as a result of individual families ramifying share any common characteristics. Though the limitations of the existing sources of information and especially the gaps in the genealogical evidence, make it difficult to be certain of the position in respect of some surnames, it seems that most of the names in question did have some common factors in their history. Hardly any were the names of major landowning families, and few seem to have been the names of peasant families in origin. Most of them, where the facts can be discovered, seem to have been the names of either landowners of moderate wealth, belonging to what at a later date would be called the lesser gentry, or the names of substantial free tenants of the franklin or yeoman class. Families so placed would be in a better economic position than bondmen, minor free tenants, or landless labourers, and would be rather more likely to have numbers of children who survived into adult life. Another common characteristic of families with surnames which ramified is that most of them had already begun to develop into several different branches by about 1400. Families whose names ramified greatly in the sixteenth and seventeenth centuries were already showing signs of such a development considerably earlier. Besides this, it is likely that genetic factors had some influence, though it is impossible to be certain about that now.

Whatever the precise causes, and the evidence is not sufficient to enable any unqualified assertions to be made on the subject, there is over a long period a marked contrast between a minority of surnames, many of them locative, which have proliferated considerably, often in the areas where they originated, and the much larger number of names which have not multiplied significantly at all. Many locative surnames which are rare in most parts of Britain, and which appear in most regions as the names of perhaps one or two families, are still today quite numerous at and around their points of origin. For this reason alone it is important to locate, if at all possible, the place from which any locative surnames under investigation have been derived. If this can be done, it will often be found that the surname, however scarce nationally, is fairly common in the district where it originated.

DISPERSAL OF SOME LOCATIVE NAMES

The discussion above has been concerned with locative surnames which have increased considerably in numbers while remaining largely concentrated in one area, but there is a relatively small group of locative surnames which became widely dispersed from an early date. Speaking generally, it is unusual in Britain for any surname, of whatever type, which originates solely in one place or one area of limited size to disperse widely at any period before the nineteenth century. Where most locative surnames are concerned, including both those which have proliferated and those which have not, it will often be found that individual names stayed for a long period clustered around their places of origin, with only occasional individuals or families appearing in other parts. Even in the nineteenth century this pattern of distribution can still be seen in the case of many names, though by then population shifts were beginning to spread some surnames more widely. There are, however, a minority of locative surnames which became widely dispersed over the country by quite an early date, often by about 1400. In some cases the reasons for this are fairly clear. There were, for instance, a series of towns along the line of the mediaeval Great North Road which gave rise to surnames already widespread in England by about 1400, and which were in many instances already showing a good deal of dispersal by about 1300. These include Baldock (a town of late beginnings, of which the place-name is, curiously, derived from the place-name Baghdad), Grantham (from which is derived not only the surname Grantham, but also probably Graham), Doncaster, and Pontefract (from which come the surnames Pomfrett, Pumphratt, and so forth). Surnames from the names of several other towns on the same highway, such as Bawtry or Boroughbridge, had dispersed by about 1400, though to a lesser extent. Busy 'thoroughfare' towns must have had many inhabitants engaged in trading and transport over considerable distances, and it is not surprising that surnames derived from the place-names concerned tended to disperse at a relatively early date. Other factors can be suggested to account for the early dispersal of some other locative names. The surname Kendal, for example, was already widespread by about 1400, and it remains today one of the few locative surnames to be found in some numbers in all regions of England. In most cases the surname is from Kendal (Cumbria), though there are other possible sources. Kendal was the centre of production of a certain type of woollen cloth which was traded extensively in England, so much so that 'Kendalman' became an occupational term for someone who dealt in such cloth. No doubt these trading connections were the chief force behind the spread of the surname.

In the case just mentioned, it is possible to put forward reasons why some locative surnames became quite widespread at an early period, before about 1400, but there are some locative names which had a similarly early dispersal without it being clear what the factors involved were. Two such surnames are Pickering (and Puckering, which is a variant form of Pickering), and Duffield. Pickering and Puckering were already to be found in most parts of England by about 1400. In the fifteenth century the name was widely dispersed, and was even present at Calais. The surname is from Pickering, a small town in North Yorkshire, and it has not been possible to find any other source for the surname. The wool trade was carried on from Pickering to some extent, but the town does not appear to have had especially wide trading connections. The surname Duffield is from either Duffield (Derbyshire), or from the neighbouring villages of North and South Duffield (North Yorkshire). The early distribution of the surname suggests that it arose separately in Derbyshire and Yorkshire. The fact that the surname had two separate points of origin is hardly sufficient to explain its appearance, before 1400, in parts of England remote from any of the places called Duffield. Both Pickering and Duffield (Derbyshire) were administrative centres for groups of estates, which might explain why surnames derived from them became rather more common locally than might be expected from the size or importance of either town, but this can hardly explain why both surnames became so widespread.

Duffield and Pickering both became widespread surnames in England during the Middle Ages, and both remain so at the present day. The dispersal of both names was the result of complex moves by a number of distinct families. It does not appear that there is any possibility of either surname having originated with a single family. It appears that, in the case of each surname, a number of separate families acquired locative surnames from the place-names in question at different periods. Something of these processes can be seen from the inevitably incomplete records that survive. For instance, a Roger de Pickering was a successful merchant at Leicester, early in the fourteenth century. Possibly he may have migrated to there directly from Pickering as a result of trading operations, or perhaps because of the links of feudal lordship between the two places (the earls of Lancaster were the overlords of both Leicester and Pickering). Roger was able to acquire land at Slawston, a rural village in south-east Leicestershire, well away from Leicester itself, and his descendants, with the surname Pickering, survived in the village for some time. Or to give another example, Sir John Puckering, who after a lucrative career at the bar became Keeper of the Great Seal (a position more or less equivalent to that of Chancellor) under Elizabeth I, was the son of William Puckering of Flamborough, in North Yorkshire, about twenty-five miles from Pickering. William was from one of the families called Pickering or Puckering which had remained in the vicinity of the town from which the surname originated. Sir John was able, thanks to his career as a barrister, to become a landowner in Warwickshire, a county with which he had, as far as can be seen, no previous connection. Repeated and complicated movements like those just mentioned no doubt lie behind the dispersal of surnames like Pickering, Duffield, and a few others, but it still remains difficult to explain why a few locative surnames soon became widespread, when the majority of such surnames are characterised by a tendency to remain grouped around their points of origin.

The need to trace the movements of families of the kind just described shows how important the information from pedigrees and from family history can be in establishing the facts about some aspects of surname history. It also shows the kind of difficulties that can confront genealogists when families migrate from one region to another.

A small number of other locative surnames have become very dispersed in the same way as Duffield and Pickering without there being any obvious explanation. For example, the surname Seagrave, or Seagrove, is from a Leicestershire village, Seagrave. The surname was already much dispersed in England by about 1500, and before that date had appeared in regions distant from Leicestershire. The village of Seagrave was never a place of any particular importance, or one of any great significance in trade. A family named Seagrave, which originated in the village in the twelfth century, became major landholders in the East Midlands in the thirteenth, but most of the people named Seagrave or Seagrove who appear in different parts of England subsequently had no traceable links with this baronial family, and it remains uncertain why the surname spread to the extent it did. Or, to give another example, a surname from the place-name Inkpen, a Berkshire village, became widespread in the south and Midlands of England, but it is not possible to put forward any reason for this.

The histories of those locative surnames which became dispersed at early periods are noteworthy because they are exceptional. In some cases it is possible to indicate the forces likely to have been responsible for the dispersal. In other cases it is not, perhaps partly because of insufficient information about the economic history of the places concerned during the Middle Ages, and about the history of inland trade generally during the same period. The history of most locative names shows a tendency to remain in an area around the place of origin, often up to at least the eighteenth century and sometimes up to the end of the nineteenth, with only occasional individuals or families appearing in more distant parts. Most locative surnames do not spread out very much before the Industrial Revolution, a fact worth bearing in mind when tracing the pedigrees of families with such surnames. Of course there are exceptions like the names discussed above, and there are instances where a surname remains mainly concentrated near its place of origin but sends out a branch which survives, perhaps for centuries, in some distant parts of the country, and possibly ramifies there. The surname Barclay, for example, present in Scotland from the twelfth century and now quite a common surname in that country, is probably in most cases from

Berkeley in Gloucestershire. Such instances, however, are rather exceptional. This characteristic of locative surnames does mean that it is particularly useful for genealogical purposes to identify the place-name from which any locative name under investigation is derived.

Even after all the upheavals and migrations of the present century, it is still true in England, and in the Lowlands of Scotland, that the locative names to be found in any region tend to be predominantly ones which have arisen from place-names present in the same region. This is especially true of those surnames that have become numerous, though there are some exceptions. There are some areas where there have been so many shifts of population that the surnames present in them no longer have very much of a local character. This has been true of London since hereditary names first began to appear, and for the last century or more it has been true of the Birmingham area. Many older industrial areas, however, such as those in the north of England, still retain many locative surnames of local origin. For many parts of the country, a look through telephone directories or electoral registers will reveal many locative surnames still existing in the county where they originated. Among the more numerous locative surnames in the Manchester telephone directory today, for instance, are Ainsworth, Bardsley, Barlow, Beswick, Butterworth, Crompton, Clegg, Entwistle, Kershaw, Meadowcroft, Oldham, Scofield, Sharples, Smethurst, Unsworth, and Wrigley, all from places within Greater Manchester. An examination of the telephone directories for many counties at the present day would furnish a similar list of surnames originating locally.

NOTES AND REFERENCES

1. E. Ekwall, 1951, *Oxford Dictionary of English Place-Names* (3rd edn.), Oxford University Press.
2. W. Nicholaisen, 1976, *Scottish Place-Names,* Batsford; M. Gelling, W. Nicholaisen, and M. Richards, 1970, *Names of Towns and Cities in Britain*, Batsford.
3. G. Redmonds, 1973, *Yorkshire: West Riding,* Phillimore, pp. 170, 172, 192–9, 204, 207–8.
4. R. A. McKinley, 1981, *Surnames of Lancs.,* Leopard's Head Press, pp. 263–5.

5. *Ibid.*, pp. 281–3.
6. Redmonds, *op. cit.*, p. 207.

CHAPTER THREE
Topographical surnames

Topographical surnames are those derived from terms for features of the landscape, whether natural (such as Ash, Brooks, Bywater, Carr, Clay, Fell, Ford, Hill, Marsh, Oakes, Pool, Ridge, Shaw, Underdown, or Wood) or man-made (such as Atlee, Bridge, Delves, Field, Furlong, Hall, Kirk, Mill, Pont, Stable, Stonehouse, Street, or Styles). Names such as Bridger, Fielder, Forder, Furlonger, or such as Borrowman, Boothman, Bridgman, Brookman, Crossman, Churchman, Hilman, Kirkman, Moorman, or Poolman have also been included in this category, because although they have at times been considered as occupational names there is evidence (discussed later) that in their original significance they were topographical. Names from the position of a person's house within a village, such as Townsend, Green, or Atwell, have also been included. Some words used as topographical terms were also the names of specific places; the names Combe, Holme, Beer, Hurst, and Holt are examples of this. Combe, from a word for a valley or hollow, is now and has for long been a quite common surname in the south-west of England. Combe as a topographical term was widely used in south and south west England, and there are a number of places so named in the same regions; it is usually impossible to say in the case of any particular family with the surname whether the name is from one of the places so called, or from the use of 'cumb' as a topographical term. Similarly, Holme, from a word for an island or a stretch of dry ground in a marsh, is also used as the name of a number of places, many of them in eastern and northern England, where the surname was present from an early date. Beer (often from a word meaning 'grove', though there are other origins for the surname in some cases, including 'bear') may not readily come to mind as one of the more common place-names, but it is the name of many places, most of them only small, and most of them in south-west England; the surname is likely to be derived in a good many cases from one or other of the place-names concerned, but it may also be from a topographical usage. Holt, from a word for a wood, and Hurst (or Herst, Hirst), from a word for a wood or a wood-covered hill, both occur as place-names in several regions, but the surnames from both words may be from one of the place-names in question, or from the use of the words concerned as topographical terms. Surnames such as these, where the classification is in doubt and where it is generally not possible to determine what the origin of the name is in any one case, have been dealt with here rather than in the chapter on locative surnames.

It can be seen from evidence set out earlier in the introduction that topographical surnames were originally much more common, in proportion to the whole body of names in use, in some parts of the country than in others. Surnames in this category were more common in the south eastern counties of England than in any other region. Sussex especially had a large and varied collection of topographical names, with rather fewer in Kent, Surrey, Essex, and Hampshire. Other parts of southern England had fewer, proportionately, during the Middle Ages, and the Midlands and East Anglia distinctly fewer. The north of England, except for Lancashire, had relatively few topographical names during the same period. This was probably also true of southern Scotland, though it is more difficult to get a general view of the surnames in use there than it is in England. Topographical surnames seem to have been rare in Wales and in the Gaelic-speaking parts of Scotland. The reason why some areas such as Yorkshire or Cornwall had relatively few topographical names was probably that in these areas there were many people with locative names from hamlets, farms, or other small settlements. Where much of the population lived in nucleated villages, as in many southern and Midland counties, it would be natural if people had names from the position of their houses in the village or from some topographical feature near their houses; in a county where there were many small settlements, it was no doubt an obvious course to designate any individual from the name of the place where he or she lived.

The number of topographical terms that have given rise to surnames is very large, despite the disappearance at various times in the past of a good many such names. One reason for the large number of names is that some were derived from dialect terms used in certain regions only. The use of such words was confined to limited areas, and it follows that the surnames derived from them were at first restricted geographically, though some of them later dispersed. Apart from these considerations however, the number of terms in use in any one area often seems surprisingly large, so that it is quite possible to find in a single county a whole batch of words meaning, say, 'marshy ground', another sizable group meaning 'valley', and a third collection meaning 'pit, excavation'. The reason for this is that the words in each group were not exact synonyms; each had a precise significance of its own for people at the time when surnames were being formed. For those who used these terms, such matters as whether there was a water supply in a valley, whether it was steep sided, or whether it had extensive flat land in the bottom were points of great practical importance, as were such points as whether a marsh dried up sufficiently in summer to afford pasture, whether peat could be cut from it, whether it held fresh or salt water, or whether trees or brushwood grew in it. Most topographical terms, therefore, were used with a precise meaning, and conveyed at the time a very accurate sense of the landscape feature involved.

Language, of course, is never static, and in the process of time some topographical terms underwent various shifts and changes of meaning. A good many words which gave rise to topographical surnames and by-names also occur as elements in place-names. However, in many cases the use of such elements in place-names dates from a period long before hereditary names developed. Most topographical surnames seem to have originated in the period between about 1150 and 1350, though rather later in the north of England and the Scots-speaking parts of Scotland. Many place-names came into existence at much earlier periods, and in the intervening time changes of meaning had taken place in the case of some words. To give an example, the element in place-names now usually spelt 'field' occurs in a good many place-names, usually as the last syllable; this is from the Old English word 'feld', which at one time had the meaning of 'open country' (as distinct from woods, fens, and so forth). By the time topographical names came to be formed, however, the meaning of the name had undergone some alteration, had acquired the meaning 'cultivated land', and was being applied to the open fields of villages. In considering the meaning of topographical surnames, therefore, the meaning that words for features of the landscape had at the period when hereditary surnames were evolving has to be considered. This is not necessarily the same as the significance of the word in modern English, or as its meaning at some much earlier time, such as the epoch when many place-names were being formed.

Most of the words from which topographical surnames have been formed are still in use in modern English, and as such are generally recognisable, even if their meaning had shifted in the last few centuries. Many of the surnames cited at the beginning of this chapter are understandable by people with no more than a knowledge of present-day English. Some of the words involved, however, are no longer in use, some were always dialect words with a restricted circulation, and others have undergone significant changes or meaning since topographical names originated. For example, the word 'well' has given rise to the surname Wells (though this is from a place-name in some instances), Atwell, Welman, and Weller, and in a few cases Will or Wills (though these are often from diminutives of William), and Wilman (though that is sometimes from a personal name). The word, however, at the time when hereditary names were developing, did not mean a well in the modern sense of the word, but a natural spring or a stream. The word 'ker', which is the original of the surnames Kerr and Carr, had the specific meaning of marshy ground with trees or scrub growing out of it. There are still around the East Anglian marshes stretches of woodland of this character, with place-names such as Spong Carr, Wigg's Carr, Decoy Carr, Buckenham Carrs, and so on, but 'carr' or 'kerr' does not convey any such precise meaning to most English-speaking people at the present day, and most people would be unable to attribute any meaning to Carr or Kerr as surnames. Or, to take another instance, the word furlong was not always used in its present sense as a measure of length. In fact, it was not until the reign of Elizabeth I that it was finally established by law that a mile consisted of eight furlongs, though the furlong had been used earlier as a measurement of distance. The word furlong was often used to mean a subdivision of an open field, and it is probably from this meaning of the term that the surnames Furlong and Furlonger (Vurlonger) come. Such names were probably given either to people who lived next to a division of the open fields, or, more probably, to people who had substantial holdings of land in the furlongs of the fields.

Other topographical surnames from words no longer in general use in modern English, and not easily recognisable, include Delf, Delph, Delve, and Delves (from a word for a pit or excavation), Slaughter (from a word for a bog; the name might also be from the place-names of localities in Gloucestershire, place-names derived from the same meaning of the word; the name might also be from the occupation of butcher in a few cases), Hithe (a landing place, but perhaps also from a place-name in some cases), Aldret (an alder grove), Tay, Tey, or Tye (an enclosure), Crouch (from residence near a cross, perhaps a market cross, or one or the crosses erected in some parts to mark parish boundaries), Hese or Hease (brushwood), Goggell or Gogill (a quagmire), Toothill, Tootall, Tootle. and Totle (all from a word for a look-out hill, though there has been some confusion with surnames such as Thurkell, Turtle, Tuttle, Thirtle, and so on, which are from the personal name Thorkell or Thorkill), Slade (a valley), Rake, Rakes, and Raikes (a pass or narrow valley), Garston (a grassed enclosure), Twitchen (a road junction), or many others that could be mentioned.

The surnames just mentioned are all from terms, no longer in general use in English at the present day, which were once used over wide areas of England, if not over the whole country, but some topographical names were from words which were only used in particular regions. It is obvious that the topographical surnames arising in any region will be drawn from the vocabulary of topographical words in use there at the period when surnames were evolving, and this is likely to include words very generally used and dialect terms with a restricted distribution – perhaps words only used in one region, or within some smaller area. Because of this, some surnames were originally common in particular regions, while remaining scarce or totally absent in other parts of the country. The fact that some surnames in this category had at first a limited distribution is some help in tracing the origins of families with surnames of the type. The early distribution of surnames has of course now been broken up by population movements, but it persisted for centuries after surnames had been formed, was still a good deal in evidence in the nineteenth century, and even now has not entirely disappeared. There are a considerable number of topographical names from words originally confined to certain regions. Some of these are from words still in use in local dialect, though perhaps not known to most people outside the districts where they are employed. For instance, the word 'fogg' is still in use in some parts of northern England, such as the Lancashire-Yorkshire border area, as a word for the aftermath, the grass growing on the stubble after the hay has been cut. The word was used over a wider area in Middle English, but it is not one that would be readily understood with that meaning by most people today. The surname Fogg, now mainly a Lancashire one, is from the word in that sense. Other names are from words once employed in local dialects, but now disused.

One consequence is that some regions retain a body of topographical names which are still much more numerous locally than nationally, though there are few if any such names which are now entirely restricted to a single region. For instance, the north west of England has long had a group of topographical names characteristic of the region, and still even now more common there than elsewhere. These include the surnames Moss (from a term for a bog), Platt (a plank bridge), Clough (a small steep-sided valley or ravine), Booth (a herdsman's hut), Scales (temporary huts or sheds, but the surname may be at times from a place-name; the surname Summerscales is a compound of Scales, with an obvious meaning), Rode and Rhodes (a clearing or assart – that is, land newly brought into cultivation; the surnames Royd and Royds are the equivalent forms in Yorkshire), Ryland and Rylands, with variant forms such as Rilance and Roylance (from land where rye was grown), or Fell. These surnames have for long been much more common in the north west of England than in other northern parts, and were generally rare, or lacking, in other parts of Britain. Most of them are still exceptionally common in the north west at the present time. At least some of them probably originated solely in the north west. Another group of surnames was, and generally still is, found much more frequently in the north west than in any other region, but is made up of names which do occur from an early period in some other regions, though less often; these include Edge (used topographically in the sense of a ridge with a sharp crest), Shaw (from a word for a wood, but the surname is sometimes from a place-name), or Riding and Ridding (a clearing). Many of the surnames involved are from words not now in use, even in local dialects, and their meaning is not likely to be obvious to most people. The distribution of these names has not been completely shattered by the population movements of recent times, and most of them still remain particularly characteristic of the north-west region.

Similarly, there is a group of topographical surnames especially common in the south west of England, but rare elsewhere. This part of England is one which suffered relatively little immigration during the nineteenth and early twentieth centuries, though more recently the tendency for people to move to the region upon retirement has brought many outside surnames into those parts. Such south western names include Yeo (a brook), Beer, Beere, and Bere (already mentioned), Hele (a nook or corner of land; sometimes from a place-name), Twitchen or Twitching (a road junction or cross roads), Trewen (from residence besides some prominent trees, but in some cases from a Devon place-name), Shute (a strip of land, but also sometimes from a place-name), and Passmere or Passmore (from the

Old French *passe mer*, a name either for a seafaring man, or for someone who lived besides an arm of the sea; compare the similar surname Passelewe, from *passe l'eau*, probably a name for one whose home was situated across a stream or river from the rest of his village).

Sussex – a more isolated county during the Middle Ages, and indeed up to the eighteenth century, than might be appreciated from its situation at the present day – had a number of rare topographical names which seem likely to have originated there only, and which even today have not spread very much outside. These include Costedel (from a type of cottage), Wister (the holder of wist or virgate), Stanstreet (from the Roman road once known as the Stonestreet), Soundry ('at the sundered, or detached, piece of land'), or Forbench (a bank or ledge in front of a house). Furlong was a word widely used in England as a topographical term from at least the thirteenth century onwards, but the surname Furlonger, and the variant form Vurlonger, seem to have arisen only in Sussex, a development to be connected with the exceptionally large number of surnames in that county formed from a topographical term with '-er' added.

There are, too, some topographical names that were originally widespread in the north of England and in southern Scotland, but were scarce or absent in other regions of Britain. The name now spelt variously Hislop, Hyslop, Haslop, and Heslop ('hazel valley'), one now quite numerous in parts of southern Scotland, seems originally to have been confined to that region and to the north east of England, though it is now to be found in most parts of Britain, and is a surname which has proliferated markedly in numbers. The surname Pullar has more than one origin (in some cases it began as a nickname, 'pull Hare'), but as a topographical name ('pool bank') it seems originally to have been confined to some parts of Scotland and to the north of England. It has long been associated with Perth. The surname Strath ('wide valley') has for long been well established in parts of east Scotland, but does not seem to have originated in any other region, and is still generally scarce in England.

Most regions in England, and in the Scots-speaking parts of Scotland, had at first a body of topographical names which were quite common locally but were absent or lacking elsewhere. This is especially obvious in dealing with counties such as for instance Devon, Sussex, or Lancashire, each of which was somewhat cut off at the period when surnames were evolving, but it is true to a lesser degree of most parts of Britain, though topographical surnames were

rarely formed in Wales or in the Gaelic-speaking parts of Scotland.

A few topographical names may have the appearance at first sight of being occupational; for example, the surnames Pott and Potts, fairly common names in south east England, are from a word 'pott', which had the meaning of 'pit' or 'hollow', though the name Potter always seems to be an occupational one in origin; the word 'binn' was another term meaning 'hollow', and in at least some cases the names Binns and Binn are from this use of the term (though Binns is from a Yorkshire place-name in some instances); the name Binner has sometimes been thought to be an occupational one for someone who made bins, but it is often from the word 'binn' in the topographical sense, with the suffix '-er' added, as in Bridger, Fielder, etc.

The origins of some other topographical surnames are perhaps not immediately obvious. The name Horn, or Horne, for example, is often from residence near a curving, horn-shaped, spur of land; compounds such as Woodhorn have a similar meaning. It must be uncertain whether Whitehorn is a similar case, or whether it is a nickname in origin. Hook is usually from residence near a hook-shaped bend in a river or stream, and Hooker has the same meaning. Some surnames ending in '-head', which might appear to be nicknames based on physical characteristics, are in fact topographical names, from residence at the head of a valley. Broadhead is often, perhaps always, a topographical name of this kind. Whitehead is in many cases from a former locality in Lancashire, near Burnley, now apparently lost, at the head of a Pennine valley; the surname was for long numerous in that area, and it is still one of the more common surnames in east Lancashire. Surnames such as Sidebottom, Long-bottom, or Shufflebottom, sometimes the source of slight embarrass-ment to sensitive bearers of such names, are from residence in valley bottoms. Shufflebottom, or Shovelbottom, is from a Lancashire place-name, now Shipperbottom, originally Schyppewallebothem, 'valley of the sheep wash'.

In addition, some topographical names are from terms in the French language. Some of these are from words borrowed from French into English at relatively early periods, and still in use in modern English, such as the surnames Stable, Castle, and Chambers. Such names are easily recognisable today, and probably arose in England, rather than being brought into the country by migration from France. The origins of some other surnames may be less obvious. The name Place or Plaice, for example, is from a French topographical term, either from 'place' in the sense of a market place, or from a term for an enclosure with quick set hedges. (Possibly in a

79

few cases it may be from the species of fish.) Roach or Roche is a topographical name from residence near a prominent rock. Boys, Boyce, Boice, and similar forms are usually from the French *bois*, and have the same meaning as the English wood. Other surnames, still present in England, but derived from French topographical terms, include Cowdray ('hazel copse', but possibly from one of the place-names formed from the topographical term, such as Cowdray in Sussex, or the French place-names Coudrai or Coudray), Fallas or Fallis (from *falaise*, 'cliff', or possibly from the French place-name Falaise), Fraine, Frayne, and Freyne ('ash tree'), Frater ('refectory', probably for a lay servant in a monastic refectory; *not* from the Latin word for 'brother'), Lisle and Lyle ('island', with the French definite article), Marris ('marsh', or from the French place-name Marais). Pomeroy ('apple orchard', or from one of the French places called La Pommeraye or La Pommeraie), or Such, Sutch, and Zouche ('tree stump'). Though these names are from French terms, at least some of them arose in England and their presence in this country is not solely caused by migration from France.

It might appear, at first sight, that it would be easy to perceive the meaning and origins of topographical surnames, and indeed many are from words still in common use and are recognisable without too much difficulty, but as can be seen from what has been said, that is not always the case. The above observations cover only a small proportion of the surnames in this category which need elucidation, and anyone interested in the meaning and origin of a surname of the type would be advised to check the name against what is said in one of the standard dictionaries of surnames (for which, see the 'Advice on further reading' at the end of the book). Some useful additional information about the rarer topographical surnames can be obtained from works on local dialects.

SURNAMES SUCH AS BRIDGER OR BRIDGMAN

An examination of any source which lists large numbers of surnames in most parts of Britain will show the presence there of a good many surnames formed from a topographical term with the suffix '-er' added, such as Bridger, Brooker and Broker, Churcher, Croucher, Downer, Fielder, Forder, Gater, Hooker, Grover, Stapler, Streeter, Waterer, Weller, and many others, and also of a similar group of names made up of a topographical term with the suffix '-man' added, such as Boothman, Bridgman, Brookman, Churchman, Crossman, Denman, Hilman, Wellman, and so forth. The total number of surnames in these groups is quite large. Many of the surnames involved have the appearance of being derived from words for occupations, and indeed some have been assumed to have such an origin. There is a certain natural tendency to think that any surname ending in '-er' must be from a word for an occupation, but in fact it is not as straightforward as that. The early history of such surnames, both those ending in '-er' (Bridger, etc.), and those ending in '-man' (Bridgman, etc.), shows that they are topographical, derived from living near the feature of the landscape which makes up the first element in the name. Thus Bridger and Bridgman are from living near a bridge, Croucher and Crossman from living near a cross (such as a market cross), Wellman and Weller from living near a spring or stream, and so forth. The clearest indication of the true origin of names belonging to both these types comes from the evidence that when such surnames were first being formed, in the thirteenth and fourteenth centuries, names in '-er' or '-man' were used interchangeably with forms without such suffixes, so that, for instance, a single person might be called sometimes, atte Bridge, sometimes Bridger and sometimes Bridgman. Many examples of this can be found in Sussex, a county where topographical surnames and by-names were exceptionally numerous from an early date. Thus, for example, Robert atte Linch ('at the hillside'), a fourteenth century resident at Madehurst in that county, is also mentioned as Robert Lincher; in the same way Walter atte Barre, a Sussex man living about 1300, is also named as Walter le Barrer; John atte Trandle ('at the circle', a name probably from a large circular earthwork in Sussex, near Goodwood), another fourteenth century Sussex man, is also referred to as John Trandleman; William atte Lote ('at the land divided by lot, a fairly common practice in the Middle Ages for assigning strips of meadow), in Sussex at the same period, is also mentioned as William Loteman. Many examples of this sort can be found, and it is clear that in the thirteenth and fourteenth centuries it was not felt that there was any significant difference in meaning between, say, Lincher and atte Linch, or between atte Trandle and Trandleman. It follows from this that surnames formed from a topographical term with either '-er' or '-man' ought to be considered as having a topographical meaning, and not an occupational one. In fact the forms for such surnames continued to be flexible as late as the sixteenth and seventeenth centuries. George Athoth ('at the heath'), a landowner at Wivelsfield in Sussex during the seventeenth century, for example, was also known as Hother; Thomas Hope (whose name was from the topographical meaning of 'hope', probably signifying 'raised land in a marsh'), was also known as Hopper. Researchers who push their investigations back into the sixteenth or seventeenth centuries should be aware that this variability of forms in topographical surnames may complicate matters, particularly in the south-east of England where such surnames were more common than elsewhere.

Such evidence shows that surnames such as Bridger, Bridgman, etc., were in origin topographical, but many surnames in this group, especially those ending in '-er', have at times been considered as occupational, in error. Binner, for example, already mentioned, comes in at least some cases from the use of 'binn' as a topographical term. The surnames Hoper and Hopper, in later times often confused with, and assimilated to, the genuinely occupational name Hooper, are normally from the use of 'hope' as a word for a feature of the landscape. Waterer is from residence by a stream, lake, etc. Flasher is from the term 'flasshe' (a lamp or pool), and Flashman, a name with a villainous significance from *Tom Brown's Schooldays*, has the same origin, while Flusher is a variant of Flasher. Hammer is from the word 'hamme', meaning a water meadow or damp ground alongside a stream, though Hamer is usually from the name of a place in Lancashire. Marker, a surname which has several possible origins, is sometimes from residence at a mark, or boundary. Perryer, which has sometimes been supposed to mean 'quarrier', is usually a name with the same meaning as atte Perye, 'at the pear tree'. Titchener and Tichner are from Twitchen, already mentioned.

It would be possible to give many more examples of surnames which appear at first sight to be occupational, but which are in fact by origin topographical. Surnames, of course, can in some cases have more than one origin. Because of this, it is important to trace any surname as far back as possible if its origins are being researched, and to bear in mind the general character of surnames in the region where any name under investigation first developed, if that can be ascertained. To give but one example of the ambiguities that can exist, the surname Winder is at times from the topographical term 'atte Wynde' ('at the winding path, alley, stream, etc.'), and this is the usual meaning when the name originates in the south east of England. There are, however, several places named Winder in Cumberland, Lancashire, and Yorkshire, and when the surname occurs in those regions it is often from one of the place-names in question. In addition, it has been suggested that Winder is an occupational name, from the task of winding wool, though evidence for such an origin seems to be lacking.

Complications such as these, though only affecting a minority of surnames, have to be reckoned with not only in considering what the original meaning of a name was, but also in considering the part of the country in which any name is likely to have arisen in the first instance.

The suffixes '-er' and '-man' seem only to have been added to simplex topographical terms (that is, terms made up of one element only), as in all the examples given. Topographical terms made up from more than one element never seem to have acquired either suffix. Townsend, for instance, though it is one of the more common topographical names, never occurs with '-er' or '-man' added. As far as can be seen from the evidence, the two different suffixes do not seem to have conveyed different meanings at the time when surnames were being formed. It does not seem, for instance, that Bridger meant something different from Bridgman, or that Hiller meant something different from Hillman. It is difficult to be certain about this, as it is only very exceptionally that there is any evidence about just how surnames were acquired, or about just what the precise meaning of any surname was. Just possibly, there was some difference in the shades of meaning which each type of name originally had, but if that was so, it cannot now be detected from the way the names were used. A somewhat similar situation existed in the case of occupational names. Pairs of such names existed – for instance, Smither and Smithman, Capper and Capman – in use side by side in the same areas and at the same periods, without there being any obvious difference of meaning involved. It is not a question of regional differences in the types of surname or by-name present in different parts of the country. Pairs of names, such as Bridger and Bridgman, Brooker and Brookman, and so forth, existed side by side in the same counties, from the time when such names first begin to emerge. In fact both types of name have long been especially common in south-east England, more so than elsewhere. There is also no sign that differences of social class were involved. It does not seem that persons named. say, Brooker, were of higher status than those named, say, Brookman, or anything like that.

Historically, surnames of the type of Bridger, Bridgman, and so forth were formed relatively late. It seems unlikely that any hereditary names of either type arose much before 1200, though isolated by-names occur earlier. Many such surnames or by-names occur during the thirteenth century, but the formation of new names of both kinds continued into the fourteenth and fifteenth centuries, even in areas like the south east of England where the acquisition of hereditary names by most of the population was early. There was a distinctly regional character about the distribution of both types. From the thirteenth century both were most common, in proportion to the whole number of names in use, in the south east, and especially so in Sussex. Both types are found, though less frequently, in the Midlands, East Anglia, and the south west (though for some time rare in Cornwall). There are very few instances of surnames from a topographical term with '-er' in the north of England, or in the Scots-speaking parts of Scotland, and it is doubtful if such names ever originated in any of those regions. It seems probable that the few examples found in those parts were the result of migration. A few surnames in '-man' appear in the north of England from the thirteenth century onwards, and seem likely to have arisen there. The original distribution persisted over a long period, and even in the seventeenth century the south east of England was still marked by a high proportion of surnames of both types. Even today, surnames of the type such as Bridger, Fielder, and so on remain relatively rare in the north of England.

A small number of surnames have been formed by adding '-er' or '-man' to the names of places. This seems to have been the result of a usage similar to the use of the word Londoner to refer to someone living in the capital. There was never any very large number of surnames or by-names formed in this way, none of the individual names ever became numerous, and a good many such names which can be found at one period or another in the past have become extinct. Names formed from a place-name with '-er' seem mostly to have originated in the south and Midlands of England, and to be from place-names in those regions. Few originated in the north of England, mostly ones which developed at a relatively late date, after about 1500. A few surnames of the type are still in use today, such as Risbridger or Rushbridger (from one of the places called Rice Bridge, Ridgebridge, or Risebridge, all in the south east of England), or Cresweller (from one of the places called Cresswell or Creswell).

A similarly small number of surnames exist that were formed from a place-name with '-man' added. Some names of this type which once existed never became hereditary, and only a few survive to the present day. Most known examples of such surnames or by-names originated from place-names in the north of England, and it is probable that the great majority of such names were formed there, and only very rarely in any other part of Britain. (It is doubtful if the name Kendalman, already mentioned, is an example of a surname of the kind under discussion, as it seems to have been an occupational term.) A few surnames in the group survive to the present day, such as Penkethman (from Penketh in Lancashire), or Fentiman (from one of the places called Fenton, probably in fact from Church Fenton in West Yorkshire), but none of them is at all common. They are now not limited to northern England, but have dispersed to other regions.

It is probable that names such as Penkethman, Fentiman, and so forth were not in fact locative or topographical names at all. It has been shown that the name Fentiman, originally Fentonman, began with someone who was probably a tenant in Yorkshire of a family called Fenton,[1] and it is probable that other surnames of the type began in a similar way. Penketh, for example, is an old-established locative surname in Lancashire, formed from a local place-name, and Penkethman probably meant originally 'tenant or servant of a man surnamed Penketh', rather than 'the man from Penketh'.[2] What makes this more likely is the existence of a group of surnames formed from a personal name with '-man' added, such as Addiman (from Adam), Harriman, Hickman (from a pet form of Richard), Jackman, Janman, Mathewman, and so forth. This is another small group of surnames, nowhere at all numerous, but rather more common in the north of England than elsewhere. These surnames are discussed in the chapter on occupational names.

A few surnames ending in '-man' are in fact derived from place-names ending in '-ham', and are the result of surnames undergoing changes in the course of time, so that their origins have been obscured. Thus, for instance, Deadman or Dedman is from Debenham in Suffolk, Hadman from Hadenham in Buckinghamshire, and Tudman from one of the East Anglian places called Tuddenham. Swetman or Sweetman is sometimes from Swettenham in Cheshire, though it is sometimes from an Old English personal name, and though Swettenham survives, unaltered, as a surname. The appearance of such surnames can be misleading, but only a small number have been modified in this way, and these are usually listed in the standard dictionaries of surnames.

PRESENCE OF FINAL '-S' IN TOPOGRAPHICAL SURNAMES

A high proportion of the topographical surnames in use at the present time end in '-s'. Names such as Mills, Brooks, Bridges, Downes, Woods, and so forth are very common. In some cases names in '-s' exist, while forms without the final '-s' are either very rare, or have completely disappeared; Styles, for example, now survives as a surname, while Style or Stile seems to have become very rare, or to give another example, forms such as Sands, Sandes, and Sandys are now much more common than Sand. Surnames such as Mills, Bridges, and so on arose in some cases from situations where there were several mills, bridges, etc., close together. Names like Sandes or Sandys possibly arose from the presence at points along the coast of large expanses of sands. Topographical surnames in the plural can be found during the thirteenth and fourteenth centuries, but they are scarce at those periods, and in fact up until after 1500 the great majority of surnames in this category are without a final '-s'.

Many surnames of the type acquired a terminal '-s' after having existed as hereditary names for several generations without any such ending. A good many examples of this happening can be discovered if families with topographical surnames are traced in parish registers, especially in the period between about 1550 and 1650. If this is done, it can often be seen that families often have surnames in the singular form, that then spellings in '-s' begin to appear, at first spasmodically, but gradually becoming more common, until, after perhaps a century during which there have been fluctuating spellings, the forms in '-s' become the usual ones, and the singular forms fall into disuse. Such developments can most easily be seen in the south east of England. where topographical names are exceptionally numerous, but they are not confined to any one region. It is less easy to obtain evidence about what is happening in such matters for the time before parish registers became available, but a fair number of examples can be found during the fourteenth and fifteenth centuries of individuals with topographical surnames or by-names which are given sometimes with a final '-s', sometimes without it, and there are a few cases where it can be seen that families at those periods gain an '-s' to surnames which earlier did not have such a termination. Occasionally, too, instances can be found of families with surnames which acquired an '-s' as late as the eighteenth century. It does not appear that the final '-s' in topographical names is ever a possessive ending, of the kind which occurs in surnames such as Williams, Roberts, etc.

Such developments obviously create a complication in tracing the descents of some families especially during the sixteenth and seventeenth centuries, when the changes concerned are particularly common. One result is that topographical names which seem at first sight to be plural, such as Banks, Brooks, Rhodes, Groves, Fields, Styles, Mills, Stables, or Downes, for example, are now as common as the corresponding names without a final '-s', or even more so. Before about 1350 topographical names with '-s' are scarce, and most of those which do occur are in fact plurals. By the seventeenth century the position had greatly changed, and forms with '-s' had become quite common, a position which prevails today.

As is apt to be the case when dealing with the evolution of surnames, it is easier to observe what is happening to names, than to explain why development occurred. The acquisition of a final '-s' is not confined to topographical surnames, though it is particularly frequent with names in that category. Some place-names which are from terms for features of the landscape and so on show the same development. For instance, the locality Barnes in south London, which has given its name to Barnes Bridge, was originally without the final 'es'. In Derbyshire, the locality known as the Riddings was called Riddinge in the seventeenth century, and in the same county Riddings Park was Riddinge Park in the seventeenth century.[3] Some surnames derived from personal names have acquired an '-s' or '-es' at the end after existing for generations without such endings, though this may be due to the influence of the many existing names such as Williams, Roberts, and so forth, with a possessive '-s', and some locative surnames also acquire an '-s' or '-es' ending which was not originally present. The same development can occasionally be seen in names in other categories. The surname Cocks or Cox has arisen in some cases through the addition of '-s' to the occupational name Cook, in some cases through its addition to the nickname-type surname Cock, and in some instances through its addition to 'cock' used as a topographical term ('hillock'). The causes of these developments remain obscure, but researchers ought to reckon with the complications which such changes create, especially when tracing pedigrees in the sixteenth and seventeenth centuries.

ATTACHMENT OF PREPOSITIONS TO TOPOGRAPHICAL SURNAMES

When topographical surnames are found in the twelfth, thirteenth, and fourteenth centuries, they are often preceded by a preposition, most frequently by 'atte', 'atter', or 'atten', less often by 'under', 'over', 'by', 'beneath', or 'above'. Up to about 1400, and occasionally later, surnames in the category are sometimes preceded in documents by French prepositions and articles, such as 'de', 'de le', 'de la', or 'del'. In most parts of the country prepositions of any kind had ceased to be used by about 1500, though in some counties, such as Surrey and Sussex, they were still being widely used during the sixteenth century. In a minority of cases prepositions have become fused with surnames, to produce names such as Atwell, Atlee, Agate, Agutter, Bywater, Bygroves, Underwood, Underdown, Overbeck, Overend, and so forth. When the preposition has survived more or less intact in this way, the nature of the surname involved is usually clear enough. In a great many cases the preposition has been discarded without trace. In particular, the prepositions 'above' and 'beneath', quite commonly used in mediaeval topographical names, have frequently disappeared. Some traces remain in surnames like Bowater ('above the water'), Bowbrick ('above the brook'), and Bufton ('above the village') (usually Boveton or Aboveton in mediaeval sources). Some surnames which are now simply 'Town' were once 'Above town' or 'Beneath town'. It is when fragments of prepositions have survived, attached to topographical terms, that the forms of surnames have sometimes been affected in a way which obscures their origins. This is true to some extent in the examples just mentioned, but there are many other cases. In some instances the last letter of 'atten' has become attached to the surnames, so that names such as atten Ash, atten Oak, atten Alder, have become Nash or Naish, Noaks, Nokes, Noke, or Nock, and Nalder, Nolder, or Nolda. The surnames Nye and Ney are from atten Eye, 'at the low lying land'. (The French surname Ney has a quite separate origin.) Noar, Nowere, and Nowers are from atten Ore, 'at the bank, shore, or slope'. The 'r' of 'atter' has in some cases become attached in the same way, so that, for example, atter Ea ('at the stream') and atter Eg ('at the island') have both given rise to the surnames Rea, Ray, Ree, and Rye (though the last is sometimes from the Cinque Port place-name, and Ray is sometimes from the Old French word for 'king'). The 'd' of the French preposition 'de' has at times become attached to surnames from French place-names, to produce modern English surnames such as Danvers, Daubeny, or Dangerfield, but it has also become similarly affixed to a few topographical names, so that, for instance, de Ash has become Dash (the compounds Dashwood and Dashfield arose in the same way). The French 'de le' or 'del' have survived in a few names, such as Dalafield or Delbridge. The name Delamere, now spelt variously Dallamore, Dollymore, etc., in some cases, is sometimes from a French place-name, and in these instances seems to have originated in France, but the surname was also formed in England, with the meaning in some instances 'of the mere (or pool)' and in others 'of the moor', the two words having become confused at an early period. In all these cases, and in some further ones where similar developments have taken place, the fusion of parts of prepositions with surnames has produced surnames of which the origins are not readily detectable at first sight.

Topographical surnames are at the present day very varied and numerous. Though not characteristic of Wales, or the Gaelic-speaking parts of Scotland, they are over most of Britain one of the larger categories of surname. The study of such names can tell us what the local vocabulary of terms for features of the landscape was, a vocabulary which in many areas will include some dialect terms confined to one region of the country. It can also tell us what topographical features appeared significant to contemporaries when, perhaps in the thirteenth or fourteenth century, they thought about a word or phrase to describe a neighbour's place of residence. For anyone interested in the history of a county's dialect, or that of its landscape, topographical names provide one source of information, and one which has not always been as fully utilised as it might be. Such names do provide some insights into the landscapes of particular areas, and they are worth looking at from that point of view, apart from their interest to those studying family history. Amateur students of local history might find it a useful exercise to collect the surnames in this category found within a county, or some smaller area such as a hundred, and to examine them to see what light they throw upon the local landscape in mediaeval times.

NOTES AND REFERENCES

1. G. Redmonds, 1973, *Yorkshire: West Riding,* Phillimore, pp. 143-52.
2. P. H. Reaney, 1967, *Origin of English Surnames*, Routledge and Kegan Paul, pp. 200–2.
3. K. Cameron, 1959, *Place-Names of Derbyshire*, Cambridge University Press, vol. 2, pp. 382, 384.

CHAPTER FOUR
Surnames derived from personal names

One important category of surnames is that which comprises surnames derived from what are usually called personal names, or 'first', 'Christian', or 'baptismal' names. These include surnames derived from personal names without any suffix or prefix, such as Paul, Petre, Lewis, Godwin, Ailwin, Thomas, Llewelyn, Finlay, and so on; surnames from personal names to which the suffix '-son' has been added, such as Thomson, Robertson, Williamson, Donaldson, or Dobson, and with these may be included surnames from an occupational term with '-son' added, such as Clerkson or Smithson; surnames from a personal name with a possessive '-s' added, such as Johns, Roberts, Williams, Toms or Thombs, or Harris; surnames from personal names with the prefix 'Fitz-'. such as FitzWilliam or Fitzalan; the numerous Scots surnames with the prefix 'Mac-'. or abbreviations of the prefix; and Welsh surnames which were originally prefixed by 'ap' or 'ab', but which today usually begin with 'P' or 'B', such as Pritchard, Probert, Bowen, and so forth. Surnames in these groups will be the subject of this chapter.

It is stating the obvious to point out that in any community where surnames are in the process of formation, the surnames that develop from personal names will depend on the body of personal names currently in use in that community. Surnames derived from personal names usually begin as by-names from parents' personal names. Men with by-names such as Toms, Dickson, or Harris were originally the sons of Tom, Dick, or Harry. People with by-names such as Godwin, Jackson, Bowen, or FitzWalter were originally the children of men whose personal names were Godwin, Jack, Owen or Walter respectively. In a large majority of cases, surnames derived from personal names are from masculine ones, but some are from feminine personal names. The causes for this are discussed later in the chapter. By-names originating in this way, from the personal names of fathers, or less frequently of mothers, in some instances developed into hereditary surnames, and descended to future generations. Just what surnames arose from personal names depended therefore, on just what stock of personal names was in use in the community when surnames were developing. It will help to explain certain features of surnames in the category under discussion if the history of personal names in Britain during the relevant period is briefly set out.

The number of Old English personal names in use before the Norman Conquest was very great. Many Old English personal names were 'dithematic', that is, they were formed by fusing together two words, in use in speech, to form a compound with two elements. The number of names which could be formed in this way was of course virtually unlimited. The formation of such personal names was not confined to England, but was a common feature of Germanic languages. In the great majority of cases, the personal names recorded in England before 1066 were those of people of some considerable rank and wealth, and it is not easy to be sure what the names of the peasant population were. There may well have been sharp differences between one region and another in the personal names in general use, but the evidence is insufficient to enable any accurate assessment to be made.

The Viking invasion brought in many Scandinavian personal names, which became established mainly in the areas of Scandinavian settlement, such as East Yorkshire, the East Midlands, East Anglia, the coastal parts of north west England, the Hebrides, the northern isles, or the Isle of Man. Scandinavian personal names also became established in Normandy, where some were modified under the influence of French phonetics. By the time of the Norman Conquest, Scandinavian personal names had spread outside the main areas of settlement, and were sometimes used by people who were not Scandinavian in descent. In addition, some Continental Germanic names (that is, names from one or other of the Germanic languages in use in Europe, but names not found in Old English) appear in England before 1066, though they seem to have been rare. After 1066 the invaders introduced a further stock of personal names. Many of these were Continental Germanic names which were widely used in northern France at the period. These included many masculine personal names which are still popular at the present day, such as William, Richard, Henry, or Roger. Other names introduced from Normandy at this time were Scandinavian, modified in some cases under French influence. Yet others were from the Celtic Breton language, names then current in Brittany, and brought in by the considerable Breton contingent among the Conqueror's followers. These included Alan and Brian (both still much used as personal names and the source of such surnames as Allen, Bryan, Briant, etc.), Harvey (though that is a name with more than one possible origin), and some others which have long been disused as personal names, but from which surnames still existing have arisen – such as: Wymark; Gernagan, from which comes the surname Jerningham; Judhael, from which come the surnames Jewell, Joel, Joule, Jolson, and Jekyll; Menguy, from which came Mingay and Mingey; Conan, still in use as a surname; and Tanguy or Tanneguy, from which come Tingay, Tengue, Tanguy, etc. Besides all this, Biblical names such as John, Thomas, or Adam, which were in use in France at the period, became more common in England after 1066, after having been previously rare in the country, at least as the names of laymen. Some further personal names also became common in England for the first time after the Conquest, such as Philip and Alexander, both ultimately Greek in origin, though they were in use in France at the period.

The combined effect of all these influences was that the number and variety of personal names in use in England after the Conquest was for a time very great, but this situation gradually changed. By about 1150 it was already the case that most landowners of any standing already had personal names which had been introduced after the Conquest, and by the same period, too, some of the peasant population, both free and unfree, had already begun to use the newly introduced names. Old English and Scandinavian personal names became much less used during the period from about 1150 to 1250, and by 1250 some such personal names had gone out of use altogether, and many others, though still in use, had become much rarer than formerly. Two Old English personal names, Edward and Edmund, continued to be popular. Both were the names of saints well known at the time, Edward the Confessor and the martyred Edmund, king of the East Angles; both saints were the object of important cults, and both names were used in the thirteenth century and later by the royal family, with whom the cult of the Confessor was closely associated. By about 1350 many Old English and Scandinavian personal names had disappeared entirely, and others had become very rare, but changes in the personal names in use took place unevenly. In some parts of northern England and in East Anglia Old English and Scandinavian names persisted to a greater extent than in the south and the Midlands, and were still fairly common between about 1250 and 1350, with the result that numbers of surnames derived from such personal names developed in those regions. Furthermore, whatever the position may have been before the Conquest, there is enough evidence to show that in the period between about 1100 and 1300 the distribution of Old English and Scandinavian personal names varied very greatly from one region to another, with some names being much more common in some regions than elsewhere. In some regions there were only sparse and scattered survivals of Old English or Scandinavian names by the late thirteenth century. In Sussex, for instance, the 1296 lay subsidy assessment lists about seven thousand taxpayers, and if the two personal names Edward and Edmund are left aside, there were only thirty two taxpayers with Old English personal names. These returns of course only list people paying direct taxes and do not include the poorest part of the population who may have had a rather different proportion of Old English names, but it is evident that in Sussex most Old English personal names had become scarce or disused. At the same period in Lancashire, however, a considerable number of Old English and Scandinavian names were still being widely used. Some personal names survived in small areas after they had become generally disused elsewhere, often because they continued to be used by a small group of interrelated families. In Lancashire, for example, the personal name Thurstan, Scandinavian in origin, continued to be used by a landowning family, the Tyldesleys, and some related families, long after it had fallen out of use generally, and it persisted in the county into the sixteenth century. This development is significant for the history of surnames, for personal names which survived in this way were especially likely to give rise to surnames, perhaps because personal names which persisted like this were rare and distinctive. In central Norfolk, for instance, the Old English personal name Eadmann survived into the fourteenth century, and the surname Edman or Ediman developed from it in that area. In north east Norfolk, the personal name Guthram or Guderam was in use in the late thirteenth century, and the surname Guderam developed in the same area. The history of surnames has consequently been influenced by the details of survival of some personal names.

The process by which most Old English and Scandinavian personal names were given up, and replaced by a group of names which had mostly been introduced after 1066, was thus both prolonged and not very clear cut. Although one major factor in the process was certainly the standing and renown that attached to the names brought in by the invaders, and especially to those used by the royal family, this is not a complete explanation of what happened. Between 1066 and about 1300, very many male personal names either fell into disuse or became very rare. Though most of the names concerned were Old English or Scandinavian, some new names brought in after the Conquest were lost, too. For instance, the Old French name Paien was fairly common in the twelfth century, but subsequently became very rare, though it survived long enough to become the origin of the surnames Payne, Pane, Pagan, etc., and to form the second element in FitzPaine. Similarly, the Breton name Judhael, already mentioned, was quite common in south west England during the twelfth and thirteenth centuries, but became rare after about 1350. By about 1250 it was already the case that in England a small number of male personal names had become very common. These are all still widely used at the present day: William, John, Thomas, Edward, Henry, Richard, Ralph, Roger, Adam, etc. The linguistic origins of this group of names are varied. Most other male personal names, whatever their origins, had become either disused or scarce in the country as a whole. A somewhat similar development can be found in some Continental countries at approximately the same period. There seems to have been a general decline in Germanic languages in the practice of forming new names by compounding words in general use. One result of all this was that it became very usual to have several men in one village with the same personal name, for this favoured the increasing use of by-names as a means of distinguishing one man from another.

Most of what has just been said applies to male personal names. There is much less evidence about female names, and it is also true that female personal names are less important in the formation of surnames than male ones. By the thirteenth century a few female names had become very common – Anne, Elisabeth, Jane, Rose, Alice, etc. – and most Old English and Scandinavian female names were becoming scarce. During the late thirteenth and early fourteenth centuries, at a time when new male personal names had virtually ceased to be created, new female names were sometimes invented, sometimes fanciful ones. Sir John Arundel, a Somerset landowner, named a daughter Arundella; Miranda, sometimes said to have been invented by Shakespeare for the heroine of *The Tempest*, occurs in Devon in the fourteenth century, and seems to be one of the female first names created from a Latin root at this period. Such neologisms were unusual, however. Occasionally rare feminine names from Greek or Latin were brought into use; the Greek name

Olympias, for instance, was used for a time by some landowning families in south-east England. These usages too were uncommon, and the number of female personal names generally used was by the thirteenth century quite small.

The situation described above, where a small number of personal names came to be used very widely while all other personal names became rare or totally disused, had a great influence on the character of surnames derived from personal names, for most surnames in that category were formed after the middle of the thirteenth century. The situation about personal names remained without much change from about 1300 until after 1500, when new influences started to take effect. Puritanism led to the appearance of many new personal names, often drawn from the Old Testament. The practice also grew up of using surnames as personal names, at first mainly among aristocratic or gentry families. William Camden, writing early in the seventeenth century, remarked on this as being a fairly new practice in his day.[1] This sometimes led to people being saddled with Christian names which were not particularly euphonious, like the eminent lawyer, Sir Harbottle Grimston, for instance. It also led to the surnames of some well-known aristocratic families becoming established as Christian names, many of them still in use now as first names. Douglas, Dudley, Keith, Neville, Sidney, Stanley, and Stuart are all examples of this, though their origin as surnames is probably not generally realised. By about 1500, however, few new surnames were coming into existence, and these changes, though significant in various ways, had few consequences for the history of surnames.

This broadly is the history of personal names in England during the period when most surnames were being formed. In the Scots-speaking parts of Scotland a similar course of development seems to have occurred, though there is less evidence for Scotland than for England for the eleventh and twelfth centuries, and it is more difficult to know what the personal names of the general body of the population were, as distinct from those of such persons as landholders. During the twelfth and thirteenth centuries many Old English and Scandinavian names were still being used in Scotland, while some Gaelic personal names were also to be found in Scots-speaking areas. However, the same period saw the establishment in Scotland of many landholding families which were either French in origin or were English, but were using personal names brought into England after 1066. Partly no doubt through the influence of such families, the small body of male personal names which had come to predominate in England also became very common in Scotland. Many Old English and Scandinavian names, however, remained in use in Scotland longer than in England. In the Gaelic-speaking parts of Scotland, Gaelic personal names appear to have remained generally in use throughout the Middle Ages. In the Hebrides, where there had been considerable Scandinavian settlement, some Scandinavian personal names long continued to be used. In the Orkneys and Shetlands, which were under Norwegian control until they were pledged to Scotland in 1468 and 1469 respectively, many Scandinavian names continued in use.

In Wales, a body of Welsh personal names remained in use throughout the Middle Ages, and many of these eventually gave rise to surnames. Some Biblical personal names were also present in Wales, and many of the personal names which had become common in England by the thirteenth century also spread to Wales, though without becoming as predominant there as in England.

This general history of personal names in Britain must be kept in mind when considering the character of surnames in the category under discussion. Surnames of the type may be divided for the purpose of studying their history into six groups:

1. Surnames derived from personal names without any suffixes or prefixes, such as Matthew, Paul, Petre, Thomas, Godwin, Jane, Ailwin, Owen, Llewelyn, Finlay, Duncan, and so forth.
2. Surnames derived from a personal name with the suffix '-son' added, such as Robertson, Williamson, Jackson, Donaldson, Finlayson, Ferguson.
3. Surnames derived from personal names with the addition of a possessive '-s', such as Roberts, Williams, Andrews, and so forth.
4. Surnames from personal names with the prefix 'Mac-', or abbreviations of it. This group includes some surnames where the prefix was once present but has been discarded in the forms now in use.
5. Welsh surnames originally prefixed by 'ap' or 'ab', now often beginning with 'P-' or 'B-', such as Probert, Pritchard, Price, Bowen, Broderick, and so on.
6. Some other surnames from personal names, not included in any of the above groups, including surnames with the prefix 'Fitz-', such as FitzGerald, FitzWilliam, FitzPatrick, and so forth.

Each of these types has its own history, and the general history of surnames derived from personal names will be clearer if each type is discussed separately.

SURNAMES DERIVED FROM PERSONAL NAMES WITHOUT ANY SUFFIX OR PREFIX

No certain instances of stable hereditary surnames derived from personal names are known in England before 1066, and surnames in that category seem to have been scarce before the Conquest in Normandy, where most of the small number of surnames in use originated from place-names. By-names from personal names did exist in northern France during the eleventh century, and were not rare, so that the spread of by-names, and later surnames, of the type in England may owe something to French influence. By the early twelfth century, surnames or by-names from personal names were beginning to appear quite frequently throughout England, and by the end of the same century were being used in the Scots-speaking parts of Scotland. The great majority of surnames or by-names from personal names occurring in England before 1200 were formed from personal names without any prefix or suffix being added. Thus, for example, the widely used personal name Godwine produced a surname or by-name Godwin or Goodwin, the personal name Aelfgar gave rise to the surname or by-name Aelgar, and to later forms such as Algar, Elgar, Ager, and Auger, the personal name Hemming to the surname or by-name Hemming, and so on. Such names were formed by taking the personal name of a father, or less frequently mother, and using it as a by-name, which might or might not become hereditary in the course of time. Some surnames or by-names prefixed by 'Fitz-' existed in England between the Conquest and about 1200. but were very much less numerous than those formed from personal names without any such prefix.

Deficiencies in the nature of the information make it difficult to follow in detail the evolution of hereditary surnames from personal names during the twelfth century. During the thirteenth century the amount of information becomes greater, but it is still not always easy to see what is happening. One factor in this is that surnames from personal names were less common among landholders, the best documented part of the mediaeval population, than among sections of the community lower down the social scale. It is possible to find a good many examples, spread across most parts of the country, where a son has a by-name formed from his father's personal name. Thus, for instance, Roger Ramkill of Woodplumpton in Lancashire, living about 1150 and later, had a by-name from his father's first name, Rafnketill, a Scandinavian personal name. Rather later, Adam Dudeman of Rochdale in the same county had during the late thirteenth century a by-name from the personal name of his father, Dudeman, an Old English name. Adam's two sons inherited the name Dudeman, which at this point can be seen to be developing into a hereditary surname. At Oxford, a family with the hereditary surname of Burewold were descended from an inhabitant of the town with the personal name of Burewold, who was living probably about 1150. Herman of Breckles, living in Suffolk early in the thirteenth century, had a son whose name was Luke Herman, and Luke in turn had a son named Richard Herman. In this case too the beginnings of a hereditary surname can be seen. It would be possible to cite very many instances of a similar sort from various parts of England, and it is clear that in most, and probably in all, regions of the country, personal names were very frequently giving rise to by-names, which in some cases evolved into hereditary surnames, from at least about 1100 onwards. There were considerable differences between regions in the frequency with which such surnames developed. In the north of England, where surnames from place-names were very numerous, surnames from personal names formed a much smaller proportion of the whole body of surnames than was the case in the south, the Midlands, and East Anglia.

It is not possible to say with any precision what proportion of families in any one region acquired surnames of this type, though comparative figures have been given in the Introduction. Nor is it possible to say in exactly what period such surnames, or the bulk of them, arose. However, many surnames formed from personal names without any prefix or suffix are derived from personal names which were either disused or rare by about 1300. The great majority of these had gone out of use altogether by, at the latest, about 1350. Most of these were Old English or Scandinavian personal names. Surnames of this type are much less frequently derived from the small number of male personal names which had come to dominate English nomenclature by about 1350. This is no doubt partly due to the fact that surnames or by-names from personal names were not common among the landholding clases, which adopted names newly brought into the country after 1066 more rapidly than did other sections of the community. From the large number of individual cases where families can be seen to be acquiring surnames of the type under discussion, and from the history of the personal names involved, it seems likely that most surnames of the type concerned evolved in the period between about 1150 to 1300. A few cases can be found where such surnames were formed rather earlier, and some surnames of the type continued to be formed during the fourteenth century, though not often, but most such surnames probably developed between the middle of the twelfth century, and the end of the thirteenth.

One consequence of this is that many such surnames are derived from personal names which have long been discarded, and are not in use today, so that the origins of the surnames involved are less obvious than might be supposed. For example surnames now in use, and derived from Old English personal names, include Allnutt, Allward, Ailwin, Brightiff, Brixey, Cobbold, Edrich, Elphick, Godwin, Seaman, Seavers, Woolnough, and Wooldridge; surnames from Scandinavian personal names include Allgood, Ingold, Kettle, Orm, Tooley, Tovey, and Thurkell, with other forms of the same name such as Turtle and Thurkhill; and surnames from personal names which were introduced into England after the Conquest, but which had become very rare, or had been lost, by about 1350, include Ansell, Baldry, Durrant, Everard, Fulcher, Goddard, Hammond, Herlwin, Otway, and Rayner. Few if any of these are immediately recognisable by an observer without specialised knowledge as surnames from personal names, for in such cases the originating personal names are nowadays unfamiliar. It is, however, the case that some surnames of the type are derived from personal names still in general use, and can generally be recognised without much difficulty.

Relatively few surnames of the type under discussion are from pet forms or shortened forms of personal names (what are sometimes called 'hypochoristic' forms). There are a few cases such as the surnames Dick, Hodge, and Hobb, from hypochoristic forms of Richard, Roger, and Robert respectively, but none of these is really common at the present day. In contrast, surnames ending in '-son' are very frequently from hypochoristic forms of personal names. It is not easy to trace the growth of hypochoristic forms because they are seldom used in documentary sources, which tend to give names in their full form. It is however possible that many hypochoristic forms found in surnames did not come into use until the thirteenth century, by which date the number of male personal names in general use was tending to contract and it was becoming useful to have a range of hypochoristic forms to help distinguish one individual from another. If, for example, there were several men called Richard in a village it may have been convenient to call one Rick, one Dick, one Hick, one Hickock, and so forth. Surnames or by-names in '-son' were rare before the late thirteenth century, a development discussed below, and this may explain why so many of them evolved from hypochoristic forms.

From the twelfth century onwards in England, diminutive forms of personal names were created by adding '-cock' to shortened forms of personal names to produce personal names such as Adcock from Adam, Battcock from Bartholomew, Bawcock and Bowcock from either Baldwin or Baldric, Hancock from Henry, Hitchcock from Hick, a hypochoristic form of Richard, Silcock from Silvester, or Wilcock from William. A number of surnames developed from the diminutive forms so created, and some of these have survived to the present day, and are not especially rare, such as Hancock, Hitchcock, or Wilcock. There has been some confusion between such surnames ending in '-cock' and surnames ending in '-cot' or '-cote', which are derived from place-names. The surname now spelt Jeffcote or Jephcott, for example, is from a form of Geoffrey, and the surnames now spelt variously Ellicock, Elcock, Ellacott, Ellicott, and Hellcat are all from the personal name Ellis or Elias, one quite common in the twelfth and thirteenth centuries. (This is also, of course, the origin of the surname Ellis.[2]) It is also the case that some surnames ending in '-cock' originated as nicknames from various species of bird: Heathcock, Peacock, Woodcock, and Grewcock ('crane'), for example. In most instances, the personal names to which '-cock' was added were ones brought into England after the Conquest.

In a similar way, from the twelfth century onwards, '-kin' was added to shortened forms of some personal names, to create diminutives, producing such personal names as Atkin or Adkin (Aitkin is a Scots form) from Adam, Dawkin from Daw, a shortened form of David, Hankin, probably from Henry, Hodgkin from Hodge, a pet form of Roger, Hopkin from Hobb, a pet form of Robert, Simkin from Simon, Thomkin from Thomas, Watkin from Walter, Wilkin from William, and so forth. The practice of adding '-kin' to personal names appears to have originated in Flanders, and to have spread from there to England, and to the Scots-speaking parts of Scotland. Some of the earliest individuals with either personal names, or by-names, ending in '-kin' found in England were in fact Flemings. In the majority of cases, the personal names to which '-kin' was added were ones introduced into England after the Conquest. The diminutives of personal names thus created by adding '-kin' gave rise to a number of surnames, many of them still existing at the present time.

The bulk of manuscript evidence surviving for the period between the Conquest and about 1300 consists of legal or administrative documents of a formal character, and pet forms or short forms of personal names do not normally occur in such documents, any more than they would be expected in similar records at the present day. In consequence, hypochoristic forms of personal names, such as Atkin, Adcock, Wilkin, Wilcock, and so on may have been much more extensively used in speech than would appear from the existing documentary sources. The increasing number of by-names and surnames ending in '-cock' and '-kin' which can be found from about 1250 onwards indicates that this was the case. By-names and surnames of the kind just mentioned were at first predominantly those of people in humble circumstances in the great majority of instances. Until after 1400 it is rare to find substantial landowners with such names, though in the course of time the effects of social mobility gradually altered this situation. This means that names of the sort under discussion are those of sections of the population which tend to be badly documented. These considerations make it difficult to trace the early history of such names in detail. It is also not possible to say with any confidence how such surnames were distributed in the early stages of their development. Most surnames ending in '-cock' or 'kin', however, are from personal names which by about 1150 were already in general use in most parts of England. Surnames in this group are, in consequence, not usually connected with any one region in origin. It also seems very unlikely that any of the surnames in this group can have originated with a single family. Early references to most surnames of the type concerned are too scattered for that to be at all probable.

Certain other endings found in some surnames derived from personal names originate from hypochoristic forms of personal names introduced into Britain after the Conquest. These include the final syllables '-et', '-ot', '-mot', '-on', and '-in', all still at the present day often found as the last syllables of surnames. Some of the surnames in question are from feminine personal names, such as Marriott and Mollett, both from hypochoristic forms of Mary, Emmett and Emmot, both from Emma, though Emmot is sometimes from a place-name, Emmott in Lancashire, Evett, Evatt, and Evitt, similarly from Eve, or Ibbot, Tibbott, and Bellott, all from pet forms of Isabel. More, however, are from masculine personal names, such as Drewett from Drew, a personal name brought in after the Conquest, but one which had become rare by about 1300 (this is the origin of the surname Drew), Parrott, Perrott, Perrel, and Perrin, all from forms of Piers, Tebbitt and Tebbutt from Theobald, or Hewlett and Howlett, both from Hugh. The present-day forms of some such surnames are not readily recognisable as being from personal names at all, such as Amlott from Ameline, Avelin or Aveling, from the long-disused personal name Avo, Arnott, Harnett, and Harnott from

Arnold (though Arnot or Arnott are from a Scots place-name in some instances), Willett and Willott from William, Willmot or Wilmot also from William, Pannett, Paynell, Pannel, and Pennell, all from the now obsolete personal name Paien or Pain, Collett from a hypochoristic form of Nicholas, Huggett, usually from Hugh, though occasionally from the Yorkshire place-name Huggate, Huwett, Hewett, Howett, Hewlett. and Howlett, all generally from Hugh, Higget from a pet form of Richard, Hodgett from Hodge, a pet form of Roger, and many others. Not all surnames ending in '-ot', '-et', and so forth belong to this group; Hickmott, for instance, is a surname of relationship, of a type discussed later in the book. Arlott is from a word which originally meant 'lad, youth', and Naldrett is a topographical name, 'at the alder grove'.

The presence in England of surnames such as those just mentioned is not necessarily due to migration from France or elsewhere on the Continent, even though the suffixes just mentioned are French in origin. Pet forms of personal names with such suffixes were in use in England during the twelfth century and later, so that surnames or by-names of the type being discussed could well have developed in this country, while it is of course also the case that French was the language normally used by landowners and the higher clergy in England from the Conquest until at least 1300.

Surnames or by-names from personal names without suffixes or prefixes were never confined to any one social class, though certain restricted types of surname within this general category were. A few instances can be found from an early period of landholding families with surnames of this kind; the Bainard family, for instance, large landholders in East Anglia and elsewhere in 1086 and later, had a hereditary surname of this type. In general, however, such surnames were originally scarce among large landholders. On the other hand, surnames or by-names from personal names, without any prefix or suffix, were common among the better-off sections of town populations from the twelfth century onwards, and among small freeholders in the countryside, from the same period. There is little evidence about serfs' names before about 1250, but when evidence does become available after that date, surnames or by-names of the type can be seen to be fairly common among bondmen too.

Surnames or by-names of the type in question can be found in any part of England from the twelfth century onwards, and were not rare in any region, but there were marked differences between regions both in the proportion of the total body of names in use which fell into this category, and in the way in which many individual surnames were distributed. Regional differences in the proportion of names falling into each of the main categories have already been discussed in the Introduction, and it has been shown that surnames from personal names were much more common in some areas than in others. The category of surnames from personal names can be divided into six groups, as already described. So far as England is concerned, only surnames of the first three of the six types described above occur with any frequency for any period before about 1500. Tables 2 and 3 give

TABLE 2

County	1	2	3
Buckinghamshire, 1332	235	3	8
Devon, 1332	138	< 1	< 1
Dorset, 1327	169	< 1	21
Kent, 1334–35	211	3	2
Lancashire, 1332	16	14	< 1
Leicestershire, 1327	161	5	8
Oxfordshire, 1327	202	< 1	39
Shropshire, 1327	161	8	38
Staffordshire, 1327	137	4	18
Suffolk, 1327	285	2	3
Surrey, 1332	140	< 1	< 1
Sussex, 1332	142	1	< 1
Warwickshire, 1332	153	4	48
Worcestershire, 1327	235	3	46
Yorkshire, 1379	66	62	< 1

In tables 2 and 3, figures are given for numbers of persons with surnames or by-names from personal names without any prefix or suffix (column 1), with surnames or by-names from personal names with '-son' added (column 2), and for surnames or by-names from personal names with a possessive '-s' added (column 3); per thousand individuals listed in each source. ('< 1' means 'less than 1'.) The sources are taxation returns for selected counties in various parts of England, for the dates as given. The figures given for names in '-son' include names from a personal name and '-son', from an occupational term with '-son', and from an existing surname with '-son'. The figures are for numbers of individuals, not for numbers of surnames. Some surnames or by-names derived from personal names do not fall into any of the three categories listed, and have been excluded. It is not possible to put forward figures for Wales or Scotland that would be useful for comparison.

TABLE 3

County	1	2	3
Buckinghamshire, 1524	219	38	77
Cornwall, 1664	284	4	81
Devon, 1524–25	258	4	13
Dorset, 1662–64	185	10	79
Gloucestershire, 1608	182	8	124
Herefordshire, 1663	184	3	140
Lancashire, Salford Hundred, 1524	45	63	2
Nottinghamshire, 1641–42	159	93	23
Oxfordshire, 1641–42	151	21	152
Rutland, 1552	157	43	31
Shropshire, 1672	143	12	241
Staffordshire, 1666	109	63	82
Suffolk, 1524	240	28	41
Surrey, 1662–64	141	6	49
Sussex, 1524–25	227	11	27
Wiltshire, 1576	160	9	95
Worcestershire, 1603	115	14	151
West Yorkshire, 1588	81	122	8

figures for individuals with surnames or by-names in each of these three types. The figures given in Table 2 are for dates in the fourteenth century, when names were either not hereditary or had not been hereditary for very long, and show what the position was at a period when surnames were still in the process of formation. The figures given in Table 3 are for dates in the sixteenth and seventeenth centuries, when the formation of new surnames had become rare in England. All the sources used list large numbers of the population, but it has not been possible to use a single source for all the counties listed. The reservations that must be made about statistics compiled in this way have been discussed in the Introduction. It has not been possible to provide details for every English county, because suitable documentary sources are not available for all of them. However, the counties chosen are sufficiently numerous, and distributed widely enough throughout England, to provide a reasonably complete view of the position in each region. The position in Wales and Scotland was so different that comparisons would not be meaningful.

It can be seen from these tables that there were significant differences between counties. These are most notable in the case of surnames ending in '-son' and in '-s', two categories further discussed later in this chapter. As far as surnames or by-names formed from personal names without any suffix or prefix are concerned, the most obvious feature is the relatively low proportion of such names in northern counties. The main reason for this is the preponderance there of surnames from place-names. Apart from this, it can be seen that by the fourteenth century surnames or by-names of the type were present in all the main regions, and that they were not particularly rare in any part.

In addition, some individual surnames of the type were much more common in some regions than elsewhere. Not enough research has been done to produce lists showing how every surname in this category was distributed, useful though that information would obviously be to genealogists and family historians. Some surnames in the category were already widespread by about 1300, and cannot be linked to any one region exclusively. Many examples of such surnames could be given. Among those which were present in most parts of England well before 1300 were, for instance, Alexander, Allen, Andrew, Austin (a shortened form of Augustine), Bartholomew, Brian and Briant, Clement, Ellis, Gilbert, Goddard, Godwin and Goodwin, Hammond, Humphrey, Jarvis and Jervis or Gervase, Lambert, Laurence, Martin, Matthew, Mitchell, Osborne (though this may be from a place-name in some cases), Payne and Pain, and Vincent. However, some surnames were common in certain regions, but scarce or lacking entirely elsewhere. The following list, which does not claim to be comprehensive, shows which surnames were much more common in one or two English regions than in others up to about 1500, giving under each region some of the surnames which occurred locally with especial frequency. Further investigations into the history of individual surnames, particularly the rarer ones, would no doubt enable additions to be made to the list, and readers who have carried out research into some of the less common names may well be aware of some surnames, not mentioned here, which were in origin confined to one region, or to a smaller area such as a county. Surnames, of course, were liable to migrate away from their place of origin at any period, and after about 1500 in particular the original distribution of names tended to be gradually broken up by population movements. Nevertheless, right up to the nineteenth century many surnames remained largely concentrated in the counties or regions where they had originated centuries before. The list given below may, therefore, give some help to genealogists or family historians trying to discover the part of the country in which some individual surname first arose.

In the list, surnames have been given in the form most generally employed today, and this is sometimes rather different from the spelling of the personal names from which the surnames in question were derived. If a surname was particularly common in more than one region, it has been listed in all the regions concerned. The distribution of some surnames was spread over two or more contiguous regions. For instance, some surnames were common over an area which extended from the southern part of the west Midlands into south west England, and in some cases into the east of south Wales as well. The exact spelling of some surnames has of course changed since 1500. It is also the case that some surnames which did not at first have a final '-s' acquired such an ending after about 1500, so that surnames like Adam, Simon, William, and so on became Adams, Simmonds, Williams, and so on; this is a development considered later in the chapter.

Surnames derived from personal names, without any prefix or suffix, which were especially common in some English regions before about 1500:

South east (Kent, Surrey, Sussex, Hampshire, Berkshire) : Allard, Ancell, Ailwin, Bartlett, Daniel, Edmund, Elphick, Goldwine, Harward, Humphrey, Ingram, Osborne, Seaman, Tomset.

South west (Cornwall, Devon, Somerset, Dorset, Wiltshire) : Oliver, Andrew, Batten, Drew, Harvey, Hosking, Hutching, Isaac, Jack, James, Jeffery, Jenkin, Perrin, Philip, Rawlin, Simon, Stephen, William.

East Anglia (Norfolk, Suffolk, Cambridgeshire, with Essex): Albon, Alger, Ansell, Benselyn, Brightiff, Cobbold, Dosing, Downing, Everard and Everett, Godfrey, Gunnild, Harman, Hobart and Hubbard, Rayner, Seaman, Thurkell, Toly and Tooley, Utting, Jeny, Kettle.

West Midlands (Gloucestershire, Herefordshire, Shropshire, Cheshire, Staffordshire, Warwickshire, Worcestershire, Oxfordshire) Allaway, Drew, Hancock, Harding, Hathaway, Hemming, Herbert, Hyatt, James, Pearce, Morgan, Meredith.

East Midlands (Derbyshire, Nottinghamshire, Lincolnshire, Leicestershire, Northamptonshire, Huntingdonshire, Bedfordshire, Buckinghamshire, Hertfordshire, Rutland) Alison, Andrew, Godfrey, Harniss, Hubbard, Ingall and Ingold, Jekyll, Marriott, Neale and Nield, Norman, Pell, Rayner, Sampson, Utting.

North east (Yorkshire, Durham, Northumberland) : Auty, Batty, Bowcock, Dolphin, Jowett, Oddy, Parkin, Story.

North West (Lancashire, Cumberland, Westmoreland) : Bibby, Bulcock, Gregory, Oddy, Orm, Otwell, Sagar, Silcock.

London has been excluded from the above list, owing to the way in which the capital tended to draw in surnames from a wide catchment area. It has been necessary to use the ancient counties, as most mediaeval records are drawn up on the basis of the then existing counties.

Some of the factors which produced these variations between regions can be detected. It is not surprising that surnames from Scandinavian personal names were relatively common in East Anglia, the east Midlands, Yorkshire, and parts of the north west, for these were all regions of Scandinavian settlement. This explains why such surnames as Auty, Kettle, Orm, or Thurkell occur frequently in some regions from an early date, while being rare or absent in others. It is also not surprising that surnames from Welsh personal names, such as Morgan or Meredith, were often found in the west Midland counties bordering on Wales. However, the uneven distribution of many surnames from Old English personal names, or from personal names brought into the country after 1066, cannot be explained on similar lines. The popularity of Old English personal names, and of the personal names introduced after the Conquest, varied locally from region to region, in the period when most surnames of the type under consideration were evolving, and it is probable that this was the principal factor influencing the distribution of such surnames. The very incomplete nature of the evidence for the personal names of ordinary people, especially for the period before 1200, makes it impossible to give any reliable statistics about the frequency with which individual personal names were used in each county or region. From what can be seen of the distribution of both personal names, and of the surnames derived from them, it was the case that, as might be expected, the more frequently used personal names in any region tended to give rise to surnames which were correspondingly numerous. There were certainly exceptions to this rule. It has been pointed out, for instance, that the personal name Edmund was very popular in East Anglia during the Middle Ages (and in fact later as well), as a result of the cult of the East Anglian King Edmund, but that surnames from the personal name, Edmund, Edmunds, Edmonson. were always rare in the region.[3] However, despite some cases like this, it does seem to be the case that, generally, the more popular a personal name was in any region, the more surnames developed from it.

The early history of surnames from personal names without any suffix or prefix in England can be discovered in its main lines, but it is more difficult to find out what the circumstances were in the Scots speaking parts of Scotland, where sources for the early Middle Ages are less copious than in England. Some surnames or by-names of the type were certainly being used in Scotland in the thirteenth century, though it is impossible to say how many of them were hereditary. By the fourteenth century such names were widespread in the Lowlands of Scotland, though not so common, proportionately, as in the south and Midlands of England. It is uncertain when surnames of the type ceased to develop in Scotland, but from the fourteenth century onwards many surnames or by-names formed from a personal name with '-son' added can be found there, and it is probable that in Scotland, as in the north of England. surnames derived from personal names which arose after about 1350 were usually surnames in '-son'. In Wales, as already described, the evolution of surnames followed a different course from that found in England. Surnames or by-names from personal names were very common in Wales, and were proportionately more common than in almost any part of England.

The use of by-names from personal names seems to have been widespread among Welshmen from at least the thirteenth century. Welshmen with such by-names, usually from personal names which were Welsh in point of language, can be found frequently in the English counties on the Welsh marches from that period onwards, and there are less frequent references in other parts of England. It is doubtful, however, if such names can be regarded as ones of a type adopted by Welsh people under the influence of English naming usages, and in imitation of England, where surnames and by-names in this category were already widely used by the thirteenth century. By-names of this type were not confined to Welshmen settled in England, or to the Welsh border areas, but occur in parts of Wales well away from the English border. The Merioneth lay subsidy roll for 1292–93, for instance,[4] contains many examples of such names. In Wales itself, such surnames were probably not hereditary before at the earliest the sixteenth century, though some Welsh surnames of the type became hereditary in England earlier. Some surnames or by-names from Welsh personal names, such as Cadygan, Morgan, Meredith, Owen, or Maddock, were already by about 1350 estab-lished hereditary surnames in counties on or near the Welsh border, such as Shropshire, Herefordshire, and Gloucestershire. Such names occur at the same period in other parts of England, though much more sparsely, and in the course of time became increasingly widespread. Before 1600 surnames from Welsh personal names can be found in almost all parts of England.

The origins of many surnames are obscured by one characteristic of the hypochoristic forms of many personal names, that is, the pet forms, diminutives, or 'short' forms of names. Where many personal names were concerned, hypochoristic forms came into use which rhymed with the first syllable of the full personal name. Thus, for example, the first syllable of Richard is Ric, and this was used as a short form of Richard, and gave rise to a group of surnames, Rick, Ricks, Rix (though Rix or Ryx is a topographical name in some cases), Ricketts, Ricketson, Rixson, and Rixon; Dick and Hick both rhyme with Ric, and Dick of course is still used as a hypochoristic form of Richard; Dick has given rise to the surnames Dick, Dickie, Dix, Dickson or Dixon, Dickin, Dickins or Dickens, Dickinson or Dickenson, and Dicketts; from Hick there are Hicks or Hix, Hickson, Hickin, Hickock, Hitchcock and Hitchcox, which in some cases has developed into Hiscock, Hiscocks, Hiscott, and Hiskett; names like Hitchin, Hitchings, etc., are often from Hick, but there has been some confusion with surnames from the place-name of Hitchin, in Hertfordshire. Hick in some cases was modified to Higg, and this is the origin of such surnames as Higgs, Higgins, Higgett, Higson, and Higginson. The surnames in this range are all ultimately derived from the single personal name Richard. It should perhaps be said that Higginbottom is not a name in this group, but is from a Lancashire place-name, Oakenbottom, 'oak tree valley'.

Other personal names are the origin of a similar variety of surnames. Robert can be shortened to Rob, from which come Robb, Robbs, Robson, Roblet, and Roblin; Robin, a diminutive of Robert, is the origin of Robbins, Robinson, and Robison; the form Bob, now widely used as a pet form of Robert, does not appear to have been used during the period when surnames were being formed, but Dobb and Hobb both rhyme with Rob, and have between them been the origin of a whole batch of surnames, Dobb, Dobbs, Dobbie or Dobey, Dobson, Dobbin, Dobbinson, Dobins, Hobb, Hobbs, Hobbis, Hobson, and Hobbins. Similarly, the surnames Hodge and Dodge are from hypochoristic forms rhyming with the first syllable of Roger, and from them are derived Hodges, Hodgson, which has in some instances developed into Hodson and in others into Hodgeon, Hodgkin, Hodgkins, which has sometimes developed into Hotchkiss or Hodgkiss, Hodgkinson, and also Dodgen, which has sometimes become Dodgeon or Dudgeon, Dodgson, and Dodson.

Many other personal names have possessed a similar collection of hypochoristic forms, which have in turn become the origin of surnames. The personal name William, widely used during the period when surnames from personal names were developing, has given rise to a series of surnames beginning with 'Will-', developed from hypochoristic forms, and many of these surnames are now common. It is very doubtful if Bilson is a case in point, as Bill is not known to have been used as a hypochoristic form of William at an early date. Surnames which have originated in the ways described above may present some difficulties when attempts are made to trace them back to the relevant personal names. It is perhaps not immediately obvious that Hixon or Hodson mean 'son of Richard' or 'son of Roger', but some light can be thrown on such problems by keeping in mind the way in which rhyming hypochoristic forms grew up from personal names. Apart, however, from the fact that there are a good many surnames now existing in the country which are from personal names long disused, and unfamiliar to present day readers, some surnames from personal names have been so altered over the centuries as to disguise their true origins. For instance, the personal name Leofric, which had ceased to be generally used by about 1300, and which is now known to the general public, if at all, only as the name of the earl who was Lady Godiva's husband, is the origin of the surnames now spelt Leverick, Leverich, and Leveridge. The more familiar name Alfred is the origin of the surnames Alfrey, Allfree, and Affray. The surnames Godrich, Goodrich, Goodrick, and Goodridge are from the Old English personal name Godric. It is not possible to mention all the cases in which the spelling and pronunciation of modern surnames differ substantially from those of the personal names from which the surnames in question derive, for examples are too numerous. The necessary information about the origins of most such surnames can be found in the standard dictionaries of surnames mentioned in the 'Advice on further reading' at the end of the book.

SURNAMES FROM PERSONAL NAMES WITH THE ENDING '-SON'

Before the Norman Conquest, there are cases of by-names occurring in England formed from personal names with the addition of the Old English word *sunu* ('son'). There are also some examples of by-names formed by adding -*sunu* to occupational terms or to nicknames. By-names ending in -*sunu* were not confined to any one region of England. So far as can be seen from the available evidence, such surnames did not develop into stable hereditary surnames of the modern type, nor do they ever seem to have been numerous. These remarks must be made with the reservation that the evidence for the period before 1066 provides the names of a very small proportion of the population, mostly those of people in the upper reaches of society, so that it is difficult to be sure of the exact position. By-names in -*sunu* continued to be used after the Conquest, but were rare.

Before 1066 there are some instances of men being identified as the son of some person by the use of the Latin word *filius*. Between about 1100 and 1300 such designations are very common in all parts of England, usually in the form of, for instance, *Johannes filius Edwardi* for 'John son of Edward'. It is often uncertain just what English, or after 1066 possibly French, phrase is being translated by this Latin formula, or even if it is anything more than a phrase put in to help identify individuals by scribes who actually drew up documents, and it is best when tracing the history of any one family, or of some particular surname, to refrain from using as evidence the names of people given in the Latin formula just mentioned. Normally the Latin phrase is not a translation of names such as Richardson, Robertson, Williamson, and so forth. Occasionally it can be seen that families with surnames beginning with the syllable 'Fitz-' (FitzWalter, FitzGerald, and so on), are being rendered, in documents written in Latin, by the use of this Latin phrase. For example, the members of the Devon landowning family Fitzpaine, are often mentioned in Latin documents of the twelfth and thirteenth centuries with their surname translated by the Latin phrase *filius Pagani*.

Surnames formed from a personal name with the addition of the word '-son' (Robertson, Harrison, etc.) are very numerous in all parts of England, and are today also fairly widely distributed in Scotland and Wales. A small number of by-names formed in this way can be found in England from the late twelfth century onwards, but such names were scarce, and none of them originally appears to have been hereditary. Between about 1270 and 1350, however, such names became very much more numerous in some parts of Britain. During that period names of the type became very numerous in Yorkshire and Lancashire, and occur rather less frequently in other counties in the north of England, parts of the north Midlands, and in southern Scotland. By about 1350 they had become a common type of name in most parts of northern England, and in many cases had become hereditary surnames. Examples of such names can be found in the south Midlands and East Anglia at the same period, but they were much fewer than in the north. In the south of England such names were still less common and in some south-eastern counties, Kent, Surrey, Sussex, and Essex, such surnames were distinctly rare. By about 1350 such names were already fairly common in southern Scotland. From about 1350, names formed from a personal name and '-son' made up a much larger proportion of the total body of surnames and by-names in use in northern counties than in any of the other English regions.

Surnames or by-names in '-son' appear in the Scots-speaking parts of Scotland from the late thirteenth century onwards, but it is not clear when they started to become hereditary. Such names do not appear to be as numerous in Scotland as in the north of England during the Middle Ages. However, names of this type were at first not much used by the larger landowners, but tended to be those of the less affluent classes, who were less well documented, so that rather more names of the type may have been in use than would appear from the sources of evidence. Some names in this category became quite numerous in Scotland, but in some cases this was due to Gaelic names being Anglicised. Ferguson, for instance, now quite a common Scots surname, is usually an Anglicised form of MacFergus, and Finlayson is an Anglicised form of MacFhionlaigh.[5] Apart from such cases, where the first element in a surname is a Gaelic personal name, a few surnames in this category seem to have arisen exclusively in Scotland, and not in England; the surnames Henderson, from Henry, and Patterson from Patrick, for example, seem to be entirely Scottish in origin.

Not only were such surnames particularly characteristic of the north of England, but within that region they were very largely at first the names of either small free tenants, or of unfree tenants, and originally they were hardly ever the names of substantial landowners. As time went on, social mobility gradually broke up the early distribution of names between the different social classes, but in the thirteenth and fourteenth centuries the class distribution of such names was very marked. It is necessary to consider how such a situation arose in the first place. The rapid increase in the numbers of such names in northern England during the period of about 1270 to about 1350 was caused by the acquisition for the first time of hereditary surnames by many families of bond tenants and small free tenants. Up to that point hereditary surnames had been rare in the north of England outside the class of larger landowners. This situation about the rapid increase of names in '-son' extended into parts of the north Midlands. The reason why such surnames or by-names were much less common in the rest of the Midlands, and in East Anglia, was that in those regions the same two social groups were at the same time acquiring surnames of a different type, formed from a personal name with a possessive '-s' added, such as Williams, Roberts, Harris, and so forth, a category of surname discussed later in the chapter. In the south east of England, where the development of hereditary surnames had proceeded rather more rapidly than in other regions, both surnames in '-son' and those with a possessive '-s' were for a long time scarce, no doubt because many families at all social levels already possessed surnames by the late thirteenth century, when surnames in '-son' and in '-s' first started to become common.

There was in fact something in the nature of a boundary running across the north Midlands, to the north of which surnames ending in '-son' became numerous, and to the south of which surnames in '-s' became common. There was never at any period a completely rigid division, with surnames or by-names in '-son' being very common in some regions and totally absent in others. During the fourteenth century, surnames or by-names in '-son' were common in north Staffordshire, but scarce in the south of the county where names in a possessive '-s' (Williams, Roberts, and so on) were common. A few names in '-son' can be found in Shropshire at the same period, mostly in the north of the county, but they were much less numerous than names in '-s'. In Shropshire, however, the position is complicated by the presence of many surnames or by-names from Welsh personal names. Names in '-son' were scarce in Leicestershire at the time, but common in Nottinghamshire, Lincolnshire, and parts of Derbyshire. This basic situation persisted over a long period, only very gradually and partially modified by migration. Names in '-son' were for long much more numerous in northern England than in other regions of the country, but some instances can be found from the late thirteenth century onwards in other parts of England, and it does not seem that this was due entirely to migration from the north. Even in the south east, where names in '-son' were still scarce as late as about 1600, some surnames of the type arose. It can be shown, for example, from a detailed examination of Sussex surnames, that some names in the category arose in that county, though such names were for long exceptional there.

It has sometimes been suggested that the prevalence of names in '-son' in the north of England is due to the influence of Scandinavian settlement in the region, but the area where surnames of the type were very common does not coincide very well with the area of heavy Scandinavian settlement. For example, judging by place-name and other evidence East Leicestershire was an area that experienced heavy Scandinavian settlement, but no single case has been discovered in which it can be proved that a surname in '-son' originated in that area, and surnames in the category were still scarce there as late as the sixteenth century. On the other hand, in north Staffordshire, an area where Scandinavian influence was less pronounced, names in '-son' can be found in large numbers from about 1300 onwards.

How big the differences were between the various English regions can be seen from the statistics set out in Table 2 above. These are drawn from fourteenth century taxation returns for counties in various English regions. In order to prevent the table from becoming unwieldy, figures have only been given for a selection of counties, but the inclusion of further figures would not have changed the picture significantly. The counties for which figures are given are representative of each of the main regions. Counties are not ideal units for analysing the distribution of names, as there are sometimes major differences between areas within a single county. Staffordshire has already been cited as an example of this. It is, however, difficult to deal with the distribution of names without using counties as the basic units, because almost all the records useful for such purposes were drawn up on a county basis.

Once surnames became fixed and hereditary, the original distribution tends to be gradually blurred by population movements. Despite this, many characteristics of surname distribution were very persistent. Table 3, above, is drawn from a variety of sources which, for the sixteenth and seventeenth centuries, list large numbers of the population. The table shows that surnames in '-son' were still mainly concentrated in the northern counties.

Since surnames in '-son' did not start to appear in any numbers before the late thirteenth century, the personal names from which such surnames were formed were of course those which were in use during that period and later, and these were in the great majority of cases names which are still in use at the present day. All the fairly small number of male personal names which were in general use during 1300 to 1500 gave rise to surnames in '-son' – Richardson, Williamson, Johnson, Robertson, etc. – and these were mostly names which were already widely distributed throughout the north of England by about 1350, and which by that date were appearing in other English regions, though more sparsely. As might be expected with surnames derived from personal names which were very widely used, each such surname seems to have been from an early date the name of a number of quite separate families. It is rarely, if ever, the case that there are grounds for supposing that any of the surnames formed from one of the more common personal names with '-son' was ever the surname of a single family. Although a large majority of surnames in '-son' existing at the present day originated in the north of England, most of them were widely distributed within that part of the country from an early period, and cannot be allocated to any smaller area within the region.

One characteristic of surnames formed from personal names with '-son' is that a high proportion of them are formed from hypochoristic, or 'short', forms of personal names. A search through a telephone directory for any part of England will show how true this still is for those surnames in '-son' which survive to the present day. As has already been pointed out, very many surnames have been formed from hypochoristic forms which rhyme with the first syllable of the more common personal names. Surnames such as Dixon and Hickson, from hypochoristic forms of Richard, Dobson, Robson, and Robinson from Robert, Dodgson and Hodgson, from Roger, or Wilson and Wilkinson from William, are still very common. The fact that so many surnames in '-son' have developed from hypochoristic forms of personal names is itself a piece of evidence about the way in which such surnames arose in the first place. Hypochoristic forms of personal names do not appear in mediaeval documents very often. This is not surprising, given the formal nature of most surviving written sources. Indeed, surnames are often the earliest and fullest evidence for the existence of hypochoristic forms. It is reasonable to deduce that surnames developed from hypochoristic forms were originally by-names used in speech, and not originally written down, and that in some cases such by-names evolved into hereditary surnames. All the indications are that names in this category began as spoken by-names in the vernacular, and many of them may well have been in use for some time, verbally, even perhaps for a generation or two, before being written down.

A few surnames which might seem at first sight to fall within this group in fact belong elsewhere. Tyson, for instance, is from an Old French word for a firebrand, and is really a surname of the nickname type; Dallison has usually developed from D'Alencon, a surname from a French place-name; Clawson is from one of the places called Clawson or Claxton; Frodson is from a Cheshire place-name, Frodsham, and is a variant which developed in south Lancashire, probably during the sixteenth century; Mayson may sometimes mean

'son of May' but it is often a spelling variant of the occupational name
Mason (there is also a place in Devon called Mayson); Pinson is from
an Old French word meaning 'finch', used occasionally as a first name
in mediaeval England. Other surnames now ending in '-son' which
are in fact from place-names include Tatterson, a late developing
form from the place-name Tattershall, and Gummerson, which is
often from the place-name Gomersall. In some cases there has been
confusion between place-names ending in '-stone', and surnames
ending in '-son'.[6] Some place-names in any case end in '-son' in their
present day form – for instance, in the county of Devon alone, there
are at the present day sixty-two places, mostly small hamlets, which
end in '-son' in the present forms of the place-names including such
names as Batson, Cottarson, Hampson, Hudson, Morson, Wilson,
and Yeatson.

There are a relatively small number of surnames formed from an
occupational term with '-son', such as Clarkson, Smithson, Milner-
son, Masterson, Cookson, or Kempson. There are also a small
number of surnames which have been formed by adding '-son' to
by-names or surnames already in use, such as Ballardson, Grayson,
Lambson, or Spinkson. These include a few from surnames or
by-names derived from, place-names, such as Kendalson or
Cravenson. Neither of these types is by any means so numerous as
the surnames formed from a personal name and '-son'. In general the
history and distribution of both types resembles closely that of
surnames from personal names with '-son'. Both types were originally
to be found mostly in the north of England and in the Scottish
Lowlands, though some examples can be found in other parts of
England. Both types, too, seem to have arisen among the same social
classes as surnames from a personal name and '-son'.

A large number of surnames in '-son', whether formed from a
personal name, an occupational term, or an existing by-name or
surname, first appear in the period between about 1270 to 1350.
During this period it is possible to find a great many instances where
such names become hereditary, while names in this category which
appear before about 1270 seem to have usually been non-hereditary
by-names. It is probable that a good many surnames in '-son' which
still survive today originated between 1270 and 1350. However, the
formation of new surnames of this type continued over a long period.
Some such surnames developed during the late fourteenth century
and the fifteenth. By about 1500 most families in England already

possessed surnames, but in some areas the development of new surnames in '-son' still continued. In fact, when new surnames arose in the north of England after about 1500 they were usually of this type. In some of the more isolated parts of south Lancashire, new surnames in '-son' were still being formed up to about 1650, but this was exceptional.

It may seem surprising that there is no group of surnames ending in '-daughter', parallel to names ending in '-son', all the more so since there are surnames from feminine personal names in England, and since surnames of a corresponding type do exist in some European languages. The fact is that during the Middle Ages by-names in '-daughter' did exist in the north of England. Women's names are much less fully documented in mediaeval records than men's, but during the fourteenth century it seems to have been fairly common in Lancashire and Yorkshire for women to have by-names ending in '-daughter'. The use of such by-names continued into the fifteenth century, but seems to have become less common after about 1500. Such by-names were still being used in part of south Lancashire up to about 1650, but this was unusual, and in most areas such names had ceased to be used well before that time. In a few cases such names may have been hereditary for a generation or two, as occasionally they occur as the names of men who had presumably inherited them from their mothers or some earlier female ancestor, but the growth of the convention that children should take their father's surnames prevented any general development of hereditary surnames of the type, and so far as is known, no names in '-daughter' have survived to the present day.

In some northern counties from the thirteenth century onwards examples can be found of men with two by-names in '-son', such as instance, William Robynson Dobson, Roger Aleynson Hoggeson, or Roger Hughson Hoggeson, all fourteenth century Lancashire men. Such double names are genealogical, giving the name of a man's father, followed by the name of his grandfather. For example, Thomas Jonson Amotson, also in Lancashire at the same period, was the son of John Amotessone, and no doubt the grandson of a man with the rare personal name Amot. Where such double names are found they do provide some useful pedigree information. They were, however, rare and restricted to the north of England and seem to have gone out of use by about 1500, so that their value for genealogy is in fact slight.

SURNAMES FORMED FROM A PERSONAL NAME WITH THE ADDITION OF A POSSESSIVE '-S'

At the present day there exist a great many surnames made up of a personal name with a final possessive '-s', such as Williams, Roberts, Rogers, Harris, and so on. A few such names have now come to be spelt with 'x', such as Dix or Rix. Such surnames are now often thought of as being mostly Welsh, and it is true that they are today common in Wales and among people of Welsh extraction living in England. The prevalence of such names in Wales, however, is a relatively recent development, only dating from the sixteenth century and later. This type of surname originally evolved in England. Such surnames were for centuries much more common in some English regions than in others, and traces of this distribution are still discernible at the present day. The history of surnames in '-s' is in fact parallel to that of surnames in '-son'. A few by-names with '-s' appear from the eleventh century onwards, but instances are scarce before about 1270. It is uncertain if any such names were hereditary before the late thirteenth century. From about 1270, however, such names start to become much more numerous, and by about 1350 they were already very common in some parts of England. The distribution of such names was by no means even, either geographically, or among the different social classes. In the great majority of cases, names in '-s' were originally those of small free tenants, bond tenants, and the less affluent members of town populations. These groups had for the most part been without hereditary surnames until after about 1270. Bondmen, indeed, seem often to have no surnames or by-names at all, until about that period, but to have been known by their personal names only. Geographically, such surnames or by-names when they first start to appear in numbers were much more common, as a proportion of the whole body of surnames or by-names in use, in the south west Midlands than in any other part of England. Gloucestershire, Oxfordshire, and Herefordshire all had relatively large numbers of such names by about 1350. In Shropshire there were rather fewer names of the type, but still a good many. By the same date such names were distinctly less common, but still fairly numerous, in the south-east Midlands and in some southern and south west counties, such as Dorset, Somerset, and Wiltshire. In East Anglia they were still less common, though not at all rare. In the south east of England they were originally scarce. Very few such surnames can be found in the north of England before about 1500 and even at later periods surnames of the type continued to occur sparsely in that region. It is doubtful if any such hereditary surnames developed in the northern counties at all. In Yorkshire some cases can be found of surnames from personal names, which had existed, sometimes for centuries, without a final '-s' acquiring an '-s' or '-es' ending at a relatively late period, often in the sixteenth or seventeenth centuries. This is part of a more general development, discussed later in this chapter.

The reason why very few surnames in either '-son' or '-s' grew up in the south east of England is no doubt that in the region hereditary names became widespread at a rather earlier date than elsewhere. The majority of the population had hereditary surnames by the late thirteenth century, when in some regions surnames in '-son' or in '-s' were becoming common. As already remarked, there was in the Middle Ages a marked division between the north of England, the north Midlands, and the southern and central parts of the Midlands, with names in '-son' occurring frequently to the north, and names in '-s' to the south. This division between the two different types of surname did not coincide with the lines of division between the various Middle English dialects.

People tracing the origins of particular surnames may find it useful to remember that surnames in '-son' mostly originated in the north Midlands, the north of England, or southern Scotland, and only rarely in the south of England or the south Midlands. Surnames in '-s' often originated in south or central England, with the south west Midlands the area where they were most common. The general history of surnames in '-son' and in '-s' seems clear, though the factors which led certain classes to acquire names of these types remain obscure, but the later history of surnames in '-s' is complicated by several developments.

One such complication is caused by the widespread adoption of surnames in '-s' by Welshmen at a relatively late period. From the sixteenth century onwards surnames in '-s' gradually became common in Wales, where the adoption of hereditary names was still not complete by the eighteenth century. Welshmen migrating out of Wales in the sixteenth century and later seem often to have adopted names in '-s'. Such migration was not confined to counties bordering on Wales. London recruited its population from a large area, including distant regions such as Wales, and there is evidence of numbers of Welshmen settling in the Thames valley. The Tudor subsidy rolls for the counties in that region contain many examples of taxpayers with Welsh surnames and with Welsh personal names. Surnames in '-s' which originated in Wales are therefore liable to be found in some parts of England from the sixteenth century onwards.

A second complication is the tendency of surnames in some categories to acquire a final '-s' or '-es', often at a relatively late period, so that some surnames today have an '-s' or '-es' termination which was originally lacking. Surnames formed from personal names without a suffix, which had existed for centuries without a final '-es', tended to acquire one. Many instances of the surnames of individual families gaining a final '-s' or '-es' can be found if the descents of families are traced in parish registers for the period 1550 to 1650, so that for instance the surname Richard would become Richards, or the surname Petre would become Peters. Researchers who carry their investigations back to that period may find it useful to remember that families with surnames ending in '-s' – Williams, Roberts, Richards, and so on – had in some cases surnames without '-s' earlier – William, Robert, Richard, and so on. Evidence for such changes becomes copious after about 1550, because parish registers are availabe for many places and supply a great deal of information, but instances can be found of families with surnames, originally without an '-s', acquiring such an ending as far back as the fourteenth century. It might be thought that the reason for this development is that surnames were influenced by the presence from the fourteenth century onwards of many surnames ending with a possessive '-s', but it is doubtful if this is the correct explanation. Examples can be found in the north of England, where surnames in '-s' were for long rare. The phenomenon of surnames gaining a final '-s' at some late period is not confined to surnames derived from personal names; many instances occur in surnames from topographical terms, as has already been described in the chapter on topographical names. One result of all this is that surnames in '-s' are considerably more numerous, proportionately, in the seventeenth century and later than at earlier periods.

In most parts of southern England many instances can be found between about 1250 and 1500 of women with surnames or by-names ending in '-s'. This has already been mentioned. There is an obvious parallel between this usage in respect of women's names in one part of England, and the growth of surnames formed from a personal name with '-s' in the same regions.

In a small number of cases, surnames formed from an occupational term with '-s' are really topographical in origin. Names such as Vickers, Smiths, and so forth seem in some cases to have originated as patronymics, and to have meant 'son of the smith', and so on, but frequently they were topographical, derived from residence at or near the vicarage, smithy, etc. In individual instances it can be difficult to discover how such surnames arose.

There are some surnames which end with the syllable '-son' followed by a possessive '-s', such as Johnsons, Robertsons, and so forth. A few surnames like this can be found in Herefordshire and Gloucestershire during the seventeenth century and later, but such names have always been scarce. They seem to have arisen through surnames formed from a personal name with '-son' migrating into a region where surnames in '-s' were very common, with the result that surnames in '-son' acquired a final '-s' which was not originally present. As far as can be discovered, this is a development which only took place in the south west Midlands.

SURNAMES FORMED FROM A PERSONAL NAME
WITH THE PREFIX 'MAC-'

Surnames with the prefix 'Mac-' originated in Ireland, the Gaelic speaking parts of Scotland, and the Isle of Man. We are not concerned here with Irish or Manx surnames except in so far as such names appear in Britain. Surnames, or more probably by-names, with '0' prefixed to the personal name of the grandfather, or earlier ancestor, of the bearer of the by-name, can be found in Ireland from the tenth century onwards. Surnames or by-names with 'Mac-' prefixed to the personal name of the father of the bearer of the by-name or surname seem to have been rather later in origin in Ireland, but were already in use by about 1000 A.D. It seems likely that such names were not at first hereditary, and that the development of by-names of both types into hereditary surnames was a long process, like the evolution of hereditary surnames in England. The process appears to have begun in the thirteenth century, and to have continued over a long period. The early history of names in 'Mac-' in Scotland is not well documented, and at first such names were found almost entirely in the Gaelic-speaking parts of the country. It is not always easy to be sure of the precise limits of the Gaelic-speaking areas at any one date; there were regions where both Gaelic and Scots were spoken by significant parts of the population, and there were areas where there was a mainly Gaelic-speaking population, but a landowning class that spoke Scots. There were districts in the central and eastern highlands, and in Galloway, where there was a corresponding mixture of different linguistic origins. In addition to this, there had been considerable Norse settlement in the Orkney and Shetland Islands, the Hebrides, parts of Caithness, and some places on the west coast, and also in the Isle of Man, and this led to the introduction of some Scandinavian personal names which in turn had some effect on the surnames which eventually evolved in Scotland.

Most surnames in the Gaelic-speaking parts of Scotland, whether prefixed by 'Mac-' or not, seem for centuries to have been those of clans rather than of individuals or of families. The extension of the power of some particular chief into new districts could lead to the inhabitants of those parts adopting the name of the chief's clan. In some areas the population might find it advisable to join whichever clan was predominant locally, and to adopt the name of the clan. Changes of name by whole communities in this way were still taking place in the sixteenth century.[7] If there ever was a period when all the members of a clan were blood relations, developments of the kind just described must have meant it ceased to be the case from some early period. It does not appear that most of the population of the Gaelic-speaking areas had hereditary surnames of the modern type before the eighteenth century. Even at that late period some surnames were still not stable.

Not by any means were all Gaelic surnames prefixed by 'Mac-'. Some well-known and numerous Gaelic names were of a different nature, such as Campbell and Cameron, both surnames of the nickname type. There were also some Gaelic occupational names, as has been already mentioned. It is also true that some landowning families had surnames which did not originate locally, and were not Gaelic in origin, but which are nowadays associated in many people's minds with the Highlands, and which indeed are now common in most parts of Scotland. The surnames Gordon and Fraser are examples of this.

It is sometimes impossible, when dealing with surnames in the category under discussion, to be sure whether a surname is Irish or Scots in origin. A considerable number of surnames occur in both countries. Further, there was never any period when there was no movement between the Gaelic-speaking parts of Scotland and Ireland. Apart from the more sizable migrations, such as the migration of Scots, mostly from the Lowlands, to the north of Ireland during the seventeenth century, or the large-scale Irish migration to various parts of Britain during the nineteenth, there was always a certain amount of movement. In addition, when Gaelic surnames are found in England and Wales they often do so in forms which have been Anglicised to a greater or lesser extent, which makes the task of identification more difficult.

The second element in surnames beginning with 'Mac-' is most frequently a personal name, in the majority of cases a Gaelic personal name. In view of the considerable Scandinavian settlement in parts of Scotland, it is not surprising that at times the second element is a Scandinavian personal name; MacIver, MacManus, MacRanald, MacKettrick, and MacLeod are examples of this.[8] There is a limited number of instances where personal names of varied linguistic origins, but generally ones widely used in English during the Middle Ages and later, form the second element in surnames of this type; MacIsaac, MacJames, MacKillop (from Philip), and MacWilliam are examples of this. Some such names seem to have originated as late as the sixteenth century. In a relatively small number of cases the second element is a Gaelic or English occupational term; MacPherson, MacStalker, MacIntyre, MacTaggart, MacLitster, MacLeister, and MacMaster are examples of this.

When Gaelic surnames migrated into England, they were subjected to influences which often brought about substantial alterations. In some cases the second element in names in 'Mac-' has been Anglicised, often by replacing a Gaelic element with some English word which bore a vague resemblance in sound. Thus, for example, the surname MacAmbrois ('son of Ambrose') has become Maccambridge, MacShuibne has become MacQueen, MacJarrow has become MacGeorge, and MacFetridge has become MacFrederick. In some instances when people migrated from Gaelic-speaking to Scots-speaking areas, or into England, Gaelic names were translated, so that MacDonald became Donaldson, MacIain became Johnson, and so forth. More drastically, Gaelic names were sometimes exchanged for Scots or English ones which had some similarity, but which had quite different origins. Weir, for instance, was sometimes substituted for MacNair, or Cochrane for Maceachran.[9] In some Gaelic names, too, the first two letters of 'Mac-' came to be discarded, leaving a name beginning with 'C', or in some instances 'K'. Thus MacOwen has become Keown or Cowan, MacCurtin has become Curtin, and so on. This development was especially typical of names originating in the Isle of Man, but as in the above examples it has occurred in some Scottish Gaelic names.

Very few Gaelic surnames, whether from Scotland, Ireland, or the Isle of Man, occur in England and Wales during the period before about 1500, and during the same time Gaelic names were not common in the Scots-speaking parts of Scotland. Although Gaelic surnames or by-names can be found in increasing numbers in most parts of Scotland from the sixteenth century onwards, it was not until the eighteenth century, and particularly after the 1745 rising, that Gaelic names started to appear in considerable numbers in those parts of Britain outside the Gaelic-speaking areas. Even so, the scarcity of Gaelic surnames in most parts of England and Wales for any period before about 1800 is notable. It was not until the nineteenth century that Gaelic surnames, whether Scots, Irish, or Manx in origin, first became really common in most English and Welsh areas. Even then Gaelic names were still relatively scarce in some parts of Scotland. H. B. Guppy, drawing on evidence for the end of the nineteenth century, drew up a list of thirty three names which he found were then the most common names in the Border counties of Scotland, and this did not include a single name beginning with 'Mac-'.[10]

More recently, names in 'Mac-' have become very widespread in England. The present-day telephone directories of such south coast resorts as Brighton or Bournemouth list large numbers of people with such names, despite the geographical remoteness of such places from any Gaelic-speaking areas.

SURNAMES PREFIXED BY 'AP' OR 'AB'

It has been explained that the use of genealogical designations, in the form 'A. ap B. ap C.' and so on was very common in Wales until the sixteenth century, and to a less extent later. There is no need to repeat here what has already been said about this usage. The existence of many by-names formed by a personal name prefixed by 'Ap-' or 'Ab-'[11] has led to the rise of a group of surnames which were originally those of Welshmen, but are now widely spread throughout Britain. These surnames have evolved from by-names such as Ap Roger, Ap Owen ('son of Roger', 'son of Owen'), and so forth. In the great majority of cases the initial 'A' has been lost, leaving surnames which begin with 'P' or 'B'. In English records of the sixteenth century and earlier, names retaining the 'A' at the beginning are sometimes found in such forms as Apryce, Abadam, etc. Although it is impossible to find evidence in many individual cases, it is probable that these were usually not stable, hereditary names. A great many surnames, consisting in their present forms of a personal name prefixed by 'P' or 'B', can now be found widely dispersed in Britain. Some of these have been formed from personal names introduced to Britain after the Norman Conquest, including many male personal names still much in use. The surname Probert or Propert, Pritchard or Prichard, Probin (from Robin), and Proger or Prosser are examples. In other instances surnames have been formed from Welsh first names. The now very widespread name Price (Pryce, Pryse) is usually from the Welsh personal name Rhys, though it has been suggested that Price might sometimes be an English occupational name. Preece is from another form of the same personal name. Bowen is from the widely used Welsh personal name Owen. Prydderch is from the Welsh personal name Rhydderch; the surname under English influence has in some cases become Protheroe[12] and many variant forms of the surname can be found during the seventeenth and eighteenth centuries, especially in English parish registers. Broderick is from Roderick, a personal name of Germanic, not Welsh, origin, which seems to have been considered as equivalent sometimes to the Welsh name Rhodri, sometimes to Rhydderch. In a good many of these instances it is no doubt not too difficult for someone without any knowledge of Welsh to form some suspicion of what the personal name involved is, but there are cases where this is not so. Prosser, for example, as already cited, is from Roger; Prinold and Prinnalt are from Reynold; and Prandle is from Rannulf or Randolph (none of the three personal names involved being Welsh).

It has already been explained that from an early date Welsh names occur in England, and that although most numerous in the border counties, or in areas easily accessible from Wales, they can be found in smaller numbers in other parts of England.

The point has just been made that the personal name Roderick, one not Welsh in origin, was considered as the equivalent of the Welsh personal names Rhodri and Rhydderch. There are one or two other cases where personal names originating outside Wales were taken as the equivalent of Welsh ones, and this has had some consequences for the growth of Welsh surnames. For instance, the personal name Louis or Lewis, seldom used in England during the Middle Ages, was thought to be the equivalent of the Welsh Llywelyn, or Llewelyn, a personal name much used in Wales, and this led to Llywelyn being replaced by Lewis in some instances. As a result, Lewis has become a common Welsh surname, and is particularly numerous in south Wales. In a similar way, Edward came to be considered as equivalent to the Welsh personal name Iorwerth (itself the origin of the surnames Yorwerth, Yorath, Yarworth, and possible Yarwood) so that Iorwerth was replaced at times by Edward. This in turn led to Edwards becoming a common Welsh surname, especially in north Wales.[13]

SURNAMES PREFIXED BY 'FITZ-'

The prefix 'Fitz-', which today appears with a limited number of surnames, is from the French phrase *fils de*, and may be compared with the 'Mac-' found in many Scots and Irish names. It has sometimes been thought that such names normally began as those of illegitimate children, but this belief is mistaken. It seems to have arisen from the relatively late practice of royalty bestowing such names on acknowledged natural children. The first person to do this seems to have been Charles II, many of whose natural children were given the surname of Fitzroy. He was followed by his brother, James II, who called his illegitimate children FitzJames. The practice continued into the nineteenth century. King William IV, who was the duke of Clarence before his accession to the throne, called his natural children FitzClarence. The last person to resort to this usage, apparently, was Queen Victoria's cousin, George, duke of Cambridge, whose equestrian statue now adorns Whitehall. He called his natural children FitzGeorge. It would appear to be this practice, in use from the seventeenth century onwards, which led to the association between names in 'Fitz-' and illegitimacy.

Apart from these exceptional late examples, most surnames in 'Fitz-' originated before about 1300. The well-known aristocratic family of Fitzalan, for example, derived their surname from Alan son of Flaad, who was living early in the twelfth century. The FitzOsberts, landowners in East Anglia, derived their surname from an Osbert who was living in 1166. There were some exceptions; a baronial family, the FitzWalters of Dunmow in Essex, only acquired FitzWalter as a stable hereditary surname early in the fourteenth century, after having used both FitzWalter and FitzRobert as by-names for several generations. This, however, was unusual, and most surnames in this group arose before 1300. During the twelfth and thirteenth centuries many cases occur of names in 'Fitz-' being used as by-names. Robert FitzParnell, Earl of Leicester (died 1204) derived his surname from his mother, the Countess Parnell, who seems to have been an exceptionally forceful lady. Richard Fitznigel, bishop of London from 1189 to 1198, was the natural son of Nigel,

Bishop of Ely. It is unusual to find such by-names after about 1300.

As far as can be seen, names in 'Fitz-' were mostly those of landholders, who in the twelfth and thirteenth centuries were presumably French speaking. When such names are found as those of people in other social classes, they seem to be usually by-names which never became hereditary. Though these names are French linguistically, their evolution was confined to England, and no names of such a type are known to have developed in France. A few surnames in this category, such as FitzGerald for example, were taken to Ireland by Anglo-Norman families who acquired lands there, and subsequently ramified considerably in Ireland. A few names such as FitzGerald are now sometimes thought of as Irish surnames, but although established in that country for centuries, they are not Irish in origin. The second element in surnames beginning with 'Fitz-' is usually a personal name introduced into England after 1066.

There is no reason to connect any of these early surnames formed from 'Fitz-' with a personal name, as a class, with illegitimacy, even if occasionally they were the names of bastards. However, in the twelfth and early thirteenth centuries there are a few such names. usually by-names and not hereditary, in which 'Fitz-' is followed by a word for a rank or title, and these names seem frequently, and perhaps usually, to have been those of illegitimate children. Thus, Brian FitzCount, a twelfth-century nobleman, was an illegitimate son of a count of Brittany. Henry FitzCount, a late twelfth century landowner in the south west, was an illegitimate son of an Earl of Cornwall. The surname Fil de Roy, later often given in the form Fillery, and today usually spelt Fildry, occurs in the south east of England from about 1250. Its origin is uncertain, but it is possible that the bearers of it were descended from a natural son of King John. There is no traceable link between these early mediaeval names and the habits of Charles II and others in naming natural children.

METRONYMICS

Most surnames derived from personal names are from male names, but there are a moderate number from female ones. These are usually known as metronymics, that is, names derived from a mother. Metronymics may be of various types. Some are from personal names without any suffix or prefix. The surname Maude is from the

127

well-known feminine first name, and the surname has developed variants such as Mahood, Mowat, and Mould; Maud is a form of a personal name which also appears as Matilda, and Till, Tillet, Tillot, and Tullett are from pet-forms of Matilda. The surname Hannibal is from the female personal name Amable (from which come the present day first names Mabel and Annabel) and not from the Carthaginian general, and Hunnable, Honeyball, and Hunnibell are variant forms of the same surname; Annott, Annett, and Annis are from Agnes or from Ann which was originally a pet form of Agnes; Parnell and Purnell are from the female name Parnell (from the Latin Petronilla), a popular feminine name during the twelfth and thirteenth centuries; Emlyn, Emblem, etc. are from Emelina; Catlin and Catling are from Cateline, the Old French form of Katherine; Cass is from a shortened form of the (originally Greek) female name Cassandra; and Marriott, one of the more common metronymics, is from a pet form of Mary.

Some metronymics are formed from a personal name with '-son' added, such as Margisson and Margerisson from Margery, Tillson and Tillotson from Matilda, Leeson, Leason, and Letson, all from Lettice, Anson and Annotson from Agnes or Ann, and Ibbotson and Ibson from a pet form of Isabel. Other metronymics are from a personal name with a possessive '-s' added, such as Annis from Agnes or Ann, Tills from Matilda, Mabbs from Mabel, or Maggs, Meggs, and Margetts, all from either Margaret or Margery. A few surnames which in their present form might look like metronymics in fact have other origins; Nelson is from the male first name Neil, not from Nell, and Polson is from Paul, not from Polly; Jones is from John, not Joan.

Metronymics, therefore, are a sizable body of surnames surviving to the present day, though fewer than patronymics. The question is why such names arose in the first place, and why some surnames were from a mother's personal name rather than a father's. It has been suggested that metronymics originated as the by-names of illegitimate children. Natural children are often encountered in the Middle Ages, at all levels from king to serf, and there is no reason to suppose that bastardy was rare. The existence of Bastard as a surname shows that it was not impossible for illegitimacy to give rise to a surname. Little stigma attached to illegitimate birth in the Middle Ages. William I, who of course was illegitimate, was referred to in documents as King William the Bastard, and the surname Bastard was that of a Devon landed family. However, evidence connecting metronymics with illegitimacy is hard to find. Really convincing examples, where it can be proved that metronymics originated as the names of bastards, have not been produced, and the present writer, in the course of collecting a great body of data about the origin of surnames, has never found a single case where the evidence proved that a metronymic arose in such a way. While illegitimacy cannot be ruled out as a possible origin, it is not proven that it is the main source for metronymics. During the Middle Ages, and later during the sixteenth century, illegitimate children were often acknowledged by their fathers, and when this was done the children often took their fathers' surnames. The convention whereby illegitimate children normally took their mothers' surnames was not fully established until the eighteenth century.

It is very exceptional to find evidence for the circumstances in which surnames of any kind arose, and if the situations in which metronymics developed are obscure, this is not surprising. There is no reason to suppose that a single cause must have operated in the origins of all metronymics. Bastardy may have been one reason, though it is impossible to prove this. In some cases metronymics may have been derived from the personal names of women who were marked out as strong characters. The case of Robert FitzParnell, Earl of Leicester, whose by-name was from his mother's personal name, has already been cited. The earl and his mother were both people of high rank, so some evidence is available about them, but such facts are not usually on record where people of lesser status are concerned. In some cases metronymics may have arisen from the personal names of women who were heiresses. In the thirteenth century Peter Picot (son of an earlier Peter Picot), a minor landowner in the Nottinghamshire-Leicestershire border area, married an heiress with the first name of Meriet; the son of this marriage used the by-name FitzMeriet. In some cases metronymics may have arisen when a widow was left, after her husband's death, with several children. By the time the children reached adulthood, their mother's personal name might have seemed more significant than that of their father, perhaps by then long dead, and the mother's name might well have been an obvious source for the creation of a by-name, which could in time become a hereditary surname.

All these factors may have operated in one case or another, but it is possible that these arguments are too elaborate. The processes by which surnames arose are generally difficult to follow, and often seem to be haphazard. If John, son of Richard, was a baker by trade and lived at Clapham, it will usually be impossible to say why he became known as John Baker rather than John Richards or John

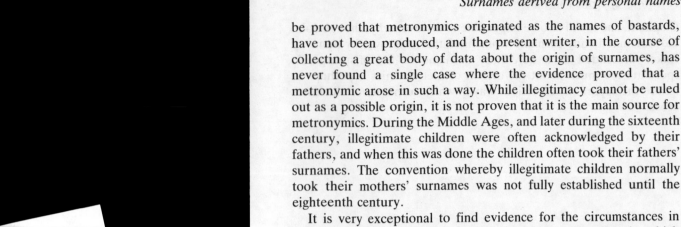

REFERENCES

1870, *Remains Concerning Britain*, p. 56.

, 1967, *Origin of English Surnames*, Routled
. 210.

72, *The Anglo-Saxon Heritage in Middle E
es: East Anglia*, C. W. K. Gleerup Lun

nes, 1970, *Merioneth Lay Subsidy Roll, 1
Vales Press, *passim*.

1979, *Surnames of Scotland*, New York
, 265.

1973, *Yorkshire: West Riding*, Phill

. xxxvii, xxxviii.

68, *Homes of Family Names in Great
lishing Company, p. 576.
the phonetics involved, see T. J. Morg
Welsh Surnames*, University of Wales

39–40, 147–50.

Clapham, and it will also be impossible to discover why, though John did not inherit any surname from his father, his own by-name of Baker descended as a hereditary surname to his offspring. To speculate too much about the origins of metronymics is perhaps to ignore the apparently capricious way in which surnames of all classes arose.

NOTES AND

1. W. Camden,
2. P. H. Reaney
   Kegan Paul,
3. B. Selten, 19
   Personal Nam
   1, p. 57.
4. K. Williams-J
   University of V
5. G. F. Black,
   Library, pp. 26
6. G. Redmonds,
   pp. 34–5.
7. Black, *op.cit.*, p
8. *Ibid.*, p. xxxix.
9. *Ibid.*, p. xli.
10. H. B. Guppy, 19
    Genealogical Pub
11. For an account of
    P. Morgan, 1985,
    pp. 10–11.
12. *Ibid.*, p. 184.
13. *Ibid.*, pp. 90–91, 1

CHAPTER FIVE
Occupational surnames

Occupational surnames are those from terms for some craft or trade, such as Smith, Baker, Shepherd, Palfreyman, Dyer, Webster, Chapman, Merchant, and so forth. It will be convenient to include in the same category surnames from the holding of office in either State or Church, such as Sheriff, Constable, Reeve, Sumner, Provost, Catchpole, Bishop, Abbot, Prior, Cannon, and so on. It is in fact very difficult to draw any distinction between surnames from occupations, and those from office, all the more because the beginnings of surnames are unknown in the case of many families. The name Bailiff (or similar ones such as Baillie and Bayliss) could arise from holding a position under the Crown, such as that of hundred bailiff, but many bailiffs were men engaged in farm or estate management, and a surname from such activities would be classified as occupational. It will also be convenient to include here surnames from ranks or status in society, such as Knight, Squire, Lord, Franklin, Burgess, Freeman, Masters, Cotter, Newbond, etc. Here, too, it is difficult to draw clear-cut distinctions. A surname like Yeoman might be considered as indicative of a rank or social position, but it might also be thought of as derived from an occupation. There are some names about which there might be some doubt if they should be classed in this type. Champion, for instance, arose in some cases from the practice by monasteries and other religious bodies of retaining professional champions to fight in trials by battle, over property rights, if necessary. On the other hand, the surname may have arisen as a nickname in some cases. It is also doubtful if surnames such as Palmer or Pilgrim ought to be included here. Whether such names should be ranked as occupational or as nicknames is perhaps a matter of opinion.

131

The use of occupational terms as by-names, to distinguish people from others with the same personal names, is a fairly obvious course, and it is not surprising that occupational by-names occur at an early date. Some by-names from Old English words for occupations can be found in Domesday Book; in the same source there are a good many by-names from Latin words for crafts or trades, and these were probably translations for Old English or Old French words used in speech. By-names, and eventually hereditary surnames, also arose from words for occupations in Welsh and Gaelic, though less frequently than in English. Occupational surnames can be found today in most European languages.

There is a certain tendency to suppose that all surnames ending in '-er' must be occupational, but this is not always the case, though many surnames in the category do have that termination. It has been pointed out in a previous chapter that some names with such an ending, like Bridger, Fielder, etc., are really topographical. Some other surnames in '-er' are also not occupational: Isbister, for example is from a Scots place-name, probably from a place in Orkney, though the place-name also exists in Shetland, while Hamer, Bamber, and Harker are from Lancashire places. Bedser is said to be from the name of a lost village, possibly in Sussex, though there is some lack of evidence for this. Docker is from a place-name, probably Docker in Cumbria, and Sturmer is from one of the places so called. Aylmer, Aimer, Gummer, Fulcher and Rayner are all from personal names that were little used by about 1300. Elmer is sometimes a variant of Aylmer, sometimes from the name of a place in Sussex, and sometimes a topographical name from the elm tree, an example which shows how difficult it can be at times to decide on the origin of a surname merely from the present-day form. Pether and Pither are from dialect forms of Peter. Pettifer is a nickname-type surname, French in language, originally *pied de fer* ('iron foot'); this is a surname which has developed into several different variants, such as Puddifer, Potiphar, and Pettiford. Telfer, Tolver, and Tulliver are all from another French phrase, *Taille fer* ('cut iron'), perhaps a nickname for a man of exceptional strength. This name has sometimes developed into Telford and Tilford. Telfer and Telford are both today quite common surnames in south and central Scotland. Gulliver is from the Old French goulafre ('glutton'). Golafre was the surname of an important landed family in the thirteenth century and later, despite the uncomplimentary meaning of the name. In some cases the name has developed into Galliford and Gulliford, Pettiford, Telford and Tilford, Galliford and Gulliford all look like locative surnames, but in fact have other origins. Telford is now a place-name in Shropshire, but this is a recent creation, derived from the name of the celebrated engineer whose surname it was. Simister is the name of a small locality in Lancashire, but it is not clear if the surname, possibly an occupational one, is from the place-name or if, as seems more likely, the place-name is one derived from the surname. The examples just given will perhaps show how necessary it is to investigate the origins of any surname carefully.

One of the more generally-known facts about occupational names at the present day is that some of them are very common. The frequency with which Smith occurs is notorious. Several other surnames of the type, such as Baker, Taylor, Cook, Turner, Miller, Clark or Clerk, Cooper, and Wright, are somewhat less common, but still appear much more frequently than the great majority of surnames in Britain. This situation is not new, but already existed by about 1300. Those occupational names which are very common now were then already very numerous, and were already present in most parts of England and in those parts of Scotland and Wales where English was spoken. One factor in producing this situation is that the trades which gave rise to these surnames were very widely practised, all over the country, yet were not exercised by a large number of people in any one place. In most villages there would be only one or two smiths, one or two tailors, and so forth, so that the occupations in question were sufficiently distinctive to mark out a man from his fellow villagers, and hence were suitable for use as surnames. Occupations which were followed by any large proportion of the population would not be appropriate for such use, for they would not serve to distinguish a man from his neighbours. This is shown by the scarcity of surnames from any of the tasks involved in arable farming, an occupation which engaged a considerable share of the population in rural areas. This contrasts with the large number of surnames derived from words for persons employed in herding different types of livestock, for these were specialist occupations, followed by only one or two people in each village.

Another reason for the commonness of some occupational names is that they were not confined to the dialect of any one region. In general, the really common occupational surnames are those from terms which were used throughout the English-speaking parts of Britain. Surnames existed, of course, that were derived from alternative words for the occupations concerned. Apart from Smith, for example, there exist the surnames Faber from the word used for 'smith' in mediaeval Latin, and Ferrar, Ferrer, and Ferrier (today sometimes variously developed into Farrar, Farrow, Faro, and Pharaoh) from an Old French word for the same occupation. In addition, there are a whole series of names from specialised forms of smithing, such as Goldsmith, Locksmith, Shoesmith (now sometimes spelt Showsmith), Naismith or Naesmith ('knife smith', now mainly a Scots name), Greensmith ('copper smith'), Whitesmith ('tin smith'), Arrowsmith (now sometimes developed into Harrowsmith and Harrismith), Sheersmith, and Marshall or Mascall (often 'shoeing smith', though the word acquired different meanings). Similarly, apart from Baker, the names Pistor and Pestor are from the mediaeval Latin word for 'baker', and there are a whole series of surnames from specialised branches of the baking trade, such as Whitbread, Blampin (also 'white bread', from the French *blanc pain*), Wastell, Wastall, and Wassall (a baker of bread from specially fine flour; Vassall, however, means a vassal in the feudal sense), Cakebread, or Wafer. (Bunn is from the French adjective *bon*.) Apart from Miller, there are other surnames from the same trade, such as Millward, Milner, or Mulliner. There are in fact surnames from alternative words for most of the trades which have given rise to common occupational surnames. Nevertheless, those occupational names which are most numerous today are nearly all from words used very widely in England, in Wales where English was spoken, and in the Scots-speaking parts of Scotland. The only occupational surname which is now really common, but which was confined to certain regions during the Middle Ages, is Walker, which was widely used in the north of England, the west Midlands, and southern Scotland, but was not much found in other regions before about 1500.

Many occupational surnames are derived from words of which the distribution was restricted to certain areas. Others are from crafts or trades which were never the work of any large number of people. Some were from occupations which by their nature were restricted to certain parts of the country. There are, for example, a number of surnames from terms for seafaring men, surnames which were originally largely confined to maritime counties, such as Cogger and Cogman from the type of ship called a cog, Floater and Flodman (both 'sailor'), Mariner and its variant form Marner, Shipman (but this may sometimes be 'sheep man'), Galliot (galley sailor, often used to imply 'pirate'), or Stearman. A few surnames in the category, at first rare, have proliferated locally in particular areas, often by the ramification of individual families. Rimmer, as already mentioned, had ramified notably in the coastal part of south Lancashire by the seventeenth century, and is still a very numerous surname in that area at the present day. Trinder ('braider') has ramified in one part of Oxfordshire. Tranter ('carrier' or 'hawker') has multiplied in Shropshire and in some adjoining districts of central Wales. Bidder (possibly for someone who summoned guests to wedddings, funerals, etc.) has become numerous in the Gower peninsula[1]. And Bowker ('fuller') has become a common surname in south-east Lancashire. The common occupational surnames mentioned above, however, have been present in widely separated areas from an early period, and there seems to be no possibility that any one of them could have developed from the surname of a single family. It is obvious that each of them must have belonged to many separate families from the beginning.

SURNAMES FROM HIGH LAY OR ECCLESIASTICAL OFFICES

There exists today a group of surnames derived from high ranks or positions in Church or State. These include names such as King, Prince, Duke, Count, Earl, or Sheriff, from secular offices, and such as Pope, Cardinal, Bishop, Abbot, Prior, Archdeacon, Cannon and Channon, from positions in the Church. Some of these names, like King or Bishop, for example, are now and have long been, quite numerous. Surnames in this group which are common today were already well established and widely distributed by about 1300. It seems obvious that these surnames, though in form occupational ones, must have been bestowed originally as nicknames. It is impossible to suppose that people with such names were actually the descendants of kings, bishops, etc. The sheer number of persons so named from an early period makes that impossible. The descendants of kings, even illegitimate children, are easier to trace than the offspring of lesser mortals, but no single instance can be found where a family named King was so called because it was of royal descent. Twelfth-century bishops occasionally had, and acknowledged, children, but no example has been found where the surname Bishop arose from such circumstances, and the name was already too numerous by about 1300 for such an origin to be feasible in all or most cases. It might be supposed that such names were in origin those of tenants, servants, or retainers of kings, dukes, bishops, and so forth, but there is no evidence for this. It may be noted in this connection that the surname or by-name Duke appears in England in the thirteenth century, though the rank of duke did not exist there until the fourteenth.

There seems to be no doubt that such surnames, though apparently occupational ones, were in fact nicknames in origin. As is apt to be the case, it is impossible to say why such nicknames were acquired. Mediaeval archdeacons had an evil reputation for legal chicanery and for extorting fees, so much so that the question of whether an archdeacon could be saved was a subject for theological debate, while sheriffs had a reputation for being oppressive and corrupt, and there seems to have been a belief that abbots were usually portly. Opinions, and perhaps prejudices, about the conduct of different lay or Church functionaries may have led to nicknames such as Sheriff, Archdeacon, or Abbot, being bestowed on individuals who were thought to be grasping, extortionate, or overweight, but it is only possible to make guesses about that. It is possible that in some cases such names might have arisen when people played the parts of kings, bishops, and so forth, in pageants or miracle plays, but there is little evidence that this actually happened, and most of the surnames concerned seem to be too numerous at an early date for this to be the explanation in more than a small proportion of the cases.

It is difficult to be sure how far down the social scale the use of ranks or offices as nicknames went. Surnames like Knight, Squire, Page, or Vavassour are, in some cases, those of actual knights, squires, etc., at early periods such as the twelfth and thirteenth centuries, when names were newly formed, and were often not hereditary. In such examples it must be supposed that the names derived from the real status of the persons whose surnames or by-names they were. On the other hand, examples can be found at the same periods of men in humble positions, including serfs named Knight, Squire, and so forth, and in these circumstances it seems likely that the names began as nicknames. Again, it is not possible to say why such names were bestowed in the first instance, but nicknames of this sort seem to have been used fairly freely in the lower reaches of mediaeval society, perhaps sometimes in a derisory sense. At one time the surname Halfknight was dispersed through England and parts of Scotland. This was never a common name, though widely distributed, and it now seems to be extinct. It has been suggested that this was a name for someone who held half a knight's fee by feudal tenure. Holders of halves or other fractions of knight's fees did exist, but no example has been found where any of them was named Halfknight. Instead, those found with the name were mostly serfs or others in lowly positions, and there is little doubt that Halfknight was a by-name bestowed jokingly, and probably in scorn. The same may well have been true where names like Knight or Squire were those of people who were not knights, squires, and so on.

Much the same is probably true of some names derived from Holy Orders, such as Priest (or Prest), Deacon (now often spelt Deakin; Dakin and Daykin are usually from diminutives of David), or Chaplain (Chaplin, Caplan, Kaplin, etc.). During the twelfth and thirteenth centuries instances of people being acknowledged as the children of vicars and rectors can be found, though such clergy ought to have been celibate, and the surnames in question may sometimes have been held by persons who were descended from priests, or deacons, but in some cases, again, such names occur at an early date, before 1300, as the names of serfs, who were disqualified from the priesthood. It must be supposed that in at least some cases these surnames from ecclesiastical ranks began as nicknames.

The term 'chaplain' was generally used in the Middle Ages for a clergyman who was an ordained priest, but who did not hold a post (such as that of a rector or vicar) with the cure of souls. This term covered the numerous clergy who were chantry priests and so on. It is likely that the surname Chaplain arose in many instances as a nickname. The word 'clerk' was usually applied to clergy in minor orders. Clergy below the rank of subdeacon were allowed to marry, and were quite a large body of people, sometimes engaged in what would now be considered as secular activities. Hence the frequency with which Clark, Clerk, and Clarkson appear as surnames at the present time.

The surname Chancellor seems always to have originated as a nickname. Besides the Chancellor who presided over the royal Chancery, an office which seems to date from not long after the Conquest, the office of Chancellor of the Exchequer existed from the thirteenth century; in addition, there was a chancellor in each diocese. These, however, were celibate clergy, and there is no evidence that the surname was ever that of anyone who was so called because of descent from an actual chancellor of any sort. In fact, here again, some of the people found with Chancellor as a surname or by-name were serfs. It is only possible to guess at the qualities that may have led to the bestowal of Chancellor as a surname. The name Chamberlain, on the other hand, is much more likely to have arisen from men actually holding office as chamberlains. Great magnates had chamberlains in their households, and sometimes had officials called chamberlains in charge of manors. There were Exchequer officials called chamberlains, and the financial officers in some boroughs were called chamberlains. The number of chamberlains existing was consequently much more than might be supposed, many of them not people of particularly exalted rank.

Baron or Barron ought probably to rank with names such as Earl, Duke, or Prince as a surname from high rank which was bestowed as a nickname, and this was probably the normal origin of the name. However, the freemen of the Cinque Ports were known as barons,[2] as also were freemen of London and York, and in a few cases the surname may have originated in that way. In Scotland the surname sometimes originated with relatively minor landowners who ranked as barons.[2] In most examples the surname must have begun as a nickname, though just what qualities would lead to such a soubriquet being bestowed remains uncertain.

The surname Lord, another quite common surname, seems to have originated with people who were actually accorded that title. In the Middle Ages, 'lord' was not a title confined to members of the peerage or their sons, but was one widely given to persons of any standing, such as lords of manors or other substantial landowners, or members of the higher clergy. Surnames from positions rather lower down the social scale, such as Franklin, Yeoman, Alderman, or Burgess, seem usually to have originated with people who were in fact franklins, etc. The surname Master, Masters, or Meystre was one usually given to a freeholder with sufficient land for him to employ labourers or servants under him. In some examples, however, this name too seems to have originated as a nickname.

SURNAMES FROM TERMS FOR FREE OR UNFREE STATUS

There are a group of names which have arisen from words for free or servile status. The most common of these is Freeman. This may occasionally have been a name for someone who was a freeman of a borough or city, but the majority of examples are from rural areas, and it must originally have been usually a name for a free tenant, as distinct from a serf. There are several other surnames with the same meaning, such as Freebody or Freeland (a name for someone who held land by free tenure); Fray, Frie, and Fry also mean 'free'. Frank and Franks usually have the same significance. The surname Francombe is from the French *fraunchomme*, and is another name from free status. This name, though French linguistically, seems in at least some cases to have originated in England. In some instances it has developed into Frankham. It may be noted that both Francombe and Frankham look like locative names. The total number of people with surnames in this group is still quite large at the present day, reflecting the importance which once attached to free status, at a time when many people were serfs.

Surnames from unfree status are less common, perhaps because people were disinclined to use names which emphasised their servile condition. The most common such name has always been Bond (Bownd, etc.), though in some cases this can be derived from a personal name of Scandinavian origin. The name Newbond, today often spelt Newbon, is rare, and none of the other names from unfree status is at all common. The surname Thrale, Thrall, or Threall ('thrall') was always scarce. So was another name from serfdom, Carl, which however may in some cases be from a personal name. The surnames Cotter, Cotterel, and Cotman are from a class of smallholders who were sometimes free, sometimes unfree. Villain or Villan is from 'villein', the chief class of unfree tenant on many manors.

The existence of this array of surnames from words for free and unfree status is a testimony to how important the division between freeman and bondtenants once was. Such surnames were never confined to any one part of the country, but generally seem to have been rather more common in the south of England and the south Midlands than elsewhere. Possibly this may owe something to the fact that these were regions with considerable numbers of unfree tenants. It is probably significant that in Kent, where serfdom had disappeared by the thirteenth century, surnames from words for status were much rarer than in Sussex, where many manors had large numbers of serfs. Once surnames became hereditary, social mobility tended over a period of time, even under mediaeval conditions, to separate surnames denoting free or unfree condition from the actual status of the bearers of such names. As early as the thirteenth century, there were examples of men with names from words for unfree condition who were in fact free tenants. Presumably this was due to serfs having been emancipated. At the same period there are, more surprisingly, a few cases of men with names for free status who were actually bondmen. Presumably this arose from men who were born free having accepted servile status to obtain holdings, or through free tenants having been forced into servitude by lords of manors. By the fifteenth century a family named Threall, a surname

with servile connotations, had become landowners of some importance in north Sussex. By 1500 at the latest, by which time serfdom
was dying out, such surnames from terms for status had usually
ceased to have any connection with actual social position.

SURNAMES SUCH AS BREWSTER, WEBSTER, ETC.

Some occupational surnames, including some quite common ones,
exist in pairs; examples are Baker and Baxter, Brewer and Brewster,
Deemer and Dempster ('judge'), Dyer and Dyster or Dexter, Fuller
and Folster, Kember and Kemster or Kempster ('comber' of wool or
flax), Hollier and Hollister, Lister and Litster, Palliser and Pallister
(maker of palings), Sanger and Sangster ('singer'), Shaper and
Shapster ('tailor' or 'seamstress'), or Webber and Webster. A good
many similar sets can be found which were in use during the Middle
Ages, but which were disused by about 1500, many of them by-names
which never became hereditary. The reasons for the existence of such
names has been the subject of much debate among the experts, but
the general conclusion has been that names such as Baxter, Brewster,
Webster, and so forth were originally from the feminine forms of
occupational terms, while names such as Baker, Brewer, or Webber
were from masculine ones. In some parts of southern England names
such as Baxter, Brewster, or Webster were still mainly the surnames,
or more often the by-names, of women during the thirteenth and
fourteenth centuries, but even in these areas they were already being
used as the names of men by about 1200. In most parts of England
there are examples of names such as Baxter, Brewster, etc.,
appearing as men's names during the thirteenth century. In southern
Scotland, too, such names occur as those of men at the same period.
Since some surnames are derived from feminine first names, and
since until after 1400 instances can be found of surnames in all
categories descending hereditarily through females, it is quite
possible that some surnames such as Baxter, Brewster, etc.,
originated with women and were inherited from them by their
descendants. Women are inadequately represented in most historical
sources, and there is generally much less evidence about their
surnames or by-names than about men's. It is consequently quite
possible that names such as Baxter, etc., were considerably more
common as women's names than would appear from the existing
written sources. Even so, considering that hereditary surnames from

their first appearance, descended in the male line in the majority of cases, it is probable that most surnames such as Baxter, Brewster, etc., arose through descent from men.

The surnames Baxter, Brewster, and Webster are all fairly common at the present day, but the remaining surnames in the group are mostly scarce. This probably owes something to the fact that the descent of surnames from females was always the exception, and that in some parts of England names in this group were still predominantly those of women in the thirteenth and fourteenth centuries, when many occupational names were becoming hereditary.

OCCUPATIONAL SURNAMES FROM LATIN WORDS

One of the complications of studying the history of occupational names is that most documents written in this country before about 1500, and even some later ones, are written in Latin. It was a common practice for the writers of Latin documents to translate some occupational names into Latin, using the Latin word which had the same literal meaning as the Middle English term which was being translated, and which was being used for a surname or by-name. Thus a man whose name was William Tanner was liable to appear in a Latin document as *Willelmus Tannator* (that being the mediaeval Latin word for 'tanner'), John Miller as *Johannes Molendinarius* (the mediaeval Latin for 'miller'), and so forth. More often than not, the translation was carried out in a haphazard and unsystematic way; a writer would translate some English surnames by the Latin word which was the literal equivalent, but for no clear reason would fail to translate other occupational surnames in the same document. If several references can be found to a single individual, perhaps in a number of separate documents, it will sometimes be found that his name is given once or twice in a Middle English form, once or twice translated into Latin, and possibly once or twice in French.

It can easily be seen that this confused situation complicates the study of the early history of occupational surnames, for it is not always clear what English name is being translated by the Latin term which appears in a written source. For instance, in the example given above, it has been suggested that the Latin word *tannator*, which literally means 'tanner', could be used to translate the English surname Tanner, but unfortunately there are other surnames from the occupation of tanning; the surnames Barker (from the use of oak bark in tanning) and Tawyer, are both from tanning, and both could be translated by *tannator*. Or again, *molendinarius* means literally 'miller', and it might translate the surname Miller, or one of the other surnames from the same trade, such as Milner, Milward, or Mulliner, or possibly one of the by-names from the same occupation which once existed but have now been lost, such as Milknave or Millgroom. It is therefore impossible to be certain what name is being translated by *molendinarius*. Much the same is true of most of the other Latin words used to translate occupational names. These circumstances obviously create difficulties for studying the early history of surnames in the category. It is difficult to be sure about the early distribution of some occupational names, or to know if they occur in some areas but not in others. There can also be difficulties if attempts are made to trace the history of families with occupational names back before about 1500.

These problems will probably not impinge on many genealogists and family historians, who are concerned with more recent periods. The practice of translating occupational surnames into Latin has, however, led to the creation of a few still surviving surnames which are from Latin words for occupations. The only surname of this type which is at all common today is Faber, from the word used in mediaeval Latin to mean 'smith'. Other similar names are Sutor from the mediaeval Latin word *sutor*, 'shoemaker', and Pistor or Pester from the Latin *pistor*, 'baker'. The surname Peregrine, now sometimes spelt Paragreen, is from the Latin *peregrinus*, used to translate 'pilgrim', not strictly speaking an occupational name. This small group of names is interesting because the surnames are from written forms, which seem unlikely to have been spoken in the first place. It must be supposed that a man appeared with his occupational surname, or, more likely, his by-name, regularly translated into Latin, perhaps in some type of record in which his name occurred frequently, such as a manor court roll, and that the Latin form passed into speech as a hereditary surname, perhaps after having been used in writing for two or three generations of a family without having been employed in speech. The great majority of surnames give the impression of having originated as by-names used in speech, which came to be put down in writing eventually, perhaps after having been used for some considerable time verbally, and possibly after having been used for several generations before being committed to writing. This seems to be true, for instance, of many nickname-type surnames, or of the numerous surnames derived from the pet forms or diminutives of personal names. The small group of surnames like

Faber, Sutor, and Pester. however, shows that there were exceptional occasions when surnames were derived from written forms. The number of such surnames is, however, very small.

REGIONAL DISTRIBUTION OF OCCUPATIONAL SURNAMES

It has already been remarked that some of the more common occupational surnames were present throughout the English-speaking parts of Britain from an early date and were never confined to particular regions. There are, however, some surnames of the type which were originally found only within limited areas, and these include some names which have been and still are quite numerous. In some instances several different terms were in use to describe a single occupation, with each term being current within one geographical area and not generally found elsewhere. A situation in which some words were only in use in particular areas was not of course confined to occupational terms. This can be found, both now and in the past, in connection with a great variety of words, and has, for instance, considerably affected the distribution of topographical surnames, as already discussed.

How these circumstances have influenced the distribution of occupational surnames can be illustrated by the surnames derived from the various processes of cloth production, which was one of the more widespread manufacturing industries during the period when hereditary surnames were being formed. In fulling cloth, for example, a person engaged in the trade was usually known in the south west of England as a tucker, in the west Midlands, the north of England, and in Scotland as a walker, and in the south and east of England as a fuller. The surnames Tucker, Walker, and Fuller had at first a corresponding distribution, which was still in existence in the sixteenth century, little changed. Subsequently population movements gradually broke up the original distribution, but even at the present day traces of the original state of affairs have not entirely disappeared and Walker is still a more common surname in the north of England than elsewhere. The surname Bowker, from the process of bleaching cloth with lye, was before 1500 fairly common in two widely separated areas, Lancashire and Sussex, while remaining rare or absent elsewhere. It is still today a more common surname in Lancashire than anywhere else, though it has become rare in Sussex.

The much scarcer surnames Bleacher, Blaker or Blacker, and Blatcher are also from the same trade. All seem to belong mainly to south and south-west England, though occasional early instances can be found in other regions.

Some other surnames from the processes of cloth manufacture had a similar regional distribution. Of surnames from dyeing, for instance, Lister ('dyer') seems to have originated mainly in East Anglia, the east Midlands, the north east of England, and Scotland. Litster belongs to the same regions. Dexter, another name with the same meaning, was at first a name chiefly found in south Suffolk and in Essex, though there are scattered examples in the east Midlands. Dyer and Dyster were found mostly in the south and south west of England and parts of the west Midlands. Hewster or Heuster, a much rarer surname with the same significance, occurs mostly in Cheshire, Shropshire and Staffordshire, as far as early instances are concerned.

Surnames from the trade of spinning are noticeably rare, perhaps because it was mainly a female occupation. Spinster existed as a surname, but does not seem to have survived to the present, perhaps because it was primarily a female name. Spinner, which is found in various regions as a rare mediaeval by-name, has survived as an unusual surname, not particularly linked with any area. Thrower, a distinctly more common surname, is probably from one of the operations to produce thread, though its mediaeval meaning is uncertain. It is widely distributed in early examples. Surnames from weaving are much more common. Webb was found in the south of England, the south west, the south Midlands, and Essex with the adjoining part of Suffolk. Webster was originally the usual surname from the craft in the rest of East Anglia, the north of England, and Scotland. Webber and Weaver were both much rarer names, with only scattered examples of both.

Some other occupations gave rise to surnames which had a markedly regional distribution. Barker was the most common name from tanning in East Anglia, the east Midlands, the north of England, and Scotland. Tanner was the usual name in the southern half of England. There is a similar situation in regard to surnames from milling. Millward, now sometimes spelt Millard, was widely used in the south of England, the south west, and the west Midlands, while Milner was found mainly in the east Midlands, East Anglia, the north of England, and Scotland. Miller was widespread in the Middle Ages, but not very common anywhere. During the sixteenth and seventeenth centuries the surnames of many families were changed from Milner to Miller, with the result that Miller became a much more numerous surname than hitherto. The much rarer surname Mulliner, one of French origin, occurs from an early period scattered in various regions.

Besides cases like these, there are examples where some occupational surnames, not at first confined to any one region, have become especially common in particular areas, sometimes it seems through the ramification locally of individual families. The surnames Rimmer, Tasker, and Tyrer (probably for he who made iron tyres for cart wheels) had by the seventeenth century become very common in west Lancashire; Mashiter or Messiter (probably meaning 'maltster') became very common in and around Lancaster; Trinder ('braider') became common in west Oxfordshire; Boad, Bode, Body, and Boddy (all from a word meaning 'messenger') became numerous in Sussex; and Beadle, with variant forms such as Biddle, Boodle, Buddle, and Bodill became common in the same county. Circumstances such as these may provide clues to the areas where some families with occupational surnames are likely to have originated, though it is rarely possible to say that any occupational name must have originated in one area alone, and could not possibly have originated anywhere else.

In contrast to the examples just considered, some occupational surnames which have always been rare, and remain so now, have from the start been found in widely scattered areas, and have never been confined to one or two regions. The surname Palfreyman, for example (a name for someone in charge of light saddle horses) can be found before 1500 in Cambridgeshire, Cheshire, Essex, Lancashire, Norfolk, Northumberland, Oxfordshire, Shropshire, Somerset, Suffolk, Sussex, and Yorkshire and also in Scotland; the surname was never at all numerous, and still remains rare. Steadman or Steedman (a man in charge of horses) appears before 1500 in Essex, Huntingdonshire, Lancashire, Norfolk, Oxfordshire, Staffordshire, Suffolk, and Sussex. Stoddard, or Stothurd, Studdert, etc., another surname from a specialised occupation concerned with the care of livestock (from the herding of stotts, a word used for bullocks or horses) occurs before 1500 in Cheshire, Cumberland, Devon, Lancashire, Northamptonshire, Yorkshire and in Scotland. Coward (or Cowherd) can be found before the same date in Essex, Huntingdonshire, Kent, Lancashire, Norfolk, Oxfordshire, Suffolk, and Worcestershire. Leadbeater, another not very common surname, can be found before 1500 in Lancashire, Lincolnshire, Norfolk, Northumberland, Nottinghamshire, Staffordshire, Suffolk, Warwickshire, Yorkshire and Scotland; Spicer ('grocer') occurs before 1500 in

Cambridgeshire, Dorset, Essex, Hampshire, Kent, Lancashire, Lincolnshire, Norfolk, Somerset, Staffordshire, Suffolk, Surrey, Sussex, Worcestershire, and Yorkshire. None of these surnames was ever at all common, though some of them ramified to a moderate degree in particular areas, after about 1500. All remain fairly scarce at the present day, yet they, and many other names which could be cited, were very widely distributed from an early period, and cannot be considered as names connected with any one region, or one dialect.

Consequently, among the rarer occupational names there are many which could not conceivably have originated with a single family, or in any one part of the country, but which can be found in widely scattered examples at an early stage of surname history. Any investigation into the history of families with such surnames will of course have to take these circumstances into account. Rare occupational surnames are much more likely to be found dispersed over the country than are rare surnames from place-names. Some indication of how widespread many occupational surnames originally were can be obtained from consulting the reference given in Reaney's *Dictionary of British Surnames* (which is discussed in the 'Advice on further reading' at the end of the book), but these references are often selective, and give an incomplete view of how scattered some occupational surnames were in early examples.

Some occupational names were derived from specific feudal services, which tenants once had to perform for their lords. On some manors there were tenants who, as part of the service due from their holdings, had to sound a horn to summon people to sessions of the manor court, and this is often the origin of the name Hornblower. On some manors, mostly in the south of England, tenants owed the duty of washing the lord's sheep, an old obligation which existed before the Conquest, and this is the usual origin of the surname Washer. The name Arblaster, now sometimes modified into Alabaster, arose from the duty laid upon some tenants of doing feudal military service with an arbalast, a kind of heavy crossbow. The duty of performing military service of this sort is mentioned in Domesday. On some manors, often where the lord was a prelate of the Church (including some manors held by the archbishop of Canterbury) certain tenants were obliged, as part of the terms on which they held their land, to go into the parish church every time they passed it and to recite a paternoster for the soul of their overlord, and this is often the origin of the surname Paternoster. Names like Banner and Bannerman (usually a Scots name in origin, though now found in England) were names given to someone who carried a flag in time of war, and some tenants performed this duty as part of the services due from their holdings.

These are examples of surnames which arose from the performance of specific feudal services. There are some types of surnames which arose from a more general obligation of service or subordination. Some names of this type, those formed from a place-name with the suffix '-man' added (Fentiman, Penkethman, etc.) have already been mentioned, but there are others.

SURNAMES DENOTING A RELATIONSHIP OF SERVICE

There is a sizable group of surnames formed from a personal name with the suffix '-man' added, such as Addiman (from a diminutive of Adam), Christman, Harriman, Hickman (from a pet form of Richard), Jackman, Janeman, Jenman, or Genman, Lukeman, Mathewman, or Sandeman (from Saunder, for Alexander); there is a similar group of names formed from an occupation term with '-man', such as Kingsman, Ladyman, Monkman, Priestman, or Smithman, or from a surname in some other category with '-man', such as Corbetsman, Maidman or Maidment, Payman, Pennyman, or Tatman. Surnames formed from a topographical term with '-man' have already been discussed, and seem to have a character different from other surnames with the same ending. The point which needs to be considered is what the original significance was of surnames ending in '-man', like those just mentioned. In what respect was someone named Smithman originally different from someone named Smith, or someone named Tuckerman different from someone called Tucker, and what is the origin of names such as Hickman, Mathewman, and so on?

The general opinion of authorities on the subject has for long been that such surnames were originally the names of servants, retainers, tenants, or vassals, so that Addiman meant 'servant of Adam', Hickman 'servant of Hick', Corbetsman meant 'servant of the person surnamed Corbet', and Smithman 'servant of the smith' or less probably 'servant of the man surnamed Smith'. The word 'man' was often used in Middle English to mean a servant or dependent of some sort, or, more specifically, someone who had performed homage to an overlord. The surname Mann originates in most cases from the use of the word in this sense, though in some instances it was a name given to Manxmen who migrated into Britain. The number of cases in which it can be proved that surnames in '-man' did in fact arise in this way is small. The evidence about the name Fentiman has already been discussed. It is also true that during the thirteenth and fourteenth centuries Latin phrases such as *homo Willelmi*, *homo Bainardi*, and so forth can be found, signifying 'servant of William', 'servant of Bainard', and so on, and that these seem to have been translations into Latin of by-names such as Williamsman, etc. In Sussex during the fourteenth and fifteenth centuries the name Cobhamsman occurs in an area where Cobham existed as a surname, Janeman occurs in an area where Jane was in use as a surname, and Corbetsman occurs in an area where the surname Corbet existed. Nigel Pershoreman, an inhabitant of Oxford in 1327, was probably a servant of John de Pershore, another inhabitant of the town at the same date. In Norfolk, the surname Faderman was present in the late thirteenth century, and the name Fader ('father') appears in the same area at the same date. In Yorkshire, the name Paslewman existed at Leeds, where the Paslew family were prominent, in the late fourteenth century.[3] John Abbotsman, a fourteenth-century Lancashire man, was a servant or retainer of the abbot of Cockersand in that county. Such examples are at least compatible with the view that names such as Corbetsman, Janeman, or Cobhamsman meant originally 'servant', or tenant, etc., of the person surnamed Corbet, Jane, or Cobham. The fact remains that despite the existence of the instances just mentioned, and of a moderate number of others which could be cited, the way in which such surnames began is mainly a matter of inference, and that the direct evidence is scanty. It is, however, the case that direct evidence about how surnames arose in the first place is often lacking.

Surnames in this group were not confined to any one region, but were rather more frequently found in the north of England than elsewhere. No surnames of the type were ever really common. At the present day Harriman, Hickman, and Jackman all exist in moderate numbers. Janeman, now often spelt Jenman or Genman, is still a well-established name in Sussex, though not at all numerous; and this is from Jane as a form of John, not from the feminine Jane. Mathewman still exists in Yorkshire, where the name seems to have originated. This is in fact a small group of surnames which have never become at all numerous, but which throws some light on how surnames were being formed at a period when hereditary surnames were evolving in this country.

Not all surnames ending in '-man' which might seem to belong to this group in fact do so. The surnames Dearman (or Dorman, Durman), Dudman (or Dodman), Loveman, Osman, Oman, Whatman (or Wheatman), Whitman, and Winman, and some others, are derived from personal names. Bateman seems originally to have been formed in the same way as names like Addiman or Harriman (from a shortened form of Bartholomew), but by the thirteenth century Bateman was already being used as a first name, and its use as a surname may in some cases result from this.

Despite the fact that '-man' is the final syllable in a good many surnames of different types, and despite the fact that 'man' is a word commonly used in modern English, some surnames ending in '-man' have variant forms ending, in their present form, in '-ment'. The case of Maidment, a variant form of the name Maidman, has already been mentioned, and there are a few other examples from names in various categories. The nickname-type name Hardiman, for instance, has become Hardiment in a few cases.

A group of names of a somewhat similar character can be found among Gaelic surnames, both in Scotland and in Ireland. These are names such as Gilchrist, Gillemichael, Gilpatrick, or Gilmartin. These have the meaning of 'servant of Christ', 'servant of (Saint) Michael', 'servant of (Saint) Patrick', and so on. Many such surnames arose in Scotland. Many surnames of the same type developed in Ireland, and it may not be possible to distinguish surnames originating in Scotland from Irish ones, merely from the form in present use. Few examples of any names in this group can be found in England or Wales before about 1700, but the population movements of the nineteenth century have brought such surnames into many regions outside Scotland, and especially into English and Welsh areas where there was much industrial expansion during the Victorian period. Such names can also now be found frequently in the towns on the south coast of England to which people from all parts of Britain often retire.

Such surnames originated as Christian names, no doubt originally bestowed by parents for reasons of piety, and by the twelfth century Christian names of the type were already fairly common in Scotland. Patroymnic surnames were subsequently formed from the Christian names. In many cases the surname so formed had at first the prefix 'Mac-' (MacGilchrist, MacGillemichael, etc.). In some instances the original 'Mac-' has since been lost, and in a few other cases surnames have been Anglicised into forms such as Gilchristson. In further instances surnames have been shortened by dropping the syllable

'Gill', so that MacGillemichael has become MacMichael, MacGillfhinein has become MacLennan, and so forth. In some other cases the surname has become so modified that its original character has been obscured; Maclehose, for example, has developed from Mac Gille Thamhais ('son of the servant of Saint Thomas'). As is sometimes the case with Scots names of Gaelic origin, some such surnames were substantially altered at relatively late periods, such as the second half of the eighteenth century.

A few surnames in this group have second elements which are not personal names. Gillespie, for example, means 'servant of the bishop'. It is probable that such a name refers to a religious devotion to a bishop rather than to actually being in a bishop's service, and it is very doubtful if any such names arose from service in the literal sense of the term.

In many names of this type the second element is a first name, usually that of a saint, and no doubt when names like, say, Gilpatrick were originally bestowed as first or Christian names they betokened a special devotion to the saint in question rather than any kind of actual servitude. Such names were, therefore, different in their original significance from the English surnames in '-man' discussed earlier.

WELSH AND SCOTS OCCUPATIONAL SURNAMES

Occupational surnames from the Welsh language are in general much less common than the corresponding names in English. In Wales a high proportion of surnames, including many of the more common ones, are derived from personal names, and no occupational names from the Welsh language are as common as names such as Smith, Baker, Clark, and so on are in English. By the thirteenth century some English occupational surnames or by-names were already present in Wales, and occasionally appear in distriets which were predominantly Welsh-speaking. A moderate number of occupational surnames from the Welsh language survive at the present day, mostly still in Wales and in the English counties bordering on Wales.[4] None is really numerous. The Welsh word for 'smith', *gov*, may have contributed to the surname Gough, now fairly common in both Wales and England, but Gough is often a surname of the nickname type in origin (see Chapter 6). The Cornish surname Angove ('the smith') is from the Cornish language, a Celtic one related to Welsh. Saer, from the Welsh word for 'carpenter', survives in Wales, but is not at all numerous, and is much less common proportionately than names such as Carpenter or Wright are in England. It is difficult to say how far this name has spread into England, as it now appears in forms such as Sawyer or Sayer, which are generally impossible to distinguish from the English occupational surname Sawyer, or from surnames derived from the personal name Saer or Sayer, which was introduced into England after the Conquest, from France, and was widely used during the twelfth and thirteenth centuries, though later disused. The surname Meddick ('doctor') can be found today in most parts of Wales, but is scarce. A few other occupational surnames can still be found in Wales that are from the Welsh language, such as Goyder ('woodman'), but are rare. In general there is a marked difference between the limited number of Welsh occupational surnames which survive, and the rarity of the individual surnames, and the profusion of English occupational surnames, some of them very numerous over a long period. This is one aspect of the basic differences which existed between the way in which surnames evolved in Wales and in England.

The occupational surnames originating in the Scots-speaking parts of Scotland are in general not substantially different from the names in the same category found in England. A few names which were present in England from an early period also occur in Scotland, but have become much more numerous there than has ever been the case in England. Grieve ('manor bailiff' or 'overseer') has been present in Scotland from the thirteenth century and is much more numerous there than it has ever been in England. The equivalent name Reeve, or Reve, has long been much more common in England. Bowman. never a particularly common name in England, is now numerous in some parts of Scotland. Dempster has always been rare in England, but is widespread and quite numerous in Scotland. Dorward or Durward (literally 'door keeper') is quite a numerous Scots surname, but has always been rare in England. It is now sometimes spelt Dorwood, which has the appearance of a locative surname. The name's frequency in Scotland may be partly due to its having been the surname of a Scots aristocratic family, who held the hereditary office of door keeper in the king's household, and possibly the surname may have been adopted by some of the family's tenants. Another surname much more common in Scotland than in England is Coltherd, and its variants Colthard, Colthurt, Coulthard, and so on. The same is true of Stalker, probably with the obvious meaning of someone who stalked game, Farmer or Fermour, sometimes used for a leaseholder, sometimes for one who 'farmed' revenues (that is, acquired the right to collect them in return for paying a fixed sum to the Crown), or the names Bannerman and Naismith, already mentioned. Apart from names from Gaelic, a few occupational surnames seem to have originated solely in Scotland. Femister or Fimister ('fee master', in the sense of a man in charge of livestock), for instance, never seems to have arisen in England.

A high proportion of Gaelic names are derived from personal names, but there are some surnames from Gaelic occupational terms. Such names include some which have become fairly common in Scotland, and which have subsequently spread south of the border, and in many cases to North America as well. Among the more numerous occupational surnames from Gaelic originating in Scotland are Crerar or Crear ('sievewright'), Dewar ('pilgrim', but sometimes a locative name from Dewar in Lothian), and Gow ('smith'). Some other Gaelic surnames are less frequently found, and are still largely Scots names, with only a limited number of instances outside the country. These include Mavor or Maver ('steward', in the sense of an estate official), Grassick ('shoemaker'), now often in the forms Gracey, Grassie, and Grass, Toshack ('chief'), and Clacher ('mason'). All these are relatively rare. One or two occupational surnames found in Scotland are from languages other than Scots or Gaelic. The only one of these that is at all numerous is Lamont, or Lamond, from an Old Norse term meaning 'lawman'. It has sometimes been identified, in error, with the French La Mont. The surname Lawman, which occurs in England, has a similar origin. Lamont and Lamond are now widespread surnames in Scotland, and are particularly numerous in the southern part of the country. One or two surnames which are French linguistically became established in Scotland, probably through direct migration from France. Boyter ('box maker') is a Scots surname of French origin which does not seem to be present in England except through migration from Scotland, though Boittier survives as a French surname.

The number of occupational surnames now present in Britain is very great, and the category includes some very common surnames. Many occupational names, including some of the rarer ones, occur from an early date in widely separated parts of the country, and it is most improbable that any surname which is widely dispersed early in its history can have originated with a single family. Occupational surnames must, consequently, in the great majority of cases, have arisen in a number of separate families. A minority of occupational names were in origin localised in particular regions, but even these were tending to disperse by about 1600, so that the regional origins of names in the category are of only limited value in establishing family beginnings.

Many occupational names are from words still in use at the present day, and need little explanation. Even surnames from trades or crafts which are now obsolete are often understandable. A few names are perhaps deceptive. Bolter or Boulter, for example, is from the occupation of sifting meal. Though never a really common name, Bolter occurs in early sources mainly in the south-west Midlands and the south west of England. Bloomer is from the work of handling and smelting blooms, or ingots, of iron, while Bowler is from making, or perhaps selling, bowls. Wetherhead, which looks at first sight like a topographical name, is a development of Wetherherd, a shepherd who looked after the, usually gelded, male sheep, long valued because they produced exceptionally heavy fleeces. This is mainly a name from Scotland and the north of England. A Carder was one who carded, that is, combed out, wool. The surname Card probably has the same significance, but the Scots name Caird is a Gaelic name, from the craft of working in brass. Leaper or Leeper may originally have been sometimes a name for someone who leapt or danced, but seems often to have meant 'basket maker'. Reader or Reeder is from the craft of thatching houses with reeds, a commonly-used roofing material in some regions such as East Anglia and Essex. This is mainly a name from the east of England in origin; other surnames from the business of roofing existed in other regions, such as Thatcher, Slater, or Tyler. Raper, Rapier, and Rooper all have the same meaning as Roper, and are from the trade of rope-making. Day or Dey is from a word meaning 'dairy maid' or more generally 'servant'; originally feminine, it was already a name for men by about 1200. The modern name D'Eye seems to be a form of this, with the spelling influenced by the belief that the name is French in origin. Day was also in some cases a pet form of the personal name David. Bannister, or Banaster, the name of a landowning family in north Wales and Lancashire in the twelfth century and later is often said to mean 'basket maker'; the origin of the name has been disputed, however, and it has been suggested that the name is a form of Ballister ('crossbowman', a name of the same meaning as Arblaster), which is rather more likely as the name of a knightly family at an early date.

All these have spellings possibly misleading to someone thinking in terms of modern English words. There are quite a number of occupational surnames, most of them rare, which are from occupational terms long disused. To quote some examples out of many which survive to the present day, these include Crowther ('fiddler'), Vieler ('also 'fiddler'), and Rutter (another name for a musician on stringed instruments); Fewster, Foister, and Fuster (all 'maker of saddle trees'); Firminger, and Furmage or Furmedge (all 'cheese maker', from the French; Cheeseman, Chessman, and Chisman have the same meaning); Cheker (for an Exchequer official; Chequers in Buckinghamshire is so named from having been held by a family who were hereditary ushers of the Exchequer in the twelfth and thirteenth centuries); Frobisher, Furber, and Forber ('furbisher', or polisher, of armour, in all three cases); Ginner and Genner or Jenner ('engineer', probably for a man who made siege engines such as mangonels, catapults, etc.; some of Edward' III's siege engines were made by Nicholas Lenginour, a Leicestershire man); Jagger ('carter' or 'hawker', mainly a Yorkshire name in origin); Lavender and Lander ('launderer', often a woman's name in origin); Palliser and Pallister ('maker of palings or fencing'); Pilcher ('maker of hide garments'; mainly a Kent and Sussex name at first); Reeve, Reve, and Reeves (a manorial official; Portriff is 'portreeve', the chief dignitary or mayor of a town, a south of England name in origin); Scrimgeour, Skriminger, Scrimshaw, and Skrimshire (all 'skirmisher'; that is 'fencing master', a disreputable trade in the Middle Ages); Straker and Striker (both said to be from the duty of supervising the accuracy of grain measures, but this seems rather uncertain); Tazelar and Tesslar (from the trade of combing cloth with teasels, or dried thistle heads); or Tiddeman, Tidman, or Tittman (all 'tithingman', a minor official concerned with the frankpledge system, a mediaeval peace keeping arrangement, somewhat like a neighbourhood watch). These are only a few of the occupational names now in use which have meanings not immediately obvious to a reader without any special-ised knowledge, and may serve to illustrate the need to check the meaning of such names in one of the standard dictionaries of surnames. The great majority of occupational names now in use are listed in such dictionaries. Many occupational surnames or by-names can be found at earlier periods, especially from about 1200 to 1500, which have now been lost. They include a good many names which were always very rare, but may be encountered in documents dating from before about 1500. In general researchers into family history or genealogy are unlikely to meet with any of these, but if any difficulty arises, most of the occupational terms involved can be found in the *Oxford English Dictionary*, which is available in many reference libraries. The use of these authorities should clear up any difficulties likely to arise about occupational names. The point made at the beginning of this chapter, that not all names which look like occupational ones in fact belong to that type, should be kept in mind.

NOTES AND REFERENCES

1. T. J. Morgan and P. Morgan, 1985, *Welsh Surnames*, University of Wales Press, p. 52.
2. G. F. Black, 1946, *Surnames of Scotland*, New York Public Library, pp. 56–7.
3. J. le Patourel, 1956, *Manor and Borough of Leeds, 1066–1400*, Thoresby Society, pp. 74, 121.
4. Morgan and Morgan, *op.cit.*

CHAPTER SIX

Surnames derived from nicknames

Surnames derived from nicknames are a varied batch. A few have long been common, mostly those from obvious physical characteristics, but many surnames in the category have always been rare, and many surnames and by-names which existed before 1500 are now extinct. Large numbers of such surnames occur in mediaeval sources, but most of them have not survived to the present day. Some of these have meanings which are reasonably obvious, and about which it is not difficult to imagine how they arose; among the names which can be found, for example, are Ragamuffyn, Smarteknave, Raweknave, Thynewyt, Tothelesse, le Uncouthmon, Orpedman ('valiant man'), and Righthert. There are many others where it is only possible to guess at their original significance, and where it can only be conjectured why they were bestowed in the first place, such as Quatreoreyles ('four ears'), Gyvecorn, Fivewinterald, Moderblissing ('mother's blessing'?), Ryngotherose, or Bletherhose (for someone very talkative?). It is not surprising that some nicknames, which were just as freely bestowed in the past as they are now, hardened by degrees into more or less permanent by-names, and that some of these in turn developed into hereditary surnames. The presence of such surnames is not confined to languages spoken in Britain, and examples can be found in most European languages.

Among the minority of nickname-type surnames to be all common at present are some derived from physical characteristics. Most of these are from obvious points of appearance, Long, Short, Ballard and Pollard (both names for bald men), Grant, Small, Little, and so forth. It is probable that most of the surnames derived from colours fall into this group, such as Black, White, Gray and Grey, Blewett, probably for someone with a pale or livid complexion, or Reed,

Read, and Reid, all probably from the colour red, though there are places called Read (in Lancashire), Rede (in Suffolk), and Reed (in Hertfordshire). It is, however, difficult to be sure just why such names arose. They may, and often probably do, refer to the colour of hair or complexion. Black, for instance, is probably a name for someone with black hair, a common enough feature in Britain, or perhaps for someone with a swarthy face, just as for instance Blunt, Blundell, Fairhead, Fairfax, Faire, and Shirlock were originally names for people with blond hair. It is, however, at least possible that Black was originally a name for someone who wore black clothes, and it is just possible that the surname has a metaphorical meaning, and refers to a person's character with unfavourable implications, of the kind implied by such expressions as blackguard, blackened character, black mark, black sheep, etc. Even a name which at first sight seems obvious in its meaning can be one of which the real significance is doubtful.

There are of course some surnames from colours which do not belong in this category. Green is usually from residence beside the village green, and Redman or Redmayne is either from the occupation of cutting reeds, used for thatching in some parts, or from the place-name Redmain (Cumbria), the two names having become confused at times.

Many scarcer names from physical features exist, the survivors of a much larger and very mixed body of often rare surnames or by-names, many of which have long since died out. A few of these are from the French language, though it is uncertain whether they were imported from France, or whether they evolved in England at a period when some sections of society there were still speaking the Norman-Picard dialect of French. Foljamb ('bad leg'), now sometimes modified into Fulljames, Beljamb ('fine leg'), now usually in the form Belgian or Belgion, Pauncefoot or Pauncefort ('round belly'), Giffard (probably 'fat cheeks'), Fisdelou ('wolf face'), Large, or Joliffe and Jolly are examples of this. Many more such surnames are English, such as Barfoot (possibly for someone who went barefooted as a penance, but there must have been people who were shoeless through poverty), Blacklock and Blakelock, Blackbird (originally 'black beard'), Crookshank and Cruikshank, Cripps and Scripps (both meaning 'curly haired'), Greathead (probably a nickname, though some similar names such as Whitehead, Broadhead, and Roughhead or Ruffhead are in at least some cases locative ones), Hoare ('grey haired, hoary'), Lambshead, Langbain ('long bone', presumably for a lanky individual), Langbant ('long bairn'),

Longfellow, Smallbone, and many others, none of them really common names today. Surnames from physical characteristics can be found among Welsh and Gaelic names too. The Welsh surname now usually spelt Gough, or less commonly Goff, is usually from a Welsh word meaning 'red haired', though there may in some cases have been confusion with the Welsh word for 'smith'; Gwynn is from a Welsh adjective meaning 'white', sometimes used as a personal name in Welsh, and the surnames now generally spelt Lloyd and Floyd are from a Welsh adjective used sometimes to mean grey, sometimes to indicate various shades of brown. In Scotland, the two well-known names Campbell and Cameron are from Gaelic phrases meaning 'crooked mouth' and 'crooked nose' respectively, though in the case of Cameron there has been some confusion with a locative name. There are also in English a number of surnames which refer to various parts of the body in a metaphorical way, such as Armstrong, Lightfoot, Proudfoot, or Strongitharm, or like such surnames from the French language as Fairbrass and Firebrace, both from the French *fier bras*, 'proud arm', Pettifer, Potiphar, and Puddifer, all from the French *pied de fer*, 'iron foot', and Pettigrew, from *petit cru*, 'small growth'.

Many other names are derived from personal habits, some regarded favourably, some with opprobrium. Surnames from favourable characteristics include, for example, Bellamy ('good friend', from the French), Blessed, Curtis and Curtois ('courteous'), Fairmaner, Good, Goodchild, with the French equivalent Bonafant or Bonifant (*bon enfant*), which has sometimes developed into Bullivant, Moody (*'bold'*), Treadwell, Welbeloved, Wellfare, Welkempt, Wise, and Wisdom. Surnames with an unfavourable meaning include Milksop, Startup (probably 'upstart', Pickup, on the other hand is from a Lancashire place-name), Best ('beast'), Dullard, Doll ('foolish', but Dole is probably from the practice of allotting land in doles, or shares given by lot), Gerish or Garrish ('wild, wayward'), Manclark ('bad clerk', from the French), which has sometimes become Moakler or Mockler, Maufe (originally the French *mal fei*, 'bad faith'), Wild, and Thewles, Thewlis, or Thowless ('ill mannered'). There are a number of surnames, which ought to be included, referring in a pretty direct way to sexual activity, such as Toplady, Topliss ('top lass'), Lemon and Leeman ('sweetheart, beloved'), Parramore ('paramour'), Spendlove, now usually spelt Spenlow, Sweetlove, Fullielove, and another name with the same significance, Blandamer (from the French *plein d'amour*). Besides these, there are several surnames which may well allude to such activities in a less obvious fashion, such as Pullrose, Breakspear, or Whitehorn, but of which the original meaning must be uncertain. During the thirteenth and fourteenth centuries, especially, many other surnames or by-names can be found which refer to male and female genitalia, or to sexual acts, in a blunt fashion, and these include some which were obscene by modern standards. These have now disappeared, and many of them were probably never hereditary. They are perhaps chiefly of interest as evidence for the phrases used in ordinary speech about such matters, and as showing that bawdy talk, coarse phrases, and sexual innuendos were at least as common in those days as they are today.

Apart from such surnames derived from desirable or reprehensible characteristics, there are a great number of surnames still in use, from species of mammals, birds, and fish. These include, for instance, Batt, Beever, Buck, Bull, Bullock, Catt, Colt, Cony, Doe, Hare (but this is at times a nickname from 'hair', probably for someone who had a shock head of hair), Hart, Hogg, Lamb, Leppard, Otter, Palfrey, Roebuck and Roe (Rae is a Scots form), Stagg, Steed (but this can have other origins), Steer, Whale, Wildbore, or Wolf. Some of these names, like Colt, Bullock, or Palfrey, may really be occupational ones, from the work of looking after the animals in question. There are many surnames from species of birds, such as Bulfinch, nowadays sometimes in the form Bolfin, Bussard, Chaffinch, Crane, Dottrell, Dove, Dunnock ('hedge sparrow'), Finch and Vinch, Fowle, which has developed variants such as Vowle, Foghill, Vugle, Vugles, and Fugles, Gander, Glide and Glead (both 'kite'), Goose, Hawke, Jay, Kite (and in some cases Keat and Keats are variants of Kite), Muskett, originally a name for a small hawk, and only later used for a firearm, Nightingale, Musson ('sparrow'), Nottage or Nottidge (from the nuthatch), Lark and Laverack (from the Middle English word for 'lark'), Partridge, Pheasant and Fesant, Peacock, with Paw, Powe, and Poe, all from Old English or Middle English words for the same bird, Pigeon, Puttock, also meaning 'kite', Pye (for 'magpie') and its diminutive Pyatt, Quayle, Raven, Ruddock ('robin'), Sparhawk ('sparrowhawk', but this was at times used as a personal name, and may at times be a patronymic), Sheldrake, Spink ('finch'), Swallow, Swan, Thrush, Woodcock, Wren, and of course Bird. Robin is a diminutive of Robert, and was not used of the bird during the Middle Ages. The Middle English word for parrot, 'papejai' or 'popejoy', has given rise to several surnames, Papigay, Pobjoy, Popjoy, and other variants. Apart from the surname Fish itself, there are many names from various fish species. Some of these may really be from occupations; Herring, for example, could be for a dealer in such fish, rather than a nickname. The origin of some surnames which appear to come from fish species, such as Puffer or Mackerel, is in fact doubtful. There remain many nickname-type surnames from fish, such as Colefish, Gurnard, Lamprey, Lax ('salmon'), Pilchard, Shad, Spratt, Tench, or Trout. Salmon is usually from the personal name Solomon, used fairly widely in the Middle Ages by both Jews and Christians.

Some surnames which might appear to be derived from animal species in fact have other roots. Badger is a variant of 'bagger', an occupational term for someone who dealt in commodities made up in bags, such as a corn merchant. Lion and Lyons, though sometimes from the feline, are usually from one of the places in France called Lyon. Bear is sometimes from the animal, but is often from one of the places called Beer, Beare, Beere, etc., or from an Old English topographical term, bearu, with the meaning of 'grove'. Seal is often from one of the places called Sele or Seal, but may at times have been a nickname from the marine mammal. While the literal meaning of such surnames is usually clear, it is not obvious why they were used as nicknames in the first place. Some species were associated with particular qualities; foxes were noted for cunning, peacocks for pride, lambs for meekness, kites with rapacity, sparrows with lasciviousness, doves with gentleness, and so forth. During the Middle Ages a great deal of folklore circulated about various birds, mammals, and so on. In some parts of the country there may well have been purely local folk traditions which attributed certain qualities to particular species, and such influences may lie behind the bestowal of some nicknames which developed into surnames. Some surnames of the type were probably nicknames referring to people's appearance, Crane, Heron, and Stork were probably at first nicknames for tall, long-legged individuals, while Spratt, from a proverbially small fish, was probably a nickname for someone undersized. However, though conjectures can be made about the origins of some such surnames, the origins of many others remains obscure.

Two smaller but interesting groups of surnames from nicknames are those from seasons of the year or from festivals, and those from oaths or ejaculations. Those from festivals include Noel, with its variants Nowell and Newell, Christmas or Cristmas, and Midwinter, all probably at first nicknames for people born over the Christmas season; Pack, Pakes, Paish, Pash and Paske, all from the Old French *pasques*, probably a nickname for someone born over Easter, and Pentecost or Pancost, a surname which seems to have originated in

Sussex and Surrey, and to have become confused at a relatively late period with surnames from the place-name Pinkhurst. Pankhurst, sometimes said to be a late variant of Pentecost, is likely to be from the place-name. Pentecost was sometimes used as a personal name in the eleventh and twelfth centuries, and the surname may have originated from this in some instances. Another surname of a rather similar type is the rare name Domesday, though it is not at all clear why such a name should have arisen. Winter may be from an Old English personal name, but alternatively it may in some cases be a nickname, either for someone born at that season or for someone with a cold and wintry disposition. There are one or two surnames from days of the week, such as Monday and Friday. The origin of these is uncertain. Monday or Mundy is sometimes from a personal name of Scandinavian origin, but it may arise from the fact that there were on some mediaeval manors tenants who were obliged to perform labour services on Mondays; in manorial records they are sometimes mentioned as Monday men, and this may be the origin of the surname in some cases. Friday was a day for fasting, and the surname may be from a nickname alluding to this. Summer, Summers, and Somers are probably all really occupational names, and variants either of Sumpter (a man who led pack animals), or of Sumner (a summoner, an official of the church courts who served summonses). Spring is a topographical name.

There is a small but picturesque group of surnames from oaths, greetings, or similar expressions. Some which can be found before 1500 are extinct, but surviving examples include Bonger and Bongers (from *bonjour*) and the English equivalent Goodenday, from the greeting 'good day'; Godsmark; Godshalf, Godsalve, and Godseff, all 'for God's sake'; Goodenough, probably for someone who used that phrase repeatedly; Pardew, Pardy, and Pardoe, all from the French *per Dieu*; Parfoy ('by my faith'); and Purdy and Purdew, from *pour Dieu*. Those names which are from French phrases may have originated in France, and have been brought to Britain as already established surnames. However, there were similar by-names or surnames in Britain during the period before 1500, which are now extinct, and it must be suspected that these, like some other names which are in the French language, may have originated in Britain. The phrases concerned are just the kind of fragments of language likely to have been known to people whose knowledge of French was very scanty.

What has been said above is a summary description of the main groups into which surnames from nicknames can be subdivided.

There are many surnames in the category which do not fit into any of the types just described, and which are impossible to classify in detail.

INTERPRETATION OF SURNAMES FROM NICKNAMES

In most cases the literal significance of surnames from nicknames is clear, but the real reasons why such surnames developed often remain obscure, and it is very unusual for any evidence to be available about how such surnames arose. Some surnames of the type may have been at first ironical, as some nicknames are today. The use of 'tiny' as a nickname for an exceptionally large man is not rare at the present time, and a few years ago the present writer knew a notoriously slow and dilatory bus driver who was known to his long-suffering regular passengers as 'speedy Gonzales'. It must be an open question if some mediaeval nicknames were not similarly sarcastic. Was Drinkwater, for example, a nickname for a drunkard, Gatherpenny a nickname for someone notoriously thriftless, or Wise for someone generally regarded as a bit of a fool? It is generally impossible to be certain about such points. In the twelfth and thirteenth centuries, the surname Sansavoir ('without possessions') or Sansaver appears. It was in fact the hereditary surname of a family of large landholders with much land in the south east of England and elsewhere. This looks as if the name might have been ironical, but it is difficult to be sure.

Nicknames, of course, are still freely bestowed at the present day, and existing habits about the creation of nicknames have been the subject of much research by sociologists and psychologists, mainly in connection with the practice of restricted groups such as schoolchildren or workers at some particular plant, and similar clearly defined groups which constitute societies of one kind or another. Such investigations show that nicknames today are often based on particular minor incidents, which are soon forgotten, while the nicknames themselves continue to be used. The research further indicates that the nature of nicknames is influenced by an individual's standing among the people with whom he or she associates, so that, for example, a man held in low esteem by his fellows would be likely to have a nickname stressing unfavourable characteristics. There is no way of testing how far these conclusions about present habits in nicknaming can be safely projected into the past, but common sense would suggest that practices in, say, the thirteenth and fourteenth centuries, when many nickname-type surnames originated, are unlikely to have been radically different from those prevailing now.

One of the very few instances where there is some evidence about how a surname in this category arose shows how difficult it can be to penetrate to the true origin of surnames in this category. The surname now usually spelt Trankmer, Tranckmore. or Trenchmer is from a French phrase, *trenche mer*, 'cleave the sea'. One of the earliest persons to be found in England with the name was Alan Trenchmere, a seaman and shipbuilder of Shoreham in Sussex during the late twelfth century. Alan built ships for cross-channel work for Richard I. He must have been well known as a capable shipbuilder, and may have had a reputation as a constructor of especially fast vessels. Alan's by-name, for there is no evidence that he inherited it, obviously came from his shipbuilding activities. The name seems to have become hereditary, for although no connected pedigree can be traced the name persisted at Shoreham, and elsewhere in Sussex, as the surname of people who were probably Alan's descendants.

The surname Trenchmere ramified to some extent in Sussex, but it also existed in other maritime areas such as London, Kent, Dorset, East Anglia, and north-east England as the name of what appear to be quite separate families. Though the surname is from the French language, the phrase from which it is derived must have been in widespread use in England, at least among the sections of the population who understood French, and these would probably include a good many of those engaged in trade or shipping across the Channel. It must have conveyed to people in different parts of the country a distinct image, probably of a man who was a skilful seaman or shipbuilder.

This instance shows how difficult it can be to discover how a nickname-type surname began, or what it conveyed to hearers when it was first used. So far as can be seen from the available evidence, Trenchmere was a surname which arose in England, despite being from a French phrase. No evidence has been found to show that Alan Trenchmere was a migrant from France, and nothing is known about his parentage. A good many surnames or by-names from French phrases can be found in England during the Middle Ages; some have already been mentioned, and though some of them have been lost, others have survived to the present day. Most such names found in England appear there without having been translated literally into Middle English, the fate of quite a few alien names brought into

England at the same period, and without having become badly distorted in spelling or pronunciation. It seems probable from this that some at least of these names originated in England, and that the French phrases concerned were understood by a significant part of the population. This would no doubt include a high proportion of those who were literate, and who produced the documents in which such names have come down to us. Though some surnames in French are those of landowning families and some have origins which can be traced back to Normandy or other parts of France, some surnames or by-names which are French linguistically appear as the names of people in quite humble circumstances. During the thirteenth century, for instance, among those who appear with French surnames or by-names are serfs who were bound to the soil, and whose unfree status was hereditary; such people are unlikely to have been French immigrants. Most of the surnames from French phrases to be found in mediaeval Britain were nickname-type surnames, and a few of these were quite widely distributed in England and in the Scots-speaking parts of Scotland.

The problems of understanding the true significance of surnames from English phrases are just as great as in understanding surnames from the French language. To give an example, the surname Shirwin or Sherwin has developed from Scherewind, 'cut wind'. This name, though never very common, occurs during the Middle Ages and later in most regions of England, and it also occurs in Scotland. Obviously it arose independently as the name of quite a few separate families. It must consequently be supposed that the phrase from which it is derived must have been in use over a wide area and not just locally or in a single dialect, and it must be supposed further that it conveyed to contemporaries some reasonably precise impression of any individual who was so nicknamed. It is, however, now very doubtful what the significance of the phrase was; perhaps, as suggested by Reaney and others,[1] it was a nickname for a swift runner; possibly it may have been a name for someone so thin that he seemed to cut the wind. There can be no certainty what the nickname meant when it was first bestowed in such distant periods as the twelfth and thirteenth centuries, when the name appears in early examples.

There are similar doubts about other nicknames from phrases, both French and English. The surname Quatermains ('four hands'), for example, occurs from an early period in several parts of the country, and was evidently the name of several distinct families. It must be uncertain whether the surname originated in England, or was brought in by migrants from France. Its meaning is equally uncertain;

perhaps it may have been a nickname for a particularly active or dextrous individual. Many other surnames are equally obscure in their meaning. Names like, for instance, Gotobed (?idleness, promiscuity), Standaloft (?an aloof or haughty personality), Passavaunt ('go before', ?an outrider, or somebody who tended to push in first), Pennyfather (?a miser, or someone with a reputation for having ready money), Shakespear and many others are impossible to interpret with any certainty. In some cases the occupations of those who appear with some surnames in early instances may furnish some clues. Some of those who appear with the name Wagstaffe in the thirteenth century were constables, catchpolls, or other peace officers, and the nickname obviously originated from their occupation. On the analogy of this, Shakespear might be a nickname for a man at arms, but it is difficult to explain similar names, such as Breakspear, in the same way, and doubts must remain about why Shakespeare was originally used as a nickname. Breakspear might be supposed to be a nickname from proceedings at tournaments, where spears were broken in jousting, but the participants in such activities were usually knights or squires, and the early examples of Breakspear as a name seem usually to refer to people of humbler status. It may be added that the name Jouster or Juster, which derives from the sport of jousting at tournaments appears in early instances as the surname or by-name of serfs who could not have taken part in such activities, and some humorous or facetious intention must lie behind the bestowal of such a name on a bondman. The true significance of such surnames eludes the present-day observer.

Many surnames from nicknames can be found from an early period in several different counties, or even in different regions, despite the fact that most of the names in question have always been uncommon. Some relatively rare surnames in this category can be found as early as the thirteenth century, or even the twelfth in some cases, scattered through different parts of the country. When surnames arise from nicknames, more or less concurrently, in several regions independently, it must be supposed that the expressions which gave rise to the names concerned were in widespread and general use. It must further be supposed that each such expression denoted to contemporaries some reasonably clear-cut points of character, justifying the bestowal of a given nickname on some particular person. A considerable number of surnames derived from phrases can be found, each of which was already widely distributed before about 1400. Some such surnames or by-names found in the Middle Ages have now disappeared, but among those which still survive, and which were already present in several regions by 1400, are: Sherwin, discussed above; Breakspear, just mentioned, which can be found before 1400 in Lincolnshire, Bedfordshire, Surrey, Sussex, and Essex; Drinkwater, present in Dorset, Kent, London, Shropshire and Sussex; Fairwether, found in Devon, Lancashire, Norfolk and Suffolk, and Sussex (and also appears in Scotland in the sixteenth century); Goodall ('good ale'), which appears in Bedfordshire, Cornwall, London, Norfolk, Suffolk, Shropshire, Worcestershire, and Yorkshire; Makehate ('make joy'), found in Bedfordshire, Dorset, Durham, Essex, Kent, and Sussex; Parlebien ('well spoken'; now sometimes spelt Parlby), present in Cambridgeshire, Derbyshire, Devonshire, Durham, Essex, Kent, Lincolnshire, London, Norfolk, Somerset, Worcestershire, and Yorkshire; Passavaunt ('go before': now often spelt Passant), found in Durham, Hampshire, Lancashire, Lincolnshire, Sussex, and Yorkshire; Proudfoot, which occurs in Bedfordshire, Essex, Hampshire, Lincolnshire, London, Norfolk, Northumberland, Suffolk, Surrey, Sussex, Worcestershire, and Yorkshire, and in Scotland; or Spendlove, now often Spenlow, found in Bedfordshire, Durham, Lanarkshire, Lancashire, Lincolnshire, Norfolk, Northumberland, Suffolk, Sussex, and Yorkshire. None of these surnames was ever really common, and none is particularly numerous at the present day. Indeed, several of them are now rare. All, however, can be found in several regions from an early period. The phrases from which they arose must have been part of the common currency of talk over much of the country, and probably over the whole of England and the Scots-speaking parts of Scotland. Some are from phrases which are French linguistically, but it is difficult to suppose that these were present in Britain as a result of a series of separate migrations from France, where none of the names concerned seems to have been at all common, or that the widespread distribution of such names is due to the rapid dispersal over the country of a few families with French surnames. Many such surnames must preserve phrases widely used in Middle English, and which were each applied to individuals with certain definite characteristics, thought to justify the bestowal of some particular nickname. In this they perhaps convey some flavour of the ordinary man's spoken English as it was in the thirteenth and fourteenth centuries, when most of these names arose.

Occasionally, some nickname-type surnames were created from diminutives or pet forms of surnames in the same category – a development more usual in the south east of England than elsewhere. For example, in Sussex the surname Faircock was formed from the surname Fayre with the suffix '-cock'. Lovecock and Lovekin were both formed from pet forms of the surname Love in the same county. The rare surname Notkyn is from a hypochoristic form of Nott. There are other examples of the same processes at work in the formation of surnames. Some other nickname-type surnames ending in '-cock' or '-kin' originated in the same way, such as Finchcock.

Most surnames in this category have always been uncommon, and the only ones which have ever been numerous are those from obvious physical features, such as colouring. A few surnames in the category, however, have become numerous in particular areas. In many cases this seems to have come about through single families putting out branches and increasing in numbers over several centuries. For instance, in Sussex the surname Fist, also variously spelt Fest, Fust, and Fiest – presumably a nickname for an aggressive person or for someone with more than the average tendency to throw punches– existed, perhaps at first as a by-name, in several parts of the county. It seems to have survived, however, as the name of only two or three families there, one living around Horsham in north Sussex, one around Chichester in the south west, and one around Wiston in the centre of the county. The surname multiplied with the growth of the families concerned, and by the seventeenth century had become quite numerous in Sussex, where it still survives at the present time. Another Sussex surname, Hogg, perhaps a nickname from the farm animal, perhaps an occupational name for a swine-herd, seems to have survived as the hereditary surname of a single family, living in east Sussex near the Kent border, though it occurs elsewhere as a by-name; the surname ramified in the sixteenth and seventeenth centuries to become one of the more numerous surnames in east Sussex, though it continues to be rare elsewhere. It still remains a quite common name in that part of Sussex. In Lancashire Straightbarrel, one of the many names in this category with a meaning which is quite obscure, appears to have been the surname of a single family, living in the Preston area from the early fourteenth century onwards. This name, too, proliferated markedly during the sixteenth and seventeenth centuries, and still survives in Lancashire. Or again, Stringfellow ('strongfellow') is a surname which existed, independently, during the Middle Ages in several counties. In Lancashire it first appears during the sixteenth century, having perhaps been brought in by migration from outside the county, and at that time it was present around Manchester, and in Prescott parish not far away. All the Stringfellows found in Lancashire at this period seem to have been related, and probably only one family was involved. The surname became very numerous at Prescott and adjoining places during the seventeenth century, having evidently multiplied rapidly. In Oxfordshire the surname Lamprey, from the eel-like creature chiefly known for having caused the death of Henry I, was quite a rare surname until after 1500, and was apparently that of a single family; subsequently it increased to become quite a common surname in the north and north west of the county. Several variant spellings of the name developed Lampery, Lanchepreye, Langsprey, etc. Though the name is generally rare, it does occur in other parts of England, as far as can be seen without any link to the Oxfordshire family. The meaning of this surname too is difficult to unravel. It can hardly have been given to someone who was thought to look like a lamprey. Possibly the name may contain an allusion to the lamprey's habit of preying on fish by attaching itself to its victim by its mouth, but this is no more than a guess.

Many other examples could be given of surnames from nicknames which have proliferated to a considerable degree, often while remaining mainly concentrated in one area. These circumstances are most easily detected in the case of surnames from nicknames, for many surnames of the type were originally rare, and were often the name of one single family in any particular area. In the case of surnames in some other categories, such as occupational names or surnames from the more common personal names, it is more difficult to see what is happening about the surnames of individual families because the situation is confused by the presence, even within a single county, of many families with the same surname, and in such situations the general defects of the genealogical evidence for early periods often make it impossible to separate out the different lines involved. Where common surnames are concerned, it is usually impossible to tell if individual families were ramifying for any period before parish registers became available in numbers, and even after that tracing the branches of a growing family is laborious. In the cases however, of locative surnames and of surnames from nicknames, there are a sufficient number of quite scarce surnames to provide examples of names which had ramified from single families, or from two or three families, in one area. The history of such names does throw light on what is happening to surnames generally at various periods, perhaps especially during the sixteenth and seventeenth centuries, when many surnames first began to multiply. Researchers into pedigrees or family histories should be aware that there are some surnames, rare in the country as a whole, which are unexpectedly common in some limited areas, and this is liable to complicate the investigation of pedigrees.

A look through almost any mediaeval source for England, or for the Scots-speaking parts of Scotland, will reveal the existence of very many surnames and by-names from nicknames, including many which have now disappeared. Such names convey the flavour of popular speech at the period, colourful, inventive, and sometimes coarse. Even names which have long since been lost have their interest when studying the early history of communities, and surnames from nicknames are often useful in tracing the history of families over long periods. The true meaning of many such names remains enigmatic, and it might be a worthwhile endeavour to follow up such names in particular localities in order to discover if any light can be thrown on the circumstances of their origin from investigation into such factors as local dialect, a task which could be undertaken without too wide-ranging research, by people interested in the history of their own town or village.

The real reason why many surnames derived from nicknames were originally bestowed must remain without any convincing elucidation. There is, for instance, a group of surnames which at first sight seem to be connected with wolf-hunting, such as Pricklove or Pricklow ('prick wolf'), Catchlove, Catchlow, or Getchlow, Trusslove ('truss wolf'), now often spelt Truslow or Trussler, or Bindlove ('bind wolf'), now often spelt Bindloes, Bindloss, or Binless. Besides these there is the name now spelt Pedlow, originally *pied de loup*, 'wolf's foot', which might refer to the practice of cutting off a dead wolf's foot as proof that such an animal had been slain, and Pellew or Pellow, originally *pel de lou*, 'wolf skin', which might be a nickname for a wolf hunter or someone who dealt in wolf skins. It is difficult to see some of these names being from operations which would play a practical part in wolf-hunting; trussing up a (presumably live) wolf sounds like a business of considerable danger and little profit. In addition, the existence of such by-names as Bindevil, Bindpouk ('bind goblin'), and Trussevilain, all apparently metaphorical ones, must raise doubts about the origin of such names as Truslow and Bindloss, Pricklove, Trusslove, and Bindlove can be found in early references in more than one region, and it is unlikely that any of them could ever have been the surname of a single family. The phrases from which such surnames arose must have had some implications which were generally understood in common speech over a large part of the country. Or, to give another example, it is possible to speculate about the beginnings of the surname Maiden, now sometimes spelt Maydon, a form which looks as if it might be derived from a place-name. Was this a nickname for someone generally thought to be a virgin, or was it ironical, for someone notoriously promiscuous, or was it a contemptuous term for a man thought to be girlish and effeminate? It is hardly possible to answer such a question convincingly. There are several surnames which seem to concern the handling or amassing of money, such as Gatherpenny, Pennyfather, and Winpenny, and there are further the surnames Penny and Shilling. It is not clear whether such names were nicknames for misers, or for people who were simply successful in trade, or whether they refer to the collection of rents, dues, tolls, etc. It would be possible to put forward a very long list of surnames derived from nicknames which have unknown or uncertain origins; in most cases more or less plausible conjectures can be made, but evidence about why nicknames were originally bestowed is almost always lacking. This is hardly surprising in view of the haphazard and whimsical way in which nicknames grow up at the present day, often on the basis of some chance incident or some casual facetious remark.

Surnames from nicknames are an extremely varied group, which largely defies classification. Many names in the category have always been rare, but others have ramified in one particular area, while remaining scarce, or absent, in other parts. Many surnames or by-names in this category which can be found before 1500 have been lost, and present-day language is the poorer for the disappearance of many picturesque and colourful names.

Several chapters have been devoted to discussing the main types of surnames, category by category. The great majority of surnames originating in Britain will fall into one or other of the main types which have been discussed. There are, however, a minority of British surnames which do not fit into any of the chief categories. There are also more surnames with unknown or very uncertain origins than is always realised.

The only group of surnames of any size which does not fit into any of the main groups is made up of surnames of relationship.

SURNAMES OF RELATIONSHIP

There is a small group of surnames from words for varying degrees of relationship, names such as Cousins, Brothers, Uncle, and so on. None of the surnames in the group has ever been among the really common names in the country, and all are rare surnames at the present day. Most of them are from words which are still in use in modern English, and are therefore easily recognisable. The '-s' which occurs at the end of names such as Cousins or Brothers is usually possessive, and is similar to the final '-s' at the end of names such as Roberts, Williams, etc., which have already been discussed.

How such names arose is uncertain. The most usual situation under which names of this type developed was when a property owner died without leaving children to succeed him, and his land passed to some more distant relative, a cousin, uncle, nephew, and so forth. Such surnames may also have arisen when it was necessary to distinguish between two members of the same family who had the same personal name. As is so often the case, however, there is some shortage of evidence about how in fact these surnames arose.

A few surnames of this type do not have any very obvious meaning or origin to the present-day reader. The surname Neave, or Neeve, Neve, is from a Middle English word with the literal meaning of 'nephew'. The word was, however, used at times for a thriftless or parasitic person, and the surname may in some cases have arisen at first as a nickname through the word being employed in this way. Eames (or Heames, Hemes, and also Neame) is from a Middle English word meaning 'uncle'. Both Neave and Eames occur in various parts of England from the thirteenth century onwards, and both surnames must have originated independently with a number of quite separate families. The surnames Neave and Neaves may have different origins when they have their beginnings in Scotland. Neave and Eames, though quite widely distributed geographically, have always remained scarce. Another similarly rare surname in the same group is Odam, or Odams, for a relative by marriage, either a son-in-law or a brother-in-law. At the present day this is sometimes given spellings such as Odhams, which have the appearance of being derived from place-names.

One set of surnames has been formed by adding 'maugh', a Middle English word, to a personal name, to produce surnames such as Watmaugh, Robertsmaugh, etc., or less frequently by adding the same word to an occupational term, to produce surnames such as Portermaugh. Such surnames all seem to have originated in the north of England, and there are only sporadic occurrences elsewhere. The meaning of 'maugh' is uncertain. It was possibly used in a rather vague way for any male relative by marriage. In the course of time the last syllable of such surnames has undergone various modifications. For example. Watmaugh, from a short form of Walter, has become variously Watmugh, Watmuff, Watmore, or Whatmoor. At the present time Watmough and Hitchmough, now often spelt Hickmott (from a hypochoristic form of Richard), are the only two surnames of this group which are not rare. A good many names of this type which can be found before about 1500 in the north of England, mostly in Yorkshire, Lancashire, and Cumberland, have died out. The type once included a fair number of surnames or by-names, but only a few have survived. A sprinkling of such names can now be found in most parts of Britain, but they are still rather more numerous in the north of England than elsewhere.

Many surnames of relationship are closely linked to words still in general use. The names Brothers and Cousins have already been mentioned. Cousins is now one of the more common names in this group, but this may owe something to its having become confused with two other names of distinct origins, one from the place-name Coutances (Dept. La Manche) in France, which gave rise to the surname de Cusaunce found in mediaeval England, and another surname which occurs today as Cusson or Cussen and which probably signifies 'son of Constance' or 'son of Cuthbert.[2] The word 'son' has given rise to the present-day surnames Soane, Sone, and Soanes (Soame, Soames, and Somes are from the place-name Soham, and are mainly East Anglian names in origin). The word 'daughter' is the origin of the surnames Daughters and Dauter. It has been said that it is the origin of several other surnames, including Darter, Dafter, and Doctor, but the derivation of any of these from 'daughter' has not been proved convincingly. The surnames Dawtrey, Daughtery, Daltry, Hawtrey, and Hatry are all developments from a French locative surname, de Hauterive, which was already established in England as the surname of a landed family well before 1200. As has been already mentioned, some by-names formed by affixing 'daughter' to some personal names existed in the north of England up to the seventeenth century, but have not survived. The surnames Fathers, Fader and Fadder, and Mothers exist today, but are rare. Bairnsfather, mainly a Scots name but one which originates in the north of England in some cases, is another fairly scarce name in this group.

The term spelt 'heir' in modern English has been the origin of a surname which is now spelt in a number of different ways: Ayer, Ayr, Ayres, Eyre, Hair, Hayer, and Heyer. Taking all the different forms together, this is one of the more common names from terms of relationship, but the spelling of the forms is now so varied that they are hardly recognisable as different versions of the same name. There has possibly been some confusion with surnames from the Scottish place-name Ayr, and with O'Hare and Hair, which are Anglicised forms of an Irish surname.

With surnames of relationship there ought to be included names from terms used to distinguish older and younger members of the same family. These include the surnames Senior, now spelt at times Senier, Seanor, Sayner, Sinyard, and so on, probably at first a nickname for the elder of two persons with the same personal name; as the surname is connected with the Old French *seignour* it may have been used to mean 'lord', though there is no firm evidence of the surname having been used in this way. The corresponding name Younger exists, but both it and Senior have always been fairly scarce. Young, a much more common name, was probably in origin a nickname bestowed on a son to distinguish him from a father with the same personal name. Younghusband ('young husbandman') may have arisen in the same way. The Welsh name now usually spelt Vaughan has the same meaning as Younger and was widely used in Wales when a son had the same first name as his father,[3] and the Welsh name Henn ('old') was used in the same sense as Senior. The surnames Old and Oldman both exist, but may in origin have been nicknames given to men who had survived into old age, uncommon in the mediaeval population, when the expectation of life was short. The surname Child, now quite widespread, may at times have been given to the youngest child of a family, but it was often used as a term for a young nobleman or landholder. The Scots name Ogg is from a Gaelic adjective meaning 'young'. It is now widely distributed in Britain outside Scotland.

The surnames of this type existing at the present day are the survivors of a much larger number of names which can be found before about 1500, many of them by-names which, as far as can be seen, never became hereditary. In mediaeval Lancashire, for instance, the names Childesfadre, Milnerstepson, le Wogherbrother ('brother of the wooer'; what lies behind this can only be guessed at), le Pristesbrother ('priest's brother'), and Johanesleman ('John's sweetheart'), can all be found, and many similar examples can be discovered in other counties. Though names from terms of relationship have never been more than a small proportion of the total number of surnames in use, they were one of the basic methods of distinguishing individuals, and were once more varied than the few surviving surnames of the type would suggest.

Any discussion of surnames group by group, with all the names being neatly arranged in categories, is rather apt to leave the impression that every surname can be deciphered, its meaning and origin unravelled, and that it can then be assigned to its appropriate pigeon-hole. A large majority of surnames can be satisfactorily explained, but out of the great number and variety of surnames now in use in Britain, there nevertheless remain a good many which baffle investigation and the origins of which have never been convincingly cleared up. In some cases this is probably because surnames have become so modified in the course of time, and so altered from their first form by the time that they appear in any records now extant, that their origins are no longer detectable. In this connection it must be remembered that some names are not to be found in written sources before the sixteenth century, though they may well have existed for some considerable time before that date. Many surnames still have no certain origin despite much investigation, though the names in question tend to be rare ones on the whole.

Besides surnames of which the origins and meaning are undiscovered, there are a good many surnames for which there is more than one possible explanation, and for which it is generally impossible to tell from the present day form of the surname what the origin is in the case of any particular family. For instance, the surname Mackerel or Makeral is in some cases a patronymic of Irish origin, which appears in south-west Scotland from about 1200 onwards.[4] However, the name Mackerel also occurs from the thirteenth century onwards in various parts of England, including some southern counties where Irish or Scots names are not common. In these areas it is probably a nickname from the fish – one of the considerable number of surnames from species of fish, as already discussed. Besides this, there is an Old French word, *macquereux* ('go between'), which might possibly be the origin of the surname in some instances. When the name appears in any part of Britain at the present day, it is difficult to choose between these possible origins. Or, to give another example, the now fairly common surname Barret or Barrat can have several possible origins: it might be a topographical name, derived from a diminutive for *barre*, in the sense of a barrier or gate; it might be derived from a word, found in Middle English as a borrowing from Old French, meaning 'trade, dealing', with the further implied meaning of 'fraud' or 'deception'; or the surname could be from the occupation of making caps. Again, it will usually be impossible to tell which of these possible explanations applies in the case of any family named Barret at the present day, and tracing the descent of such a family back to, say, the sixteenth century would not clear up the issue. Scarlett, another surname not especially rare at the present day, may have been a name for someone who manufactured or dyed scarlet cloth or who dealt in such material, but there is no clear evidence that the name originated in this way, or indeed that there were people who dealt exclusively with scarlet cloth, and not with material of other hues. Possibly it may have been a name for someone who habitually wore scarlet clothes, a conspicuous mark at a time when only a limited range of dyes was available, or for someone with an exceptionally ruddy complexion. These are no more than guesses, and there seems to be no direct evidence of how the surname began. The surname Roe or Rowe is in some instances a nickname from the roe deer, from which the name Roebuck also comes, and this may be one source of the surname Rae, which is usually a Scots surname; it is sometimes a topographical name, from residence in a row of houses, and it is sometimes from a place-name, Rewe, the name of several places in Devon; in some instances it is from an older form of the word spelt 'rough' in modern English; it is generally unsafe to rely on the present day spelling of a surname as grounds for chosing one of these possibilities rather than another. The surname Warren similarly has several possible origins; a family whose name was from a French place-name, Warenne (Seine-Maritime), was already established as landholders in England by 1086; the senior male line of this family eventually died out, but there may be families still surviving with surnames which go back to the French place-name. In some cases the name Warren is from residence near a rabbit warren, or from being in charge of one. This is an occupation from which come the surnames Warrener and Warrender, and it is one source of the surname Warner, which itself has an alternative source, from a personal name; rabbit warrens were a useful source of food in the Middle Ages, and were often preserved; finally, Warren has for long been confused with what was in the beginning a separate surname, from the personal name Warin, one brought to England after the Conquest, and widely used for about two centuries before going out of general use. The same personal name is the source of the surnames now spelt Waring, Wareing, etc., and is the second element in Fitzwarren. It is impossible to tell from the present spelling of the surname Warren just how it originated, and even tracing the pedigree of a family so named back for several centuries, if that could be done, would probably not clear up the matter.

Many other surnames have more than one possible origin, and there is often no way of telling how a surname arose merely from its present spelling. Tracing a pedigree back to some relatively early period, such as the sixteenth century, will often not make the matter any clearer, and no one should suppose that there is any way in which every existing surname can be instantly and reliably explained, or its original meaning set out. Things are not as simple as that. Guesswork about origins is unsatisfactory, and it is better not to indulge in it. If the precise beginnings of a surname cannot be established by adequate evidence, it is best to leave the issue open. Although the great majority of surnames have been satisfactorily explained, there remain some which have defied investigation up to this time. Occasionally it may be possible to discover fresh evidence by a thorough examination of local sources in the area where a surname first appears, and there is still much to be done in searching through the older documents in local record offices. Researchers may, however, find themselves in the position that it is not possible to discover with real certainty how a particular surname which interests them originated.

REFERENCES AND NOTES

1. P. H. Reaney, 1976, *Dictionary of British Surnames* (2nd edn.), Routledge and Kegan Paul, p. 317.
2. P. H. Reaney, 1967, *Origin of English Surnames*, Routledge and Kegan Paul, p. 81.
3. T. J. Morgan and P. Morgan, 1985, *Welsh Surnames*, University of Wales Press, pp. 58–60.
4. G. F. Black, 1979, *Surnames of Scotland*, New York Public Library, p. 526.

CHAPTER SEVEN

Some general themes in the history of surnames

The discussion of surnames category by category may omit certain issues which concern surnames of all the different types. It will, therefore, be useful to draw together here the evidence about certain points which concern the history of surnames in this country as a whole.

SURNAMES AS A GUIDE TO SHARED RELATIONSHIPS

One question which is often raised in connection with the history of surnames is whether all the bearers of one particular surname are ultimately related, and can all trace their descent back to some common ancestor living in the distant past, perhaps in the twelfth or thirteenth century, when many surnames originated. This is obviously a matter of interest and importance to people tracing their own pedigrees, or the history of their families. It is also no doubt a point of interest to people studying the history of a single surname, such as the members of one name societies, and it is a significant question for anyone wishing to use surname evidence for studying such questions as, for example, mediaeval population movements.

Even a very general study of surnames will show that some names have been so common and so widespread from an early date that it is inconceivable for them to have originated with the descendants of a single person. As has been shown in the discussion on occupational names, most of the really common surnames in that category were widely distributed from an early date, and the same is true of some of the less common occupational names. The same thing is true of some of the surnames from high offices in Church or state, such as King, Bishop, or Abbot. It is, however, the case that some of the rarer occupational surnames, though originating independently in different parts of the country, became relatively common in particular areas through the increase of single families. For instance, the surname Rymer (or Rimmer; probably a name for someone who recited verses for entertainment) occurs separately in several English regions, and the form Rimmer also occurs in Scotland. In Lancashire, however, the name seems to have originated with a single family who were living in the south east of the county in the thirteenth century and migrated to the west coast of south Lancashire. By the sixteenth century the name was already numerous in the coastal area between the Ribble and the Mersey, almost certainly through the ramification of one family. The name continued to increase in numbers there subsequently. It is still today a quite common surname in that part of Lancashire, and in all probability all the people named Rymer, Rimmer, etc., in that part of the country share a common ancestry. The surname has remained generally rare in other parts of Britain, though it does occur elsewhere. Similarly the surname Tyrer (probably from the craft of making iron tyres for wheels) seems to have originated in Lancashire with one family, in the south west of the county, around Liverpool. This surname, too, proliferated locally, and had become fairly common in that area by the sixteenth century. It still survives there at the present day, and it is likely that all the Lancashire Tyrers are descended from a single family, living in the fourteenth century. The name does, however, occur independently in other parts of the country.

In Oxfordshire, the surname Lardiner seems to have originated with a single family, resident at Oxford in the fourteenth century. It had become relatively numerous in the county by about 1600, and survives there to the present. The surname existed from an early date in several other parts of the country, as the name of people with no ascertainable links with Oxfordshire. In Sussex the name Shoesmith, now sometimes spelt Showersmith or Showsmith–a rare occupational name from the trade of making horseshoes–appears to have originated with a single family, living around Mayfield in the north east of the county. It had become fairly common in that area in the sixteenth century. This name too occurs separately outside Sussex.

Many surnames were derived from really common first names such as Thomas, Rogers, Williams, Johnson, Richardson, and so forth. Though some of them were largely confined at first to certain parts of the countrys they were too numerous and too dispersed from the time of their first appearance to suppose that any of them could be traced back to a single ancestor. The same is true of the large number of surnames from shortened or pet-forms of common personal names, surnames such as Hodges, Thoms and Tombs, Tompkins, Hitchcock, Wilcocks, Hoskins, Perkins, Hotchkiss. Wilkins, Dobson, Wilkinson, Dixon, Harrison, and many others. After investigating the history of many individual surnames, the author knows only one example where it seems likely that a surname from a hypochoristic form of a personal name could have been originally that of a single family, and this concerns the surname Thomsett or Tomsett, which is from an uncommon diminutive of the personal name Thomas. Thomsett as a surname originated in east Sussex, near the Kent border, and ramified there to a moderate degree without becoming really numerous. It subsequently spread to the London area, drawn into the metropolis like so many other surnames. It is still quite a rare surname at the present day, and not generally met with outside south east England. There may be other instances where surnames from shortened or pet-forms of common personal names seem likely to have originated with a single family, and students of the history of single surnames may be able to produce other examples, but such cases are rare.

Apart from surnames derived from personal names still in use at the present day, there are many surnames from personal names which have long since either been discarded altogether or have become very rarely used. Some of these surnames occur in many parts of the country from an early period, and obviously originated with a considerable number of separate families. For instance, the surname Godwin and Goodwin (the two forms became confused at an early date), can be found before 1400 in Norfolk, Suffolk, Lincolnshire, Cambridgeshire, Sussex, Yorkshire, Shropshire, Derbyshire, Oxfordshire, Surrey, Staffordshire, Devon, and Dorset; by the thirteenth century the surname Hammond was already a common surname or by-name in Norfolk and Suffolk, and must have originated in East Anglia alone with a number of separate families; besides this, it occurs before 1400 in Sussex, Surrey, Oxfordshire, Lincolnshire, Hertfordshire, Herefordshire, Somerset, Dorset, Devon, and Lancashire; the surname Durant (or Durand, Dorant) appears before 1400 in Lincolnshire, Norfolk, Suffolk, Essex, Surrey, Sussex, Oxfordshire, Warwickshire, Worcestershire, Derbyshire, Northamptonshire, Dorset, Devon, Yorkshire, and Lancashire. Many more examples could be given of surnames, frequently occurring and widely distributed before 1400, and in many cases still quite common today, which are derived from personal names disused, or very rare, from at the latest about 1350.

It is highly improbable that the surnames discussed above, whether the more common occupational names or surnames from any of the more common personal names, could have originated with a single family. To these must be added surnames from place-names which occur as the names of many different localities. Surnames such as Kirby, Ashby, Norton, Middleton, Preston, Drayton, Burton, and so forth can hardly ever have begun as the surnames of single families, and in fact surnames from these and other place-names can be found widely distributed from an early date. There are also, as noted in the section on locative surnames (see Chapter 2), a few surnames from place-names which became widely spread at an early period in their history and which each seem to have originated with a number of families, such as Pickering, Grantham, and Doncaster. There are, however, a great number of surnames derived from place-names which can only have originated from a single place. Many of these surnames have always been rare and remain so to the present day. Some others, like those Lancashire and Yorkshire surnames already discussed, have gradually proliferated over the centuries to become numerous in particular areas. The difficulty of finding adequate genealogical evidence for the period before parish registers came into existence, and even to a less extent later, usually makes it impossible to prove that all the people with any one locative name share a descent from a common ancestor. Some examples of surnames derived from place-names in the north of England, which each seem to have originated with a single family, have already been given in the chapter on locative surnames (see Chapter 2). It is possible to find similar instances in most parts of England and in the Scots-speaking parts of Scotland. For example, the surname Larwood, derived from a small locality in the Norfolk parish of Horstead, seems fairly certainly to have originated with a single family at Horstead, to have gradually increased in numbers there and at nearby places in east Norfolk, and before 1600 to have spread to Norwich and into Suffolk. Though never a common surname, Larwood became well established in one region, almost certainly through the ramification of one family.

Or, to give an instance from another part of the country, the surname Evershed, from a small place in the south of Surrey, appears in south Surrey, and across the county boundary in north Sussex from the fourteenth century, and the surname gradually increased in numbers in that part of the country. It still persists there to the present day as a fairly numerous surname locally, though it can now be found in other regions as well. Though genealogical evidence is not sufficient to supply a complete pedigree, this seems to be another case of a single family ramifying over several centuries. Also in Sussex, the surname Gratwick, from Greatwick, near Cowfold in that county, seems to have originated with a single family so named, existing in and near Greatwick from the early fourteenth century, and to have gradually proliferated in Sussex, where this name, too, survives to the present day.

In none of these cases is it possible to trace genealogical links which can prove that all the bearers of any one of the surnames just mentioned were all related. The evidence for pedigrees available for the mediaeval period, or even for the sixteenth century, is hardly ever sufficient to enable an investigation into such questions to furnish proof. If, however, the history of the surnames in question, and their distribution at various periods, is considered, and all the existing evidence is assembled, relationships can be traced in the cases of a good many individuals, and there seems little doubt that the spread of the surnames in question is due to single families proliferating. Examples of locative surnames with a similar history can be found in most parts of England and in the Scots-speaking parts of Scotland.

Some surnames from place-names outside Britain have similarly entered this country as the surnames of single families, at an early date, and have then spread to become relatively numerous in one particular region. For example, the surname Molyneux, one of French origin, was the name of a landed family in south west Lancashire from the twelfth century. The surname has survived in the same part of Lancashire, and though the senior branch of the family still exists there, branches from the family have proliferated at various periods to make the surname relatively numerous in south Lancashire at the present day. Though generally a scarce surname, it has spread to Cheshire and the west Midlands. To take another instance, the name Scarfield, originally de Scardeville, has existed continuously in Sussex from the thirteenth century to the present. It was the name of a landowning family in the south west of the county, and as late as the sixteenth century was still largely concentrated in that area. It has subsequently dispersed somewhat, and is now widely distributed throughout Sussex, though rare outside it. Another family with a surname of French origin, de Haut Rive, were landowners during the twelfth and thirteenth centuries in several counties, including Yorkshire, Sussex, and Hampshire. This surname persists today in a somewhat muddling profusion of forms, including Dawtry, Daughtery, Hawtrey, Hatry, Dealtry, and Dowtry, and in one form or another is present in most parts of England. It seems likely, however, that all the bearers of the name, in all its different variants, share a common descent from the de Haut Rive family, which had been in England from the twelfth century.

It can be seen that there are cases of surnames which have become fairly numerous, often in one particular county or region mainly, but which seem very likely to be names which each originated with a single family. Something has already been said in the chapter on locative names about the tendency of locative surnames in some northern counties to increase greatly in numbers within restricted areas. Some of these surnames are today very common in some parts of northern England, and though much less common elsewhere have spread to some other regions. Nevertheless, where many of the surnames in question are concerned, the evidence suggests that each of them was in origin the name of a single family. The mere fact that a locative name is fairly common in some region or county is not in itself a reason for rejecting the idea that all the bearers of the name share a common descent.

What is true in this respect of locative names is also true of surnames derived from nicknames. Many surnames from physical characteristics can be found widely dispersed already in the thirteenth century. This is true of England and the Scots-speaking parts of Scotland. Though there is less evidence for Wales where early periods are concerned, it seems that there, too, some by-names from physical characteristics early became common and widespread, and that these in some instances later developed into hereditary surnames. It is also true, as already noted in the discussion on nickname-type surnames, that some of the rarer surnames from nicknames occur from an early date independently in a number of different regions, indicating that each of them is likely to have originated with a number of separate families. In the case of surnames in this group, too, there are examples of surnames which seem likely to have been at first those of single families. The rare surname Straightbarrel, for instance (probably from a particular type of cask, and so a nickname for a stout party), existed from the fourteenth century onwards at and around Preston in Lancashire, almost certainly as the name of a single family. The surname ramified in Lancashire to some degree, but has never become as numerous as some other Lancashire surnames. The surname Maufe was that of a single family holding land in both Sussex and Northamptonshire during the twelfth century. The name was originally Malfei, 'bad faith', and is one of a group of surnames from the French language, all with unfavourable implications, which appear, rather surprisingly, as the names of landed families. The surname has ramified to some extent, but seems to have begun as that of one family, though it occurs from an early period in both Sussex and Northamptonshire, two counties some distance apart but linked in this connection through the ties of landownership. There are also cases where surnames derived from nicknames seem to have originated with a single family in one particular county or region, while arising independently in some other, often distant, areas. In such instances it is likely that there are cases where all the bearers of one particular surname in one county or region share a common ancestry, while there are people with the same surname in other parts who are not linked by blood relationships. For example, the surname Lamprey (a nickname-type surname from the eel-like aquatic creature so called), occurs in north Oxfordshire from the thirteenth century and seems to have been the surname of a single family. The surname proliferated in that county to some extent, and still persists in north Oxfordshire to the present day. Though the surname has always been uncommon, it has been found in Devon from the fourteenth century, and has persisted there to this day as an old-established though never very numerous Devon name. No connection can be traced between the Devon and the Oxfordshire families involved. Again, the surname Trenchmer, now often Trankmor or Tranchmere, seems as already mentioned to have been the name of a single family in Sussex, but it occurs separately in other maritime counties, such as Dorset, without having any link that can be traced with Sussex.

A similar position exists about surnames derived from topographical features. Some surnames from common features of the landscape, such as Hill, Ford, Field, Brooks, Bridges, Mills, Cross, and so forth, have long been very widespread and have obviously each originated with a number of distinct families. Some other surnames of the type, though much less common taking Britain as a whole, have been widespread in certain regions from an early period. For instance, the surname Clough (Cluff, Clewes, etc.) has for long been a common surname in north west England, and still continues to be so. (Clough occurs in Wales, but its presence there seems to be due partly to migration from England and partly to the Anglicising of a Welsh name with a similar sound.) The surname Moss, not from the plant which infests lawns but from a word for a bog, has long been common in the same region. Both these names can be seen from their early history to have originated with a number of separate families. The surname Combe, sometimes from one of the places called Combe (or Comb, Coombe), but frequently from the use of the word as a topographical term meaning a small valley, has for long been common over a large area in south and south-west England, and early examples of the name are much too dispersed to suppose that they are all connected to one family. Yeo, from a word for a stream, is still quite a common topographical name in south-west England, especially Devon and Somerset, while remaining scarce in other regions, and again early instances are too dispersed to suppose that they all relate to a single family. The surnames Tye and Tey, both from a term meaning 'enclosure' or 'common land', have been widespread over a long period in south-east England from an early date, and it cannot be thought that either name can relate to one family. All these, and a good many other topographical names which could be mentioned, occur from early periods in too many different places and are too widely distributed for it to be feasible to consider that any of them could have originated with one family. Even some quite rare surnames in the category, such as Nutbeam, Cockshoot, Crabtree, Sandes and Sandys, Wainhouse, Childerhouse, or Raikes (Rakes), can be found from an early stage of their existence in several different areas and must have each originated with a number of separate families. Very few topographical surnames can have begun as the names of single families. This is true even of many quite scarce names. In consequence, it is true that in the great majority of cases the bearers of any surname in this category will not all share a common ancestry.

There are very few topographical surnames which seem likely to have been at first those of single families. The surname Fairclough, now sometimes spelt Faircloth, seems likely to have started with a landowning family in south Lancashire, though from the sixteenth century it occurs in other regions. The surname Leyne, sometimes now spelt Layne, from a word for a tract of arable, and one used in Sussex for arable lying at the foot of the Downs, probably first arose as the name of a single family in that county in the thirteenth century. Flasher or Flusher was probably at first the name of a single Sussex family. The same is true of Furlonger or Vurlonger which seems, to begin with, to have been the name of a family of husbandmen in north Sussex. In Suffolk the name Greengrass, which survives today though still rare, probably originated in the thirteenth century as the name of a single family. Some other instances could be quoted of topographical surnames, none of them common at the present day, which seem likely to have been at first the surnames of single families, and the bearers of which today seem likely to have a common ancestor in the distant past, often in the thirteenth or fourteenth century. An intensive search through local records in various parts of the country would probably produce some further examples, so far undetected. In general, however, most topographical surnames appear to have originated separately with a number of distinct families.

As with occupational names, there are instances where topographical names seem to have originated with individual families in one county or region, while arising independently in other parts of the country. In Norfolk, for instance, the surname Orchard probably began with a single family in the thirteenth century, and until the sixteenth century it was a rare name in East Anglia, though found quite frequently in other parts of southern England. In much the same way the name Booth, quite a common topographical name in the north of England, seems to have been that of a single family in mediaeval Norfolk. Possibly it first arrived there as the name of someone who had migrated from one of the northern counties. The surname Stock, sometimes given as Stocks or Stockes, with an inorganic final 's', appears to have been the name of one family living in and around Rossendale, in Lancashire, and the references to the name over a long period in the southern part of that county all seem to concern this family, but the surname (from stock in the sense of 'tree stump'), has also developed independently in other parts of the country. In Sussex the surname Standbynorth, from residence in the northern part of a village, was at first the name of a single unfree family at Perching in that county. Again, further instances could be given of cases where topographical names evolved in one county or region as the names of single families, while the same surname arose, separately, in other parts of the country.

In considering whether there is any possibility that all the bearers of one surname might be descended from a common ancestor, it is necessary to examine the whole history of the surname in question in as much detail as the evidence which can be assembled permits. Although very few, if any, really common surnames can have originated with single families, the fact that a surname is at the present day quite common in one region or one limited area, and is also the name of quite large numbers of people, is not proof that the name did not at first arise with one single family. It is possible over some centuries for one family to ramify to a great extent, while sometimes remaining largely concentrated in one district. It must be remembered that there were times in the past when the population of this country was multiplying by natural increase at a much greater rate than is the case today. Some Yorkshire and Lancashire locative names have become very common locally in this way. Some families, in fact, proliferated on a great scale, with the result that their names became common in particular regions, while others, for reasons which are difficult to explain, existed over long periods of time without showing any significant increase, with the result that their surnames remained scarce. Some surnames which have always been quite rare, and still are so today, have in fact originated with several different families, dispersed through different regions, although it might be supposed from their rarity that only one family was involved.

It is unwise to attach too much importance to variant spellings of surnames in considering whether people who share a common surname also share a common ancestry. Examples have already been given at several points where surnames in one category or another have developed into a great variety of different forms. Anyone who has worked on eighteenth- or early nineteenth-century parish registers, as many genealogists and family historians have done at some stage in their researches, will know that even at those relatively late periods the spelling of many surnames is still not standardised and considerable changes of spelling, which can be observed to take place at those dates, are sometimes sufficiently drastic to obscure the origin of the surname involved. During the Victorian period minor changes in spelling were sometimes deliberately made to differentiate one branch of a family from another or to improve the appearance of the name to give it what was thought to be a more aristocratic ring. The fluctuations to be found at earlier periods are often much greater. It must be remembered that even as late as the nineteenth century there were still many people who were illiterate to the extent that they could not spell their own names. Entries in parish registers were made by parsons and parish clerks from what they knew, or could hear, of the pronunciation of any surnames, and not surprisingly this produced a variety of spellings, some of them eccentric.

It is, of course, equally important, and just as difficult, to avoid confusing two or more different names. The multiplicity of forms existing for a good many surnames can create problems here, and writers of family histories have sometimes failed to separate different surnames correctly. Some guidance on the subject can be obtained from the works listed in the 'Advice on further reading' at the end of the book, and especially from the standard dictionaries of surnames mentioned there. The variety of forms which can be found is so great that no reference book can list them all. It will be some help in avoiding confusion on this issue if all the genealogical evidence which can be found is collected and carefully sifted to produce as complete a set of pedigrees as possible. The geographical distribution of surnames can at times provide some clues. Although surnames can of course migrate from one region to another, there was over a long period a tendency for many surnames not to stray too far from their place of origin. When all these steps have been taken, however, researchers may still at times be left in doubt about what the connections of some forms are.

RAMIFICATION OF SURNAMES

It has already been observed that some surnames over a period of several centuries have ramified very considerably, either nationally, or, more often, in one region, while other surnames increase in numbers to a much smaller degree, or not at all, even in periods when the population of this country was growing by natural increase. For reasons already discussed, some occupational surnames have for long been both numerous and widely distributed and the same is true of some surnames derived from personal names in general use. These circumstances make it difficult to tell if any one family in either of these groups has ramified notably and increased in numbers, but it must be suspected that it has happened in some cases, and that the ramification has been concealed by the general commonness of the surnames in question. The surname Lord, for example, can be found from an early period in almost all parts of England (the form Laird occurs in Scotland); in south-east Lancashire the surname increased greatly in numbers between the sixteenth century and the nineteenth, and became distinctly more common, proportionately to the population, in that part than in most other regions of England. Since this is a district where many other surnames proliferated greatly during the same period–many of them local names from Lancashire place-names and some of them at least probably in origin the names of single families–it must be suspected that the increase in the surname Lord was due to the ramification of one, or perhaps several, families with the name, increasing very much in numbers over several hundred years. Tracing the pedigree of a family with an extremely common surname is very laborious, and at times may present insuperable problems. All the same, it must be supposed that among the more common surnames from occupations, or from personal names, there are instances where individual families have ramified very notably, even if the process is difficult to detect where very common surnames are concerned.

It is, however, easier to observe the course of development when dealing with rarer surnames such as many of those from place-names, from the less widespread trades or crafts, or from the less common nicknames. It is possible in a good many cases to trace the history of individual surnames and to see which have proliferated, and which ones have not. Some of the factors involved inevitably elude research. It is usually impossible, for instance, to discover the genetic factors that were at work in the Middle Ages. Generally, we cannot tell the total number of children that any couple had at that period, or whether the fecundity of some families was markedly greater than others, though it must be supposed that such differences existed, or whether the children of some families did better in surviving the high infant mortality than others. However, despite these limitations, it is possible to make some general observations about the process of ramification, based on the study of many individual surnames.

Most cases where any surname began with a single family, and then ramified, are instances where surnames had already begun to ramify by the early sixteenth century, though usually only to a small extent, and were already by that time the surnames of several different branches. Families whose names increased in this way are often families who had hereditary surnames by the middle of the fourteenth century, who survived the heavy mortality from epidemics of that period, and who began to multiply as population levels gradually recovered. Although it is not always possible to discover what the economic and social positions of the families in question were, in many instances they were either substantial free tenants, such as franklins or yeomen, or families of minor gentry, rather higher up the social scale. Such families would be in a better position than most in regard to nutrition, housing, and so forth. and their children would have had a rather better chance of survival than the average. Surnames do not usually seem to have ramified within the larger towns and cities, probably because of the higher mortality there during the early modern period.

While examples of surnames which have ramified considerably can be found in most parts of Britain, cases where the surnames of single families proliferated to a great extent tend to be found in areas where the population grew, mostly by natural increase without very much immigration from other regions, during the period from about 1500 to 1800. This is notably the case both in south east Lancashire and in parts of West Yorkshire. In most cases where the names of single families ramified largely, the surnames in question had already become much more numerous than the average before 1700. Seventeenth-century sources, such as the Protestation Returns of 1641–42 show that most surnames which occur in the nineteenth century as ones which had by then ramified extensively were already exceptionally numerous in the seventeenth century.

These remarks apply mainly to English surnames. Some Scots surnames became very numerous because they were adopted by all the followers of some important clan chief, or the tenants of some important landowning family. The processes involved in such developments were, of course, different from those just discussed. In Wales, some surnames have become very common because they are derived from personal names which were very widely used during the sixteenth and seventeenth centuries, when many Welsh families were acquiring hereditary surnames for the first time.

MIGRATION OF SURNAMES

No rigidly applicable rules can be laid down about the migration of surnames, but some general features of surname movements can be described.

Many people have in their minds a picture of the average villagers of the Middle Ages, and even later during the seventeenth and eighteenth centuries, as people who spent all their lives in the villages where they were born, and usually married within their own villages, with the result that many communities were closely inbred. Anyone who has done much work on parish registers will be aware that this is not an accurate view of the situation from the time when registers first start to survive in any numbers – from about the middle of the sixteenth century onwards – and in fact this is generally true for earlier periods as well. It is true generally in Britain that closely inbred communities are unusual. Indeed, such communities are rare anywhere in the world except in places where there are established customs favouring marriages between close relatives, such as marriage between first cousins. Even where circumstances might seem to favour inbreeding,as for instance where communities were isolated to a greater or less degree because of their geographical position, close inbreeding is much less commonly found than might be supposed. In mediaeval Europe, the scarcity of inbreeding owed a good deal to the rules of the Church which forbade marriages between couples who were at all closely related by blood or marriage. Besides this, however, the rural population in Britain during the Middle Ages, and later, was never closely restricted in movements. Even serfs, though in law unable to leave their native manors to reside elsewhere, were never restricted to a single village in the sense that they were banned from passing beyond its confines. Serfs in fact were often obliged to perform services for their lords, as carters and so on, which took them some distance from their own manors. It is also true that, at least from the thirteenth century onwards, serfs frequently removed from their native manors and went to live elsewhere, either legally with their lords' permission or illegally without it. From the period when hereditary surnames first start to appear, in fact, the population was never wholly static, even in the more remote rural areas. Indeed, one feature of the history of surnames during the Middle Ages is the way in which families moved into and out of villages over a period of two or three generations.

It is in practice unusual for families to remain in a parish for more than a few generations. Exceptions to this can be found, in rural areas mostly in the case of families either of gentry or of substantial freeholders such as yeomen, or earlier in some cases of serfs. Families such as these tend to be anchored to one place by their property holdings. In general, however, it is common for a family to move into a parish, remain there for several generations, and then move out of it. From the sixteenth century onwards this can readily be seen from a study of parish registers. The same situation can often be found earlier in places for which there are adequate sources of information, such as manorial records. This process is apt to leave the impression that surnames of any one place are in a constant state of flux. Most movements, however, were over a short distance only. If the distribution of any surname, except for those that are very common and widespread, is looked at, it will generally be found that it exists in a number of clusters, each in an area with a diameter of perhaps about ten or twelve miles, with only occasional stray examples elsewhere. This is true for any period up to the Industrial Revolution, and in the case of many names it is still true during the nineteenth century. This is most easily seen with surnames from place-names, which tend to be grouped around their places of origin, even as late as the nineteenth century, though as already discussed there are certain exceptions to this. Many instances, however, can be found among the less common surnames in other categories. The short range movements which produced this situation can be discovered as far back as the thirteenth century.

Any extensive study of the history of surnames in this country leaves a strong impression of how stable surnames have been, in the sense that surnames tend to remain in one area, though not in any single place, over long periods. Nothing about the subject is more striking than the way in which the same body of surnames tends to persist over centuries in a unit such as a county. The history of many individual surnames confirms this. Of course there are names which do not conform to this pattern, which in some cases became widespread from some early period, or which migrated away from their points of origin to become established, and sometimes prolific, in some more or less remote district, but on the whole such developments are exceptional.

Movements over longer distances do exist, however, though much less commonly than the purely local migrations shown by many surnames. Leaving aside immigration into Britain from outside, various factors can be seen to be at work. One of these is migration from rural districts into towns and cities. London was already attracting migrants from all parts of England, even distant ones like the north or the south west, as far back as about 1200, besides drawing in new migrants from abroad. Even at that early date, this was leading to the presence in the capital of surnames and by-names from many parts of England, including many locative names, often from places in the nearby counties, but including a good number from the more remote parts of England. Over a long period, it was the practice of people who moved to London, were successful there, and attained affluence to a greater or less degree, to invest in property purchases. These were often in the regions from which the individuals in question had originally come, and families which moved into London often kept up a connection with their places of origin for several generations. There were also many examples of the wealthier inhabitants of London buying lands in the areas closely adjoining the capital, in Essex, west Kent, north Surrey, and what used to be Middlesex. This led to the appearance in and around London of many surnames which had originated in distant parts of the country. As a result, London and the neighbouring areas have for long contained a great variety of surnames, many of them with origins in other parts. Even where a surname is very largely concentrated in some district in the provinces, a few instances can often be found in or near London. This is a common feature of the distribution of surnames over a long period, and is due to London's powers to attract migrants from remote parts. Many surnames from outside Britain also occur in London, and in some cases these too have spread into the adjoining county areas.

What was true of London was also true, on a rather smaller scale, of the main provincial cities, such as York, Norwich, or Bristol, which acted as regional capitals and attracted migrants from large catchment areas. These major centres tended to draw the majority of their migrants from the regions in which each of them stood, but there were smaller numbers from more distant regions, which led to the establishment in the large provincial cities in England of surnames from remote parts of the country, besides names from Wales, Scotland, Ireland, and various Continental countries. As with London, surnames which migrated into the large provincial cities sometimes migrated eventually into the surrounding countryside. At Norwich during the Middle Ages, for example, a good many surnames from Yorkshire place-names occur, many of them from places on or near the Humber, probably as a result of the coastal trade between Norwich and the Humber ports. Some of the families concerned, with surnames from Yorkshire place-names, moved out of Norwich after a generation or two, and became established in the country districts nearby, bringing Yorkshire surnames into some Norfolk villages.

The smaller provincial towns tended to draw in most of their migrants from a restricted catchment area, often one with a radius of ten or fifteen miles around each town, with only occasional instances of people who had moved over longer distances. In the borough records of many provincial towns, for example, the lists of borough freemen are full of men with surnames or by-names from the place-names of villages within ten miles or so of the borough in which they lived. In some boroughs lists of apprentices survive for the Middle Ages and later, giving information about apprentices' parentage, and where apprentices came from outside the borough it will generally be found that they came from places only a very moderate distance from the town in which they were bound apprentices. The locative surnames found in the smaller towns during the Middle Ages, or later during the sixteenth and seventeenth centuries, generally have a very local character, with only a few clearly from the names of remote places. There were of course exceptions. Surnames from places on major routes of inland trade and travel became unusually widespread, a circumstance discussed in the chapter on locative surnames, and apart from such cases occasional instances can be found in most towns of surnames which originated in distant counties, including of course some names of aliens.

Migration over long distances into rural areas was never entirely lacking for any period from the first appearance of hereditary surnames onwards. At times the causes behind such movements can be seen. Some of the more long distance movements which took place were linked to the way in which landowners' estates were distributed. For instance the Percy family, who were large landowners in the north of England, with estates in Northumberland and Yorkshire, were also the owners of lands in Sussex, around Petworth, and some movement of estate officials took place between the northern properties and the Petworth areas. Families sometimes moved from one region to another because they acquired property in a new area, by inheritance or otherwise. For example, the Hastings family, whose surname derived from Hastings in Sussex, inherited lands in Leicestershire in the fourteenth century, and long remained prominent in that county. Links of landownership in such ways explain some movements of surnames which have taken place. It is, however, the fact that in many cases where families migrated over longer distances, from one rural part to another, it is difficult to discover the factors that prompted the movement. Even dealing with relatively late periods, such as the nineteenth century, it is often not possible to tell why families migrated over considerable distances.

CHAPTER EIGHT

Surnames and local history

Most people's interest in surnames arises from work on genealogy and family history, or from research in a broader way into the history of one particular surname. Surnames can, however, provide some evidence for the history of communities in several aspects, and it is worthwhile for anyone interested in the history of their own town, county, or village to consider what information can be gained from looking into local surnames, both those present today and those present at various periods in the past.

If a large-scale ordnance survey map for almost any part of Britain is examined, it will reveal traces of human activity at many different past periods. It will show, possibly, prehistoric earthworks and burial mounds, Roman roads and the remains of Roman towns or villas, lynchets which are surviving traces of early cultivation, nucleated villages dating from early mediaeval times, Norman and Angevin castles, roads and field boundaries laid out by eighteenth-century enclosure commissioners, nineteenth-century industrial developments, and finally twentieth-century developments such as suburban housing estates and motorways. Besides all this, the place-names of any area are themselves a great store of historical information, and other features marked on the map, such as parish boundaries and field boundaries, may contain valuable clues about an area's history. A list of surnames currently in use in any community, such as a telephone directory or an electoral register, will similarly show traces of the community's past history in various forms. It may well contain surnames from personal names: some personal names of Old English origin, some names brought in during the Viking invasions from Scandinavia, or some introduced from France after 1066. It will probably contain locative surnames, some which originated in the area and have remained there ever since without moving very far, some brought in from elsewhere by population movements during the Middle Ages, or some brought in by the major migrations of the Industrial Revolution. There will be occupational surnames: some perhaps originating locally and reflecting local dialect usage, or others brought in from different regions of the country at various dates. There may be topographical surnames, some probably from regional dialect words for features of the landscape, and there may be surnames from nicknames, some long-established in the community and it may be interesting to compare these with nicknames in current use. There are likely also to be surnames from outside Britain, possibly Dutch or Flemish names introduced by migrant craftsmen in the sixteenth century: French surnames which were once those of seventeenth-century Huguenots; German surnames brought in by nineteenth-century immigration, Irish surnames which were originally those of people who came to Britain after the Famine; surnames from eastern Europe, which were at first those of displaced persons who came to Britain during or just after the Second World War; and perhaps now surnames from the Indian subcontinent. All these groups of surnames show something of a community's history, and are traces of occurrences at different periods in the past. Such evidence is worth investigating by anyone interested in the local history of any community or area.

It ought to be stressed that evidence from surnames should never be used in isolation from information of other kind. In order to get the fullest and most accurate picture possible of a community's life at any period in the past, it is obviously essential to use all the different types of evidence which are available, and to combine them to arrive at the most complete account possible. It is always a mistake to rely solely on one type of evidence to the exclusion of other material. A parish or township is in many ways too small a unit for the study of surnames as historical evidence, since families move in and out of parishes fairly frequently, and this has been true of most places in Britain for centuries. It would be better for such purposes to take a larger unit, such as a group of six or eight adjoining parishes, a modern district council area, or some unit from the past such as a hundred or wapentake. A study of such an area will often show that there was a body of surnames which persisted locally over some centuries, and after a certain amount of research a local historian will become familiar with the established names in the area under study. It may well be seen that some surnames have been present in the area from their first formation, perhaps about 1300 or earlier, and are still there today, while other surnames can be identified as having arisen locally at later periods, or as having been brought in by migration at various dates.

SURNAMES AS EVIDENCE FOR MIGRATION

The extent and nature of movement into and out of any area is obviously one of the basic factors determining its social and economic life. A community which is a constant state of flux, with families moving in, and possibly moving out again after an interval, is clearly a different proposition from one in which the population is largely stable, with only a very limited amount of immigration or emigration. Plainly, too, large population movements are brought about by correspondingly powerful factors. It is, however, very difficult to obtain adequate evidence about what is happening in regard to population movements for any period before the detailed returns from the nineteenth-century census became available. Parish registers, where they are in existence, can be used to produce much evidence about population, but they are of limited value when studying migration. In particular, if a person listed in the parish registers has been baptised outside the parish, his or her place of baptism (often the same as the place of birth), will not appear in the registers . Poor law records, especially those concerning the operation of the laws of settlement, may provide some evidence about people's movements, but such documents are lacking in many parishes, and where some of them do survive they often cover short periods only. Some other sources, such as the dealings of the justices of the peace with vagrants, may provide some information about movements, but what is available from such sources varies greatly from one parish to another, and for many places little or no information can be obtained. Surname evidence, on the other hand, is available in some form or other for the great majority of places. Parish registers, if scrutinised for a considerable period, will yield the names of a good many families in any parish. For earlier periods, when it is often very difficult to tell what is happening, other sources such as the mediaeval lay subsidies will provide lists of taxpayers which will list enough names to produce a fair amount of information, though of course no mediaeval source is likely to list the whole population. In mediaeval towns, such sources as lists of freemen or of apprentices will be a good source of information about the names of townspeople. Many other sources, such as seventeenth-century poll taxes and hearth taxes, gravestones in the older local churchyards, local censuses which exist for a few places, lists of people making Easter offerings, poll books, and so forth, will all give some evidence about the surnames of the local population, with varying degrees of completeness.

Although the availability of some types of evidence varies greatly from place to place, and although in some parishes local records have survived to a much greater extent than in others, it is generally possible to obtain a reasonably full view of the surnames present in any parish, or, preferably, over a wider area, if all the existing sources are utilised, and this in turn can provide some evidence about migration into a parish or into some wider area. It is not very useful tracing migration out of any locality. As anyone who has tried to trace a pedigree back over any length of time will know, discovering what happened when a family made a move over any great distance can be a laborious business. If a surname disappears from a parish, or larger area, it may be difficult to tell whether this is because the family died out in the male line (perhaps leaving daughters who married and did not continue the family surname) or whether the family in question had moved away into some other district. The use of surname evidence to trace movements out of any place is therefore liable to be both unproductive and time consuming, unless there is some obvious destination for migrants, such as a growing industrial town nearby.

On the other hand, surname evidence is often valuable where migration into any area is concerned. The locative surnames to be found at different periods are one obvious source of information for any date from the time when surnames and by-names first start to be found in any numbers. The complications involved in establishing which place-names have given rise to locative surnames have already been discussed (see Chapter 2), and the origins of some locative surnames in any area under investigation may well prove impossible to discover with certainty. Nevertheless, in most parts of England and in the Scots-speaking parts of Scotland, the locative surnames to be found will usually give some indication of what migration there has been into any locality – in some cases, perhaps, purely local movement over short distances; in other, less frequent, cases, movement over a longer range. An investigation of locative surnames, too, will often reveal the presence of surnames, derived from local place-names, within a parish or larger area which have remained in existence in the locality for centuries, and which perhaps persist there to the present day. In Wales and the Gaelic-speaking parts of Scotland locative surnames are very much fewer, proportionately, and consequently much less useful in establishing the facts about migration, though in some parts of Wales locative surnames from place-names in England can be found as a result of migration from England at various periods.

Apart from the use of locative names, some information can often be gained from surnames in other categories. Some topographical names were very widespread at an early date and present in many parts of Britain, but others had a markedly regional distribution which often survived, not greatly modified, until the Industrial Revolution or even later. An investigation into the surnames of any area – preferably including some examination of the names present locally before about 1500 to get to know the original character of the surnames in the area – will generally make a researcher familiar with the topographical surnames in use and enable those which did not originally occur there to be detected. Any topographical name which is not found in general use locally must be suspected of having been brought into the area by migration. Much the same is true of occupational surnames, some of which were in origin restricted to one or two regions. Some useful information about the regions where topographical and occupational names originated can be obtained from P.H. Reaney's *Dictionary of British Surnames*; this usually gives several early examples for each surname listed, and states the counties in which the early instances are found. Some further evidence can be obtained from H. B. Guppy's *Homes of Family Names*. (Both these works are listed and discussed in the 'Advice on further reading', below.)

Besides all this, it will often be possible to recognise surnames from Welsh or Gaelic when they occur in regions where English was the usual language. Rather less easily, Cornish names may be identifiable when they occur outside that county. French surnames will often be recognisable too, but their presence will not necessarily be due to migration from France at some relatively recent date. A large body of French surnames was introduced to this country in the seventeenth century by the Huguenots, and there were some religious refugees in the sixteenth. Many French surnames, however, have been present in Britain from a much earlier period. In particular, many surnames from France, including many derived from French place-names, were introduced into England between 1066 and about 1150, and some of these soon spread to Scotland. Besides this, as already explained, some surnames from the French language may have come into existence in England.

If the surnames present in any area are examined with these considerations in mind, a good deal of information about migration, or the lack of it, may be obtained, some of it for early periods when other evidence on the subject is liable to be lacking. This in turn should reveal something about how much, or how little, any community was isolated, what its range of outside contacts was, and how mobile generally the population was.

SURNAMES AND THE SOCIAL STRUCTURE OF COMMUNITIES

Surnames can provide some evidence about the social structure of towns and villages to supplement the evidence which can be obtained from other sources. Surname evidence is most useful for the period before about 1500, when surnames had not been hereditary for long periods and evidence of other kinds is often defective for many communities. People who wish to study the history of any community over the whole period of its existence will find it useful in many cases to collect the surnames in use locally from such sources as taxation returns, title deeds, and manorial records, and to see what information this evidence provides about the society being studied. Surnames can indicate how far a community was stable, and how much movement there was in or, to a less extent, out, but migration is only one part of the matter. In many villages there was during the Middle Ages and the early modern period a core of families present over several centuries, resident locally, and in many cases not changing greatly in social or economic position. In most villages these were at first a mixture of free tenants and serfs. In many mediaeval villages there were some families of free tenants, with holdings locally, which survived over long periods, and often played an important part in village life. In many villages, too, there were during the Middle Ages families of unfree tenants which, being bound to the soil and, consequently, having more restrictions on their movements than freemen, often persisted in the same place for centuries. In the fifteenth century, when serfdom was tending to decline, many families of unfree tenants became leaseholders or copyholders, but continued to live in the same villages, so that families which first appear as serfs, perhaps back as far as the thirteenth century, may appear later as copyholders or small tenant farmers in the sixteenth, seventeenth, and eighteenth centuries, perhaps persisting in the same area over that whole period. There were of course villages which were depopulated, some as the result of the fourteenth century pestilences, and some as the result of enclosure and the conversion of arable to pasture. In many villages, however, there were some families, of no great wealth or rank, which survived over long periods and played a significant part in the life of the village community. In many places this situation persisted into the nineteenth century. A detailed examination of the surnames present in a village over a long period, collected from all the available sources of information, will often show which families survived in a village, or in some larger area, while other families came and went in a much more transient fashion. Evidence like this from surnames, backed up by whatever facts are available from genealogy and the history of individual families, will reveal a good deal about the society of many villages.

In towns and cities, there was often a similar body of families, often middling merchants and craftsmen, which survived for generations, often without rising or falling very much, either socially or economically, while above them the few really wealthy families tended to move out and to establish themselves as gentry in the countryside. Long persisting families like this, often filling the various civic offices over generations, played an important part in the society of many provincial towns. In reconstructing what urban society was like, the evidence which can be obtained from the study of the local surnames, and of the history of the more permanent local families as far as it can be discovered, are important sources of information. Lower down the social scale, there were classes of journeymen and labourers, about which it may not, in some places, be possible to discover very much.

An investigation into these aspects of any community, urban or rural, will do something to reveal its character, and the degree of stability which existed within it, and surname evidence can be one useful source of information on such matters. Surname evidence may be useful in another way, in showing the extent and nature of class divisions, and providing some guidance about the extent of social mobility. When surnames first originated, there were marked differences between the different social classes in the types of surnames acquired. These differences were never absolutely clear cut; it is never possible to say, for any period in the past, that a person with one particular type of surname or by-name must have been a member of one particular social class. Nevertheless, when surnames were originating first of all, in the twelfth, thirteenth, and fourteenth centuries, they do provide some indication of social position.

If the surnames or by-names in use in English communities in the period from approximately 1100 to 1400 are analysed in class terms, it can be seen that there were sharp differences between one class and another in the nature of the names in use. A high proportion of the landholders of any real wealth or standing had locative names. It was never the case that all landed families had surnames in that category. Some few had nickname-type surnames; the Norman landholding class had a tendency to employ nicknames of a grotesque or droll character, which perhaps reflected the contemporary sense of humour, and some of these nicknames in the course of time developed into hereditary surnames, though many of the nicknames once used have not survived. A few families in the same class had surnames or by-names from personal names. Even so, almost any list of landholders of knightly or baronial rank for any date between about 1100 and 1400 will show a marked preponderance of locative names. The factors producing this situation have already been discussed (see Chapter 1). It is also true that locative names were never entirely confined to the landholding class, a matter which has also been discussed above (see Chapter 2). They are, however, much less common, proportionately, in other sections of the community. In the north of England the occupiers of isolated farms, who were often landholders on a more modest scale, frequently had locative names. People who migrated into towns from villages nearby sometimes acquired by-names from the place-names of the settlements which they had left to move into towns. This became less common after about 1350, by which time an increasing number of families already had settled surnames.

At a lower level of society, there is little difference between the surnames or by-names of small free tenants, and those of serfs. The distinction between free tenants and serfs was already clear and important in legal theory by the thirteenth century, and in practice the differences in status between the two classes had major consequences. However, both classes had surnames or by-names of much the same types. In many villages, too, some surnames appear as the names of both free and unfree people, in a way which suggests that some families had both free and unfree members. This evidence indicates that the social gap between the two classes was not as meaningful as might be expected from the legal position. Some serfs had names from skilled trades, such as Smith, Wheelwright, and so on, or even names from trading activities, such as Chapman, which shows that their occupation was not confined simply to agricultural work. In the nucleated villages of southern England and the Midlands, many small tenants, free and unfree, appear with topographical names which often seem to relate to the position of their houses within their villages, for example Green, Atchurch, or Townsend. As has already been explained, many families in both classes acquired surnames formed from a personal name with '-son' added, in the period from about 1270 onwards, while in other parts of the country, people in the same social groups acquired surnames formed from a personal name with a possessive '-s' added. From about 1300 onwards, large numbers of small tenants, free and serf, can be found with such names, which for many years hardly ever occur as the names of landowners of any real wealth. In towns in the north of England, many people can be found with names in '-son' from about 1300 onwards. Often these seem to be people who had migrated into towns from the surrounding countryside, but such surnames were formed within towns too, a process which continued in some places until after 1500. From about 1200 onwards, the population of towns included many people with occupational names from specialised crafts, as might be expected from communities where many varied trades were being practised.

Anyone interested in the history of a town or village might find it interesting to look at the names in use there with this sketch of the class differences involved in mind, especially for the period before about 1500. Once surnames became hereditary, social mobility gradually broke up the original class distribution of surnames. In many regions all such differences between classes had already been lost by about 1550, which provides some evidence about how much mobility there was between classes in the period after surnames became hereditary. In some of the more isolated areas of the north of England, class differences in surnames persisted until a rather later period. There are unexplained features about surnames from this point of view. It is quite common to find at fairly late dates, say after about 1600, families which have the same surname as that of prominent landowning families in the same part of the country, but which are not themselves families of any great wealth or standing. In many cases this results from families descended from younger sons who have come down in the social scale, and it is often a point of interest in any area to trace how many families which were large landlords in the Middle Ages have left surnames which are still present in the same area today. However, this is not the whole story about the survival of surnames belonging to leading families. During the Middle Ages there are a good many instances of people with very low status, such as serfs or labourers, with names which are those of well-known landed families in the same area. How this situation arises is not clear. Such people may have been illegitimate children. Possibly they may have adopted the names of well-known families because of the prestige such names carried. Any local investigations which might throw light on such issues would be worth pursuing.

VALUE OF TOPOGRAPHICAL AND OCCUPATIONAL SURNAMES

Topographical and occupational surnames are both of some use as evidence for local economic conditions, besides providing evidence about the vocabulary in use about such matters locally. The topographical names in use at relatively early periods, say up to 1500, come from a time when names were either not hereditary or had not been hereditary very long, and when for most parts there had not been a great deal of movement inwards or outwards. They therefore tend to have a mainly local character, with only a few names, exceptionally, which had been introduced into the area from other parts. Topographical names do give some indication of the nature of the landscape. There are obvious implications, for instance, in the presence of many surnames from words for marshy or boggy ground, or for fen country, and similarly in the existence of many surnames from words for woodlands, coppices, clearings, groves, etc. The presence of surnames from the various words for enclosures, Close, Hay, Toft, Tey, Pightle, etc., is obviously evidence for local field arrangements and agricultural methods. Something about the early shape and layout of a village may be discovered from noting those topographical names which are connected with the positions of houses within a settlement, especially if this evidence can be combined with that from other sources, such as manorial surveys or title deeds.

Some further evidence about the local economy can be gained from occupational surnames or by-names, particularly again for the period when names were relatively new and had generally not migrated far from their points of origin. It would be a mistake to suppose that the number of people in any occupation can be deduced from the number with names derived from the occupation in question. There is often little connection between the importance of an occupation locally and the number of surnames derived from it.

Some skilled crafts were distinctive because they were the work of only a few persons in any place and, consequently, were an obvious source of surnames. Smith is a case in point. It is, therefore, unwise to use occupational names as a measure of the size of any industry or craft at any place, and it is further unwise to argue from the absence of evidence and to conclude that, because there are no occupational names from some particular trade to be found in any locality, the trade in question was not pursued there. Apart from any other considerations, it must be remembered that it is not usually possible to get a full list of the names existing in any place for any period before the nineteenth-century census returns became available. The truth of this can be seen by noticing that very few surnames are from any of the operations of arable farming, despite the importance of that activity during the Middle Ages and later, and despite the large numbers of people engaged in it. So much of the population was engaged in arable cultivation that it was not distinctive enough to give rise to surnames in the usual course. However, occupational names do at least give some indication of what crafts or trades were being followed in any one village or area. In rural areas the large numbers of names which are derived from the specialised tasks of herding the different species of domestic animals provide some evidence about local agriculture, while the presence of surnames or by-names from crafts give some indication of the services available in each village. In many cases these may be simply names which would be expected in such circumstances: Smith, Miller, Wheeler, Cartwright, and so forth. In other cases, however, questions about the nature of a village's economy may be raised by the presence of surnames from more specialised occupations which would not be expected in a rural setting, such as Spicer or Goldsmith, to quote names which can in fact be found in such situations, or surnames which concern some trade not at first sight likely to be pursued locally, such as the name Salter occurring at an inland place where there were no salt deposits in the vicinity. In towns and cities there is often an array of occupational names from specialised handicrafts and trades which provide a picture, even if incomplete, of local commerce and manufacture. Occupational surnames and by-names, therefore, do provide some evidence about the economic life of village communities. They are likely to be particularly useful in the many villages and market towns for which little or nothing now survives of manorial records or town records. Some smaller boroughs, too, have little or nothing extant of early borough archives, and surname evidence may be useful there.

All such evidence of course becomes gradually less valuable as surnames become hereditary, occupational surnames no longer correspond with crafts actually being followed by the bearers of such names, and the original distribution of surnames is gradually altered by population movement. It is also true that, speaking generally, there tends to be more evidence from other sources for later periods.

SURNAMES AND LOCAL DIALECTS

Surnames are a valuable source of information about the local dialects spoken in Middle English – that is, the language spoken in England between about 1150 and 1500. Surnames provide much evidence about both the phonetics and the vocabulary of dialects, evidence which is all the more valuable because of the high proportion of mediaeval documents which are written in Latin, and are consequently of little use in the study of what was being spoken, apart from the evidence of the proper names which are mentioned. A good many English topographical and occupational terms appear as surnames or by-names before there is any evidence for their use in any other connection.

Much investigation has been carried out into Middle English dialects, those of later periods, and the dialects existing in this country at the present day, by linguistic experts. The results of such research have on the whole attracted little attention from amateur local historians or from people interested in a more general way about aspects of the past in their own part of the country. It is a matter which does not impinge very much upon people interested in local history or in family history. In fact as has been explained already, a good many topographical and occupational surnames are from words which had a distribution confined to certain regions, and the phonetics of local dialects have left their mark on the spelling and pronunciation of many surnames as they exist at the present day. This has to be taken into account in considering the history of surnames which have been modified under the influence of local dialect pronunciation. Beyond this, however, people interested in local history ought to take account of the boundaries between dialects in their own areas, for dialects are one source of information about the course of history in the period between the end of Roman rule and 1066 – a very obscure period in the history of many localities in Britain and, therefore, one for which it is important to draw on all such sources of information as there are. Dialects do not develop through mere chance, and the factors which produced them were historically significant. There were differences during the period of the Anglo-Saxon settlement between Saxon and Anglian dialects. At a later period the dialects in some parts of the country were affected by Scandinavian settlement, which has left its mark on the English language as a whole. In some areas words of Celtic origin were borrowed into the local dialects. In some areas the boundaries between the Middle English dialects have been influenced by the boundaries between the minor kingdoms which existed during the Anglo-Saxon period. Anyone interested in the early history of any locality or area should take account of what can be learnt from local dialect boundaries.

Enough has perhaps been said to show that surnames are not only of interest to people wishing to trace their forbears, or to discover the meanings of their own surnames, even though researchers into family history and genealogy may be the groups most likely to find the study of surnames useful to their investigations. A collection of surnames in use locally, beginning at the time when surnames or by-names first start to appear in numbers, say round about 1100 or 1150 and continuing up to the nineteenth century when the census returns produce a much greater volume of evidence about the population, will reveal much about the history of most localities in Britain, and such material will generally be worthwhile collecting for anyone interested in the local history of any place or region.

CHAPTER NINE
Advice on further reading

Much has been written on surnames over a long period. In the seventeenth century William Camden made some shrewd and scholarly observations about both personal names and surnames, which still make interesting reading, and during the nineteenth and early twentieth centuries much pioneering work was done by writers such as C. W. Bardsley, M. A. Lower, and L'Estrange Ewen. These earlier works are now best left on one side by amateur historians or genealogists. Many of them at the time when they were written advanced the study of surnames and their history, but they have now been superseded by later books, and inevitably some of the views advanced in them have been shown to be inaccurate or incomplete by later research.

DICTIONARIES OF SURNAMES

The works to which genealogists and family historians are most likely to turn, first and foremost, for information on family names, are the dictionaries of surnames. It should be said at once that there is no reference work to which it is possible to resort in the confidence of being able to obtain an accurate account of the origin and development of every surname to be found in Britain. It would in fact be an almost impossible task to produce a dictionary which listed every surname now to be found in Britain, including names brought in from abroad at various dates, let alone a dictionary which listed all the surnames which have appeared in Britain at one time or another. There are, however, several dictionaries of surnames which are very useful. P. H. Reaney, *Dictionary of British Surnames* (Routledge and Kegan Paul, second edition, 1976), is a large dictionary which covers the whole of Britain, though the treatment of English surnames is usually fuller than those of Wales or Scotland. Usually the earliest known forms of each surname are cited, together with a note of the sources in which early forms can be found. The etymology of each name is given. This dictionary is a very useful work of reference, and generally speaking gives more complete details about surnames than can be found elsewhere, but it does have certain limitations. One of these is that a large number of surnames derived from place-names are not listed. Many of these were omitted to save space, and on the somewhat optimistic assumption that it would be easy to identify the places from which surnames were derived by using a gazeteer of place-names. In fact, as already explained, such identifications can be complicated. The dictionary also leaves out some other surnames, and in any case only deals with surnames which have survived to the present day, and does not deal with names which once existed but are now extinct. Early, usually mediaeval, forms are given, and these are then linked to forms which exist today. Although the connections made in this way are usually reliable, there are a few instances where it seems doubtful if the mediaeval forms given are in fact the early forms of the present-day names with which the dictionary connects them. Many surnames exist at the present day in several different variants, each with its own spelling, and the dictionary does not always list all the variant forms, so that users may at points have to search some distance through the alphabetical sequence of names to find the surnames which they are investigating. Despite all this, and despite the fact that it is now in need of further revision, Reaney's dictionary remains a valuable source of reference.

Basil Cottle, *Penguin Dictionary of Surnames* (Penguin Books, second edition, 1978), has the advantage of being available in paperback. It gives the origin and meaning of each surname listed, and puts each surname into one or other category. It tends to deal with a rather larger number of surnames than does Reaney's dictionary. It has an introduction, which discusses the various types of surnames. For anyone who simply wants to discover the meaning and origin of any surname, this is likely to be the most useful work now existing. It is a book easily used and understood by amateur genealogists without any specialised linguistic knowledge.

T. J. Morgan and Prys Morgan, *Welsh Surnames* (University of Wales Press, 1985), is a very useful dictionary of Welsh surnames, which were not dealt with very fully in Reaney's dictionary. It has an introduction which deals with the development of Welsh surnames and also with the phonetics of Welsh names – a subject which English speakers are liable to find difficult. It gives forms assumed by Welsh surnames when they migrated into England, and there is a good deal of information about Welsh names in the English counties bordering on Wales. This is much the most useful work on Welsh surnames for genealogists or family historians.

The standard work on Scottish surnames is G.F. Black, *Surnames of Scotland* (New York Public Library, 1946, reprinted 1979). The treatment of Scottish surnames in Reaney's dictionary, mentioned above, is largely based on Black's work. Black usually gives the earliest known Scottish instances for each name, and he includes remarks about the families or clans connected with many surnames. His dictionary does not explain fully in every case the meaning or derivation of each name. There are occasions when he cites conflicting opinions without resolving the differences between them, and occasionally he leaves issues about origins in doubt.

The dictionaries mentioned above are the principal ones at present available, and probably the only ones sufficiently reliable and scholarly to be worth consulting. There are, however, a number of surnames which do not appear in any of them. Researchers who find themselves confronted by a surname which cannot be found in any of the dictionaries may pursue the matter further by several methods. If the surname seems to be from a place-name, an attempt can be made to identify the place in question using the methods described in the chapter on locative names (see Chapter 2). Surnames from occupational or topographical terms can sometimes be elucidated by looking up the appropriate word in the *New English Dictionary*, which is available in most good reference libraries. After all these resources have been utilised, however, there may still remain some surnames which defy explanation and which do not appear in any reference work. Some of these may be names introduced from abroad at one period or another, but some surnames which appear to have originated in this country are still unexplained, and names are sometimes found which have been so mangled by inaccurate copying or by eccentric spelling as to be unrecognisable. Anyone who works through a list of surnames, and finds one or two which cannot be explained, should therefore realise that this is a common experience, and should not be too despondent if one or two names are found for which no origin can be traced.

This book is not concerned with surnames in Ireland, but many Irish surnames are now present in Britain; many Irish surnames have been established here since the large-scale migrations of the nineteenth century, and there are a smaller number of Irish surnames which have been present in Britain for a longer time. The standard dictionary on Irish surnames is E. MacLysaght, *Surnames of Ireland* (Irish Academic Press, 1969). This work includes surnames of English, Welsh, and Scots origin which have long been settled in Ireland. It also in the case of many names, indicates the part of Ireland in which surnames are most likely to be found. Some further information about the distribution of Irish surnames as they were at the end of the nineteenth century can be obtained from R.E. Matheson, *Special Report on Surnames in Ireland* (1909). The information about the frequency and distribution of surnames in Ireland is based on the Registrar-General's statistics. The book also has some interesting observations about usages concerning nick-names, as prevailing in Ireland about 1890. Some remarks made about the linguistic origins of names, variations in spelling, and interchanges between Gaelic and English surnames, are not always sound.

GENERAL WORKS ON SURNAMES

A good many works were written in the nineteenth century about the general history of surnames in Britain. Some of this was conjectural, and is not now of very much value. Two more recent books are worth consulting on the subject. P.H. Reaney, *Origin of English Surnames* (Routledge and Kegan Paul, 1967) was, when originally published, a book which treated the subject in a much more scholarly way than anything else then available. It is now many years since this book was published, however, and it does not take account of any research carried out since it was first written. It is also true that even when the book was first published it was stronger on the etymology of surnames and the linguistic aspects of the subject than on the historical side. What is said about historical issues such as population migration, as evidenced by locative surnames, is disputable in parts. Little account was taken of genealogical evidence, and topics such as the spread of surnames through the ramification of individual families, the geographical distribution of names, or the differences in the surnames of different social classes, were not very much discussed. Despite this, the book is still a useful introduction to the linguistic side of surname history, and its publication did mark a considerable advance in studies on the subject.

The second book on the history of surnames generally which it might be useful to consult is C.M. Matthews, *English Surnames* (Weidenfeld and Nicolson, 1966). This gives a brief account of the development of hereditary surnames in England, and it discusses English surnames category by category. The origins of many individual surnames are discussed. The book does give a good general view of the evolution of English surnames (not Scots or Welsh ones), but it does not give much guidance to readers on how to set about finding out the origins of individual surnames, which was not the book's intention. The book was written twenty years ago, and of course takes no account of research published after that date. The same writer's *How Surnames Began* (Weidenfeld and Nicolson, 1967) is basically a condensed version of the earlier work.

Apart from older publications, there are several more recent works on surnames generally, some of them unlikely to be much use to someone wanting to do research into a particular surname, and to put the results of that research into some general context. Among the more recent works are L.G. Pine, *The Story of Surnames* (David and Charles, 1965, reprinted 1969), which mainly deals with aristocratic and landed families, about which it has a good deal of anecdotal material, but it does not give very much in the way of a general history of surnames. Sir William Addison, *Understanding English Surnames* (Batsford, 1978) discusses surnames region by region, but in general does not add anything very much to what can be found in Reaney's *Origin of English Surnames*. A more scholarly work is W.O. Hassall, *History Through Surnames* (Pergamon Press, 1967). This gives short explanations of the history and origins of many surnames, written in a manner comprehensible to the ordinary reader without any specialised knowledge, and it is a useful and reliable source of information on the subject. It does not set out to give a general history of British surnames.

A work of quite a different character is H.B. Guppy, *Homes of Family Names in Great Britain* (Genealogical Publishing Co., 1890, reprinted 1968). Guppy attempted to fix the original homes of a large number of British surnames by examining the names of farmers as given in the late nineteenth-century directories, supposing that farmers were likely to be less mobile than other sections of the population. He underestimated the amount of migration which had taken place before 1890, but his book is a useful guide to the way in which surnames were distributed at the end of the nineteenth century, when at least some features of earlier distribution were still discernible. Guppy discusses surnames county by county, and his book is sometimes worth consulting for clues about where to look for the beginnings of surnames. His book gives brief notes on the history of many surnames. These are usually accurate as far as they go, but they do not by any means give full accounts of the surnames concerned.

Dictionaries of surnames exist for some countries on the Continent of Europe, but few if any of these are accessible outside academic libraries, though at times they would be valuable in dealing with the origins of surnames brought into Britain by migration. One of the most useful, which is more readily available than many others, is A. Dauzat, *Dictionnaire étymologique des noms de famille et prénoms de France* (Larousse, 1951). This deals with surnames present in France, but does not deal with all the surnames existing in Britain from the French language. A number of books dealing with the surnames of particular areas or provinces of France have been published, but are not generally available in this country.

A good many books have been published in recent years which give advice about tracing pedigrees, and about how to compile family histories. There are also a large number of books dealing with particular classes of records, such as title deeds, parish registers, probate records, and so forth. Many of these are likely to be useful to readers who are setting out to trace their ancestry, or to put together family histories, but it would go rather beyond the scope of this book to discuss them, and a good deal of space would be required to deal with these subjects adequately.

Index

All references are to surnames unless
otherwise indicated

213